D1065291

THE ART OF LEARNING

THE ART
of
LEARNING

by

WALTER B. PITKIN
PROFESSOR IN JOURNALISM, COLUMBIA UNIVERSITY,
AUTHOR OF *The Art of Rapid Reading*

WHITTLESEY HOUSE
McGRAW-HILL BOOK COMPANY, INC.
NEW YORK · 1931

Copyright 1931, *by the*
McGraw-Hill Book Company, Inc.

All rights reserved. This book, or parts thereof,
may not be reproduced in any form without
permission of the publishers.

FIRST EDITION
THIRD IMPRESSION

Published by

WHITTLESEY HOUSE

A Division of the
McGraw-Hill Book Company, Inc.

Printed in the United States of America by
The Maple Press Company, York, Pa.

A PREFACE WHICH IS TO BE READ

Here is the Textbook of the New Age. It introduces you to the most important, most neglected art in the world.

Why the most important? Because on it depends every good thing in life except what comes to us by blind luck. Health, wealth and happiness are attained only through learning, which brings all inventions and improvements, all significant art and literature.

Why the most neglected of all arts? Heaven knows! But the fact cannot be disputed. Every year we Americans spend well over $2,000,000,000 on our public schools in an effort to educate 25,000,000 children. We spend more millions training teachers how to teach. But not a penny to teach those 25,000,000 pupils how to learn!

Is it to be wondered at that millions of boys and girls drop out of school, discouraged, bewildered, irritated, and ill informed? Or that most of them forget all they half-learned in the classroom five years after leaving school? Or that most intelligent adults declare that they never began to learn much until after they had been out in the world a while?

The wastage of time and life and intellect in school is a horrible crime. Some experts throw the blame on the horde of intellectual inferiors who are forced into the classrooms by our compulsory education laws. But I think the heavier burden of sin falls upon those educators who have maintained that learning is mainly a matter of personal interest, and that the way to arouse interest is to make textbooks and classroom methods as lively, as simple, and as entertaining as possible.

v

Both doctrines are half-truths. Are you interested in running? Do you like to run a mile a day? If so, will that interest and the daily mile enable you to win a Marathon race? No physical trainer encourages you to think so. He knows the severe drill in the technique of handling your lungs and legs and body muscles which is indispensable to high success in running. Do you wish to learn typewriting? Do you practice away at it daily? If so, is this a guarantee that you will master the touch system? No! Much more is required.

The Art of Learning is something more than the trick of learning some single subject or act of skill. It is less concerned with the particular material of study than with the learner and his mental abilities. Once mastered, it may be applied to almost anything. Hence it makes for versatility and quick adaptability.

Men of the New Age must learn or perish. The world moves faster, changes faster, grows more intricate; hence people must adapt to sudden shifts of scene and fortune, as so many millions now are doing. They must learn strange things, often in an unseemly hurry. Wars, mergers, stock market collapses, revolutionary inventions, tariff wars, trade depressions, and all the rest of modernity's mad turmoil impose this necessity upon all of us.

Education, as we conceive it, is a good thing. But most of us need the Art of Learning far more than we need education. This is my revolutionary doctrine. It deserves a word of explanation.

What is education? Let John Dewey, our American leader in this field, tell us. It is, says he, the learning of certain attitudes, habits and facts "which enable you to participate in the social consciousness of the race." An excellent description! But this ignores entirely the Art of Learning, which has nothing to do with the social consciousness of our race or any other. Deeper than all race

consciousness, older and more enduring than any civilization or cult, and more necessary than any religion or moral
system is man's ability to adjust to new situations. No
matter what his race or cult or clime, he must adjust or
die. And this adjusting is founded upon his capacity to
learn. The savage who seeks shelter from an oncoming
tornado is not participating in the social consciousness
of his race; he is saving his life. But to seek the best shelter
in the best way, he must learn much about tornadoes and
local geography. So, I maintain, the Art of Learning is
broader and deeper than education. For to go on living in
health is vastly more important than to share in any kind
of social consciousness. True, the herd thinks otherwise.
But those who learn much care little about herd opinions.

This book is not for school children. It has been written
to aid the following people:

1. Young men and women who, having finished their
school years, wish to push on by themselves into higher
fields of learning;

2. Older people who feel the lack of the right early drill
in the Art of Learning and aspire to overcome it;

3. Energetic, ambitious adults who, having been well
trained to use their minds, find themselves with many
leisure hours on their hands and desire to make the most of
them;

4. Equally energetic and ambitious adults who are the
victims of the New Unemployment and must become proficient in some new trade, craft, business, or profession in
order to make a decent living.

The book is emphatically not intended for sappy souls
who sigh for inspiration, in the hope of being kicked
upstairs. It is not addressed to worshippers of the Success
Cult who will read anything that promises to increase
their cash in hand quickly. Nor is it a fit volume to be

placed in the hands of pedants who fancy that true culture
consists merely of knowing what certain ancestors did,
wrote, and taught.

It is a work book. In the hands of a lusty toiler, it will
show solid profits. For every part of it has been tried
out carefully, if not by me then by other teachers and
psychologists. Some of the methods described have been
employed by thousands of learners, a few by hundreds of
thousands, and others by smaller numbers. But all have
been thoroughly tested. In this sense, the book advises
little or nothing novel. But it does bring together for
the first time the most advanced practices in the Art of
Learning.

The valuable suggestions as to books, equipment, and
procedure in learning some of the more important subjects
discussed in this book have come from many colleagues
at Columbia University, among whom the following
deserve special thanks for their thoughtful and extensive
recommendations:

In geography, Professor J. Russell Smith; in geology,
Professor Charles P. Berkey; in physics, Professor H. W.
Farwell; in botany, Professor E. W. Sinnott; in Greek
and Latin, Professors Young and McClees; in vocational
psychology, Professor Harry D. Kitson; and in chemistry
and general science, Professor Frederick Barry.

Unfortunately, some of the most valuable recommendations have proved too lengthy to be included in this volume.
So I have given only those bearing upon key subjects.
Perhaps the others may be furnished in supplementary
form to readers who desire them.

WALTER B. PITKIN.

NEW YORK CITY,
    March, 1931.

CONTENTS

BOOK III

BOOK IV

BOOK V

HOW TO GET THE MOST OUT OF THIS BOOK

Before you turn to the next page, get rid of all writing materials. At the first reading, take no notes whatsoever.

Begin reading at a place and time which make it possible for you to go straight through the entire volume without interruption except for short rests and sleep. If this cannot easily be arranged, then see to it that you read it in the longest possible installments. Don't spend, in all, more than ten or eleven hours at it.

Read it through at first just as you would skim a light novel. If you have already become expert in skimming, flit through it at top speed. Get the bird's-eye view of the whole subject. Enjoy as much as you can. Make no solemn effort to learn anything. Relax! Look upon everything in the volume as a possible source of entertainment.

As soon as possible after this first lively glance, write your impressions of the book as a whole. The longer your notes, the better. What interested you most? What puzzled you? With which points do you heartily disagree? Which phases of the Art of Learning seem to be covered too scantily? Is there anything that hits you between the eyes? Anything that applies to you with unusual force? What is the main argument of the book, if any? What are its outstanding conclusions?

If you find writing reports like this arduous, you may serve the same purpose just as well by talking the whole book over with somebody. Be sure to pick a good listener!

Next begin the first serious reading of the book. And now reverse the whole process: do not cover more than 4,000 or 5,000 words at any one sitting. And avoid studying it oftener than once a day. (This last rule will not apply to certain types of keen students. Decide for yourself whether it suits you.)

Take no notes! Write nothing except when working on the exercises at the close of the chapters. But mark passages freely.

Under no circumstances fail to do these exercises, sooner or later. They are the better half of the book. But do not try to finish them all at this second perusal. Leave some of the longer and more difficult for the final reading.

Keep all copies of your exercises. Later you should refer to them for various questions, especially those touching your own progress in learning.

After this thorough reading, you will have learned enough about the Art to apply it to your own personal problems. From now on, study the book selectively. Pick out those passages which either appeal to you most intensely or serve to correct your bad learning habits.

Spend as much time as you can in reflecting upon the principles and practical advice here set forth. But be sure to persist in drilling yourself along the lines laid down in the chapters which most deeply concern you.

If you learn fast, you may master the Art of Learning within three or four months. But not many can approach that velocity. Be satisfied if you succeed within a year.

INTRODUCTION

THE NEW ERA OF LEARNING

Four Forces Aiding Our Art.

Four mighty forces are now converging upon the art of learning, to improve it and to make it more popular than ever before. All four are major phases of the new civilization which is being shaped in the present generation. They are the new knowledge, the new leisure, the new unemployment, and the new ethics of personality.

The New Knowledge.

The new knowledge calls for no report here. Every serious magazine, book, newspaper, lecture, and radio talk is echoing it. Men are discovering strange, revolutionary facts faster and faster. The flood of novelties mounts day by day. No man can stem it, none can drink it to the full. Have you read Mr. Einstein's latest? And what about that new chemical which makes wood at once fireproof and waterproof? Petroleum has been found beyond the headwaters of the Amazon in such quantities that the politics of all South America will be transformed by it. Now they're saying that pulsations cause stars to form and to disintegrate. Bad habits may best be broken by trying to keep them going. Thus it goes, on and on. Would you keep in touch with your own generation? Then you must learn fast and learn much. In one year you must pick up more facts than Aristotle ever knew. To hold the pace, must you not become an adept in the art of learning?

The New Leisure.

The new leisure also is familiar enough to be taken for granted by most readers of this book. What a perplexing luxury it has already become! What a strange array of unpleasant surprises have come in its train! For most of the problems of leisure, tradition offers no satisfactory solutions.

From hand laborer up to captain of industry and college president, the work day shortens. Vacations lengthen; and ingenious man has even devised, in daylight saving, a trick stretching the sunny hours. Machines take over drudgery. Skilled organizers enable men to double their output in shop and factory, without exerting themselves a whit more. The human intellect is just beginning to permeate our civilization, and a single idea diffuses itself at lightning speed throughout whole continents, changing business and manufacturing in a trice. The six-hour day and the five-day week have arrived for the vanguard; soon they will become the habit of millions.

What Shall You Do?

And what will men do with their free time then? Why learn to play the piano, when your radio brings you, at the twist of a dial, finer music than ever you could finger through? Why read books, when the authors themselves chat with you through the ether and in the popular magazines? Why even learn to cook in a world where canneries engage the finest chefs to devise recipes for goodies fetched to your door in tins?

The new leisure threatens, among other things, to undermine the forward-looking traits which lift the civilized man above the savage. It has been said that "civilization is measured by the ability to forego present pleasure for the sake of future benefits." But the new leisure, having received the benefits from a thousand generations of toilers and thinkers, sees little ahead worth striving for; so it settles down to wallow in pleasures of the hour.

Now, a little wallow now and then is relished by the best of men. But to make a career of wallowing hardly seems commendable—not even to pigs. Tens of thousands of Americans understand this and seek escape from such a disaster. They begin to see that, in the long run, there is only one way out: they must train their highest traits either in hard work or in profitable pleasure such as intellectual hours may bring. And that means a new mastery of the art of learning.

The New Unemployment.

The third force, the new unemployment, is less clearly recognized. Some statesmen, indeed, imitate Herbert Hoover whenever it is mentioned; they make a sour face and insist that tales of the plague are grossly exaggerated. None the less, their own statisticians refute them behind their backs. Engineers are losing their jobs daily as a result of profound changes in the industries they have mastered. Tens of thousands of women, having spent years training themselves to teach school, are unable to secure positions. As I showed in my study of the opportunities for the highest grades of scientific and technical workers, "The Twilight of the American Mind," our civilization is finding it harder and harder to employ such persons in work that measures up to and absorbs happily their full intellectual and physical abilities. To the so-called "technological unemployment" caused by changes in the demands of industry, we add the deeper and vastly more disturbing unemployment caused by a diminishing demand for superior people in nearly all the professions, arts, and techniques, relative to the amount of work to be done.

Protective Trades.

The time is at hand when a bright youth ought to learn, not one trade, but three or four, in order to safeguard his future. The specialist in any of seven out of ten lines must cultivate not one specialty, but perhaps three, to keep himself in bread and butter. Here is a brilliant school teacher who has been compelled to learn newspaper reporting, inasmuch as she can find only part-time employment in the schools. Here is a competent chemist who becomes a photographer on the side, so that he can devote about half of his year to motion picture work, while he is idle as a consulting chemist. Here is a keen sanitary engineer who, finding no work at all in this field during the past four or five years, has drilled himself to be a moderately good editor of technical journals, a factory foreman in a shipbuilding plant, and a financial investigator for a Wall Street house. These people—all acquaintances of mine—typify the new proletariat. All poor, all watching their chances for decent work at decent pay, as a cat watches a mouse, they become perforce past masters in the art of learning. They never know at what hour they must learn a new job.

The New Individuality.

The fourth force is the new ethics of personality. Though the name may ring strangely, the thing it stands for will be recognized instantly. Ever since the World War—and perhaps as a result of that supreme imbecility—intelligent people have been rebelling more and more hotly against the ethics of the herd. Never before in modern times, perhaps, has the average man of average mind and tastes been happier in his enjoyment and approval of herd activities, serious and frivolous alike; and never before has the superior man despised more keenly the shoddy patriotism, the noisy degradation of sports, the thin schooling, and the moron contempt for solid learning which pervade most American cities, their politics, their newspapers, and their innumerable lodges. Steadily we see forming, among the three or four million people of quality, the will to be themselves. With that must go the conviction that the man who would truly live must develop, to his utmost, all of the highest and finest traits of personality. The person who has a splendid voice and would enjoy singing should train this gift and make the most of it, to his own private satisfaction, no matter whether anybody wants to listen. The housewife who feels the urge to write a novel about her girlhood ought to go ahead and write it, quite indifferent to publishers and what they will buy.

ΓΝΩΘΕ ΣΕΑΤΤΟΝ.

Now, to make the most of oneself, it is necessary, first of all, to discover one's inclinations and aptitudes. That done, one must set out, in orderly fashion and with strong will, to perfect the strongest of them. Here we come, then, to the art of learning. It is plain that, among the three million adult Americans who are carrying home study courses or attending university extension lectures, a sizable group is moved by the single wish to cultivate their own personalities along the lines of highest pleasure and accomplishment.

Here, then, are the four great forces. Is it to be wondered at that Americans are becoming the most enthusiastic of learners? Or that the art itself bids fair to rise to new high levels in our country?

BOOK I

LEARN AND LIVE!

LEARN AND LIVE

"Live and learn!"

A wise old saw. But one which I would supplement with another which, I feel, is equally wise.

"Learn and live!"

All life, from one angle of observation, is experience and action. Acquiring the experiences is all a matter of learning, even though it is as informal as a sneeze. Using what one learns to get what one wants is the fruit of learning.

Learning Is a Phase of Living.

Always the human being is learning, and his studies should always aim to enrich him as a personality. What that life more abundant means to him depends, of course, upon his own primary nature, and to a slighter degree upon the society into which he has been born. When all is said and done, he must pick and choose for himself. He must teach himself, too. The wisest men in the world cannot advise him, unless they know him intimately. The best service they can render is to inform him about the nature of personality, its expansive needs, and its creative possibilities, all of which he may then apply to himself as best he can. He must learn and live, while he lives and learns.

Your life is rich in the measure of its breadth and depth of experiences and activities. But is this not the same as saying that it is rich in proportion to what you learn and how you apply your knowledge and skill?

Do you wish to live? Then learn!

Would you like to live more intensely? Then learn more intensely!

9

Learning is the greatest achievement in the world. It is the foundation of every other achievement. And it is the very essence of human progress. He who cannot learn stands still. He who stands still goes backward. He who goes backward soon drops by the wayside, while men who can and will learn press onward.

The Law of Learning.

Every time a creature learns something, it changes itself a little. Nerves once disconnected are now hooked up. New calls come in over the line, new answers ring out, and a new deed is done. This deed changes something in the outside world. The rat which has, by long striving, found its way through the maze into which the experimenter has placed it now reaches the bread and milk. The bread and milk are devoured; and the world's visible supply of bread and milk is thereby reduced. Thomas Edison, toiling day and night for years, eventually learns how to make a little glass bulb and a filament which will glow for many hours. The first wavering dull light shines in his laboratory, and then a million men string wires forty times around the world, and night is driven from street and shop and home. The habits of two billion people are changed. Cities are rebuilt. More wealth is added to the world's hoard than the shabby empire of Napoleon would have brought under the auctioneer's hammer. And all because one man insisted on learning just which fiber of all the thousands on earth would stand up under an electric current.

From rat to Edison the law of learning runs smoothly upward, yet the heights have not yet been reached. In truth, mankind has scarcely left the salt strand of the sea which spawned us all. As a learner he is only a little higher than the fishes, measured by the astronomer's rod. For how slowly he changes himself! He still clings to hundreds of habits and ideas which his ancestors fashioned. To the ancestors these were bold novelties. To him they are holy traditions, first truths, the cornerstone of morals and society. But to the cosmic observer they are all on a par with the twists and turns of the hungry rat which gropes toward the bread and milk.

Revolutionary Learners.

Man, the learner, faces today a crisis unknown to all those ancestors. And what a strange, terrifying one it is! A few thousand of his kind whose abilities far exceed the rank and file have, in the course of the past generation or two, mastered so many new tricks that they are now changing man's environment faster than man can change himself to fit it. Will the mass of the human race be able to learn the new heaven and the new earth? Having learned it, will they then be able to throw it aside as soon as their intellectual leaders have scrapped it for a still newer outfit?

Nobody knows the answer. But every thinker must readily perceive the situation as unique in human history. Man must learn faster and deeper than ever, to keep up with the revolutions wrought by his own learning. To the dull learner, the reactionary and the esthete, this must appear as a vicious circle. To the alert and the forward-looking, it presents a fascinating problem.

Never before has the call for quick learners been so insistent. Never before have the rewards of high-speed learning been so rich. Never before has the formal learning of schools lagged so far behind the vanguard of science.

The Art of Unlearning.

This lag imposes an extra burden upon the learner. He must acquire the art of unlearning, as well as the art of learning, for a vast deal of information which he picked up in school, not so many years ago, has become obsolete—or worse. Many facts have been so transformed by the addition of later discoveries that, while still facts, their significance has changed profoundly. Other knowledge has fallen into disuse—witness Greek and Latin, which once were indispensable to several learned professions. Then too, some subjects have ceased to be either true, good, or beautiful.

Because they have been compelled, in high school and college, to wade through such unattractive courses, many of our younger adults resisted learning them; and, as a result, they lost their earlier proficiency in learning, for the habit grew rusty. Out in the world of business and society, they yearn to know much; but they find it hard to knuckle down and master subjects which intrigue them. The old school habits of skimming and evading plague them now.

"There are lions in the path," they say.

Obstacles to Learning.

Yes, there are lions in the path. Many lions!

"I am too old to learn." How many people tell you this! And how many sincerely believe it!

"I lack the ability to master that subject. It's miles beyond me." This is another lamentation.

"I'd learn it, if I could find the time," say others. "But you've no idea how frightfully busy I am."

"If I could afford a good teacher, I'd take the subject up in earnest. But it's beyond my means," say many others.

These are the four biggest, fiercest lions whose roars terrify would-be learners. Age, incompetence, busy-ness, and poverty. Just how fatal are they?

The First Lion Roars.

"You can't teach an old dog new tricks."

So roars lion No. 1.

And how shall we answer Sir Lion?

One raw winter day a stranger came tramping out the rutty, frozen back road to my old farm. Briskly he told his business. He was forty-five, the successful general manager of one of the largest factories in Ohio, and ready to quit once and for all in order to enjoy life.

"I've saved enough so that my family will never worry over the grocer's bill," he smiled. "And I've salted away just enough for myself so that, if I cannot do what I want to, I'll still be able to carry on."

"What do you want to do?" I asked.

"Write, of course!"

"Any training?"

"None—except letters to my daughter, who is still in college."

"Ever study the subject?"

"Never!"

"How about your college grades in English?"

"Never went to college!" he laughed. "All I fear, though, is that the habit of writing business letters may cramp my literary style. What do you think?"

"Nothing at all until we see how you work out. How much time can you spend on writing?"

"Eight hours a day, if necessary. I'm moving to a small coast town where I'll have peace and quiet."

Now that was about as unpromising a prospect as a pessimist might sigh for. Middle-aged business men seldom stop work without a pretty serious upset, especially if they are as robust and as alert as was this stranger. And few people can pick up the finer tricks of writing as late as forty-five unless they have an unusual foundation in some language habits. All my caller claimed to have in this respect was a passion for reading endlessly in good books. So I played safe and discouraged him.

But that scheme didn't work. He knew what he wanted. And all my dire predictions ran off his mind like the well-known drops of water off a duck's back. He resigned his high post, sold his house, and packed off to his still nook with reams of paper and two typewriters. Friends tapped their brows ominously. His wife worried, poor soul. But—

Less than two years later, he had sold his first book to a first-class publisher, and a dozen or more stories to magazines. Nobody has ever regarded him as Kipling's successor, least of all himself. He's no genius, but just a healthy human getting fun out of life in his own way. He'll never write the "great American novel." But he makes enough money to prove to his wife that he has followed his natural bent to a hair's breadth.

At the age of forty-six a woman who had long played the violin about as well as most amateurs found her hands crippled with arthritis. She had to abandon her beloved instrument. How could she find an outlet for her strong musical trends? After a period of deep blues, she hit upon the idea of composing music. She had never been so moved in all her life. She had no training in such work, though she did read music fluently and knew all the masterpieces, nor had she ever invented tunes.

She had a large household to manage and no money for private tutors. So she sat down alone with a few books on harmony and counterpoint and worked away at them while her children were in school. Betwixt breakfast dishes and noon soup she enthusiastically fingered out her little studies on the piano, which she had never learned to play.

While the volume of her compositions is small, some of her work is charming, even good enough to publish perhaps. But she has no interest in fame. Her joy springs from the work itself, which isn't work at all but the purest play.

Frederick B. Robinson, president of the College of the City of New York, takes up a new hobby every year. Once he went in for etching and did well enough to place two works on exhibit at the Brooklyn Museum of Art. Then he learned to play the cello, which he tackled on a wager.

He had previously played no instrument and knew nothing of musical theory or practice. But he believed that almost anybody who enjoyed music, as he does, could make solid progress with almost any instrument in short order by dint of intensive study. In this belief he was challenged by expert musicians. Robinson asked them to select the instrument he was to learn. They picked the cello.

Though everybody told him that at his age and with his complete lack of training he could make little headway, he went at it. After thirty days he gave a recital and was pronounced by professional critics as competent as any learner could be in that brief span.

During the past year, he has been learning sculpture. He has finished a bust of his daughter, an altogether creditable piece of work. Next year he proposes to work at landscape painting. After that, it will be either boxing, poetry, or chemistry—whichever his son decides!

But the first prize surely goes to Henry Smith Williams. Simply because he liked to study all sorts of things, and not in the least as a necessity, Williams, who is a distinguished physician with a long record of achievement in medicine, has made himself an almost equally eminent ornithologist, a student of astronomy, a writer of popular detective stories, a historian, and a specialist in radio.

Before he had learned anything about radio, a publisher invited him to write two articles on the subject. He undertook the contract, largely in a spirit of play. He began his studies around the age of fifty-five, if I recall correctly. The articles proved so good that he was asked to take charge of a radio department. After that he wrote one of the most popular books on the subject.

A large volume could easily be filled with tales like these. What a wreck they make of the moth-eaten old yarn that only the young can learn!

Old Dogs and New Tricks.

"You can't teach an old dog new tricks."

This isn't true, even of dogs. Witness Sandy. He is a collie born and bred on my farm, and perhaps the cleverest of a dozen or more which I have had. For various family reasons, Sandy missed a proper early education. When he should have been mastering his three R's, the poor fellow was practicing tail wags, barks, and chasing sticks. Thus he arrived at adulthood in a lamentable state of intellect and skill.

At the age of five—which is, in a dog's life, roughly as old as a man of thirty—some of us decided that Sandy had far too fine a wit to be wasted on the pursuit of stray cats and the guardianship of the back yard. So we ventured to train him in sundry accomplishments. In the course of six months, Sandy learned to respond correctly to a dozen or more commands given entirely in speech. He learned to jump through a hoop. He learned to sit up on his haunches, holding a morsel of food on the tip of his nose until commanded to eat it. He learned to eat when told "Yes" and to refrain quietly when told "No." He learned to charge, to retrieve, and to keep quiet. And, in most cases, he learned each trick within a week or less.

If he had been trained to do other things while a pup, this would not redound so greatly to his credit. But he had no educational habits on which to build, and that is the point of this moral tale. From all of which may we not safely conclude that many humans as old in their scale as Sandy is in his can learn fully as well as the dog?

Thorndike and his associates have demonstrated of late that most two-legged adults can go on learning most things up to the age of fifty, if they want to earnestly. Naturally they have more difficulty in subjects which require great dexterity of hand, eye, and leg. Great toe dancers probably will never start their careers at the age of forty. But work lying mainly in the realm of the intellect can be fully as well learned late in life as early; and in some cases it seems to be mastered better after the tropical years of youth have passed. At forty, you can learn a new language better than at fifteen.

Given a certain minimum of native ability, you will usually find that something can be done with it at any time before the last tooth drops out and the senile citizen clamors for his wheel chair. If developed on the basis of related habits, it is not at all remarkable. Thus, a Latin scholar who, at the age of fifty, first undertakes to learn the Spanish language can hardly brag over his success with it. For Spanish resembles Latin and so is half learned ere the scholar reads a line of it. But were this same scholar, knowing nothing of any physical science, to attack chemistry at fifty, he would be achieving something notable by its mastery.

Maturity Aids Learning.

Between the ages of twenty-two and forty, the ability to learn a systematic logically organized subject, such as a foreign language, mathematics, or any natural science, declines no more than 1 per cent per year. A man aged forty-two lags only 20 per cent behind a twenty-year-older. To this conclusion Thorndike and his associates came as a result of their prolonged experiments in teaching adults Esperanto.

But they also find that the older people make up for this slowing down by more mature backgrounds which aid them in thorough comprehension. To some unmeasured degree, they also suffer from self-consciousness and a conviction of their own inferior capacity. When these and a few other minor influences are given their due weight, the final opinion is reached that

. . . the general tendency from all our experiments is for an inferiority of about 15 per cent as a result of twenty years from twenty-two on. Learning representing an approximation to sheer modifiability unaided by past learning shows considerably more inferiority than this. Actual learning of such things as adults commonly have to learn shows considerably less.

In other words, the adult under forty-five who wants to learn a new natural science or a language or a branch of economics or social science can usually assume that he will master the subject only a little more slowly than a youth of twenty-two. He will take from 10 to 15 per cent longer than the latter to finish the task.

The Lion of Incompetence.
Lion No. 2 now roars.
"I lack the ability to learn."
This is a bolder and wilder beast than the first one. We cannot be sure that there isn't some truth in his discouraging remarks. For people do differ enormously in their native abilities, no less than in the extent to which they have trained these. It is foolish to pretend that all of us are born intellectually equal, or even on a parity as to our physical energies and our initiative. Not every young American can master calculus, simply by high diligence. Nor can we all dance like Pavlova or sing like Caruso. So why bluff ourselves about it?

But, granting all this, I maintain that, nine times out of ten, it is impossible to determine, in advance of prolonged tests, whether your supposed incompetence is due to a limited native ability; to poor early training in some related field, to lack of drill in subjects which necessarily precede the subject in which you deem yourself incompetent, to an emotional fixation rooted in some long past (and even forgotten) shock, or even to a present subconscious laziness or resistance to the proposed study. What men call incompetence is protean.

Let me wax personal again and, like a doddering old man, reminisce. When in high school I had good reason to accept, with many a sigh, my own utter incompetence in geometry. I entered the first course joyfully. The subject allured me, and I had done well in algebra; so the path looked smooth and rosy. But what a jolt I received! Within a month, I trailed at the tail of the class. Nothing went right. Every theorem jammed somewhere in my anatomy and came out in recital a poor mutilated thing.

I was flunked three times, as I recall. Then my teacher, weary of beholding my bright and shining face, passed me, just to be rid of me. And on I went to higher things, firm in the drab conviction that I had no mind for geometry or any other higher mathematics. My record in college bore out these views only too well. Thenceforth I knew my limitations and would move cautiously within them.

And yet, after ten years or thereabouts, I became interested in logic; thence I progressed into mathematics, not by way of high school courses but by way of self-education, with particular attention to the writings of truly great mathematicians, such as Dedekind, Whitehead, Russell, and others on down to Einstein. With two eminent men in the field I studied about half-way through relativity, long before the populace began to hear of it. All of which caused me to wonder about the incompetence displayed in those high school geometry classes.

I cannot wholly solve the mystery, but part of it is clear enough. The teacher had started me off wrong by insisting that all the presuppositions of the science were Gospel truths. They were facts of Nature implanted there by the Creator of the universe. And, as I remember now with grim mirth, a mild riot was precipitated by my impudent remark that, for the life of me, I could not see why lines parallel on our earth might not meet somewhere west of the Milky Way. I was roundly berated for such imbecilities. I shut up. But so too did my mind. A decade afterward, reading the treatises of Henri Poincaré, I suddenly realized one source of my past infirmities and discomfitures. The so-called axiom of parallel lines is no fact of Nature; it is a simple definition which expresses something that the geometer presupposes, with no evidence whatsoever. I failed in high school geometry because my teacher misrepresented the situation to me; and I happened to have an absurdly logical mind, instead of an illogical one.

I have known music students to come to a bad end mainly because their teachers, by sheer chance, drove them to master pieces which they did not enjoy. And probably every teacher with years of experience can cite scores of tragedies like that of the young man who, some years ago, lagged far behind his fellows in my Columbia classes. He worked hard, far into the night, but to no avail. Being poor, he could ill afford to spend ten years finishing a college course; so he dropped out after the doctors had told him that his troubles were largely physical. A few years later he wrote me to report that he had been suffering from encephalitis, had been cured, and was now racing onward merrily. So long as the cause of his mental sluggishness remained unknown, he cursed himself as incompetent.

But why go on with all the many forms of low attainment and skill due to causes other than native inferiority? Take warning from the cases just given. Be slow to pronounce yourself beneath a subject. Analyze your past training, your health, your emotional attitudes toward the subject, and all the other possible destroyers of the nimble wit. Not until you have assured yourself that these do not explain your inability should you invite lion No. 2 to devour you. Most causes of hard learning can be removed.

Father Time Is a Lion.

Roars now lion No. 3: "I haven't time to learn what I'd like to. I'm so busy!"

This loathsome beast is my pet enemy. Pardon a crabbed old metaphysician if he loses his temper for a few minutes.

The only people who truly haven't time are dead. Dead and buried. All the others who insist that they haven't time fall into a few familiar classes, to wit: fools, loafers, shirkers, and wastrels. Even invalids flat on their backs in bed have time—too much time, in fact!

I make one slight qualification to this sweeping indictment. Now and then you come upon a man who honestly denies that he has time to learn a hard subject, on the more specific ground that he will have to spend hours a day at it for years on end. This is a grave misapprehension; and it is the duty of this book to remove it, once and for all. If you know how to study, you can progress at bewildering speed.

The Profits of Half an Hour a Day.

Half an hour a day, if properly spent, will make you master of the fundamentals of almost any science or other subject *within one year*. And not more than one hour a day is required for learning even the most difficult things, whether they take one year or five.

What if a young man of average ability who had to go to work at the age of eighteen earnestly wished to continue learning so that he might hold his own, in business and in society, with highly cultured people? Suppose that he first masters the art of learning, devoting to it about six months at the rate of one hour a day. What can he then accomplish?

He arranges his schedule so that he inflexibly assigns one full hour a day to study. That makes 365 hours in a year. Five years of such orderly work would give him a thorough grasp of the essentials of physics, chemistry, biology, psychology, economics, and modern history. He would have an insight into these subjects fully as clear as that possessed by the average graduate of Harvard or Columbia.

This does not mean that, were he to concentrate upon one of those subjects exclusively for five years, he would advance just as rapidly. For, as will later be demonstrated, we learn fastest at the beginning of a new subject, and, after passing a certain stage, we necessarily slow down; finally no perceptible forward movement occurs, though we burn the midnight oil. Every specialist discovers this fact after a few years of intensive learning. It simply means that, the more you learn of a subject, the less there remains to be learned. So our young man need not despair! Slowing down is no reflection upon his intellect.

What if he went on for ten years at the pace we described? Well, first of all, his habits of learning would have been refined to the utmost, surely before the end of the fourth year; and so he would master new subjects ever faster and faster. He would find it not at all arduous to learn all the basic facts about twenty major subjects in the decade. And that would elevate him to the small, select company of choice spirits who live in a realm far above those of the intellectuals and the artists. He would be one of "those who know." Beside him a typical university Ph. D. would cut a sorry figure.

And all on one hour a day! All on the time which most young men fritter away over poker or bridge or puffing a pipe!

High School Hodge Podge.

I grieve to say that several of the strongest trends in our high school system rapidly wean the young away from such an intensive life of learning. Let me quote here a typical complaint of an American parent on this score.

A bewildered, if not infuriated father writes thus to the *New York Times:*

I have a boy 15 years old, now closing his second year of high school. As far as I can ascertain, not only has he not acquired anything of practical value, but he has actually retrogressed during the high school period.

As a grammar school student he was, if not brilliant, at any rate able to maintain an average around 95 per cent and to pass two grades in one year. As a high school student he is apparently a total loss, with an average down in the low 80's and in some subjects even lower. Naturally I am worried, particularly as I find my experience is by no means unique among parents of high school pupils.

In his two years my boy has acquired a small smattering of Latin, a worse hodgepodge of French, some "civics," history and what have you. His writing is illegible and his spelling has gone back to about fourth grade. He has practically forgotten much of his grade teaching, simply because he gets no "credits" for it in high school. In other words, his sole object is to scrape through by doing as little as may be of the unpalatable but compulsory subjects. He has no pride in his work and no anticipation of his future. He has two more years of this to go through before he "graduates"—when he will have to begin his education in real earnest.

Were the U. S. Census enumerators to pursue an inquiry in this year of grace, 1931, they would record several hundred thousand parents whose experiences and sentiments would closely resemble those of this letter. Where would these complainants place the blame?

On women teachers, on athletics, on coeducation, on mollycoddle methods of teaching, on the low grade of pupils, on the jazz age, on prohibition, on immigration, and, for aught I know, a hundred other things. But, underneath all the special causes, you will find one common worker of evil; and that is a total and catastrophic failure to train high school students in the supreme art of making every minute count to the utmost. Little girls are taught genteel leisure, little boys are raised to dawdle. All the snap, kick, thrust, and onward lunge of a truly strenuous, makeful career are missing, not alone in the curriculum but in the spirit of the teachers.

Young America is not mastering the art of learning. And a generation which grows up thus is doomed to a hard time. The lions will eat it alive (and get horrible indigestion). Nobody has so little time to achieve worth while things as the person who is furiously doing a hundred nothings all day long.

Who's to Blame?

These youngsters, however, have only their parents to blame for their plight. For the parents it has been who pay taxes for the schools and, by their silence or their apathy, give consent to the sappy system of perverting the next generation. Look at thousands of mothers. Are their days spent to profit?

Mothers?

Up at seven and to bed at midnight, Mrs. Damon Dawdle gets breakfast by eight for her husband and the three children. The family then depart for the day at work and school, and Mrs. Dawdle clears the table and plans the housework for the family maid. Dishes to do, make the beds, a small wash, lunch for the children, groceries for the day, brush up the carpets and run over the floors—and most of the work is done. Mrs. Dawdle's slave is capable and a good cook, so her mistress is relieved of the household burdens that she may go on to the higher and finer things.

A few minutes at the morning paper. Then the day's mail. An hour or so at the telephone—calling the grocer; talking with Mrs. Dephew about that committee meeting of the Ladies' Club; asking Mrs. Smithson whether that

scrap between the secretary and the president of the Western
Satellites was settled without damage; and so on, through
five or more chats. An occasional interruption by Nellie the
maid. And then time for the children's lunch.

The three of them off again for school, Mrs. Dawdle
rushes upstairs to get ready for the afternoon's bridge.
Three hours of gossip and tea, and she must get home for
the evening meal. An hour or so at dinner, the children to
bed, the evening at the radio, at the movies, with friends,
or at hit-or-miss reading, a few minutes of conversation,
and odd moments doing nothing at all, and Mrs. Dawdle's
day is done at twelve. She is all worn out, poor thing.

Had she been well bred, this Mrs. Dawdle, she might
have learned almost all that there is to know about Greek
philosophy, Gothic architecture, preventive medicine, and
apple growing in the time she spent preening herself before
her mirror, snouting into the private affairs of her neighbors, and reading the society notes in the town paper. As
for her bridge, the years it has absorbed would, if sanely
employed, have taught her nearly all that there is to know
about anything of real importance.

Fathers?

But how about a hard working man? He puts in eight
or ten hours a day at his job. He devotes to it his best energies and enthusiasms (let us politely assume). Has he time to
learn economics or Russian history or theories of esthetics?

Yes, of course! With perhaps one genuine exception in
every hundred cases. Before breakfast, during lunch hour,
on the way home at nightfall, after dinner, on Saturday
afternoon, or of a Sunday morn; somewhere will be found one
precious hour that suffices for genuine mastery. For three
years I devoted the gray minutes between half past five
and seven in the morning to the German philosophers, most
of whom were much darker than the study hour. The only

ill effects I ever felt from this heroism resulted from my believing some of their rubbish for a while.

Using Odd Moments.

Later in this book I am going to show you that there is another way of cashing in on Old Father Time. The cunning use of odd moments between larger jobs turns the trick. And if employers understood the psychology of the rapid shift of interest and activity, they would encourage workers to employ a little of their working hours in study, even though the subject had nothing to do with their jobs. Twelve five-minute snatches in the course of a work day will perform miracles of learning, given the right system of concentration. In fact, I should not hesitate to sign a contract to teach a group of factory or office workers French or astronomy or economics in twelve such flickers of time daily exactly as well as the same subjects are taught in full hourly periods in high school or college. The odds are that the factory workers would, in the long run, learn faster and better than the institutional inmates.

Again I stand ready to sign still another contract. I guarantee to teach any young American of normal physique and average intelligence any four trades such as carpentering, masonry work, or plumbing within two years, using no more time than the youth aforesaid wastes on inane trifles such as comic supplements, listening to Amos 'n Andy, and shooting craps.

What's more, I could find time to do it, and still go on learning something new myself.

When I can't do that, I shall know that the last sad rites are about to be performed.

"I Can't Afford It."

The last lion roars.

"If only I could afford a good private teacher! Or go to a fine college! But I can't afford a first-class education."

This lion is all mange, spavins, and asthma. A sorry wreck of a beast! Fear him not! His teeth are decayed and cannot even prick your skin. In these United States and in this generation, poverty is no excuse for lack of learning. It is not even a legitimate plaint over lack of good teachers and good books.

At no time in the world's history have more excellent books on almost every teachable subject been in circulation. Never before have so many public libraries opened their doors to learners who cannot afford to buy all the books they wish to study. Never before has the mechanical equipment of learning been accessible to so many millions, in the form of manual training schools, vocational classroom tools, educational motion pictures, and all the rest.

Teach Yourself.

"But who will teach me?" asks the poor youth piteously.

"The only person who ever teaches anybody. You! You yourself will teach you yourself. It is the learner who does the most."

Later in these pages, I shall argue that the method of learning is far more important than the subject learned, while the teacher may be fully the equal of the method inasmuch as he conveys the latter, with all its promise of high achievement, to the learner. Nevertheless, a man who cannot gain access to a wise teacher need not despair. For, in recent years, long strides have been taken toward standardizing the essentials of the best teaching methods; and courses based on such have been reduced to book form.

The best home study course offered by our universities and the output of the superior correspondence schools are available to any learner. They embody some of the finest learning methods. And these are, to all intents and purposes, the spirit of the best teacher. To reveal the unkind truth of the matter, I may add that some of these prepared courses for private consumption surpass the efforts of the average college teacher.

So the last lion dies with a wheeze.

Learning to Use Your Mind.

You are now going to learn how to use the most important part of yourself.

You learned how to use your legs when as a baby you acquired skill in walking and running. You learned how to use your hands when somewhat later you mastered the difficult arts of dressing yourself, using knife and fork, and drawing pictures. You learned how to use your eyes when you first took a book in hand and began to read. At that same moment you started to use you mind in a new way. But probably nobody urged you to train it then. There were too many other things you had to do!

But now you ought to learn how to use your mind; and there is no reason why you should not become as skillful with it as you are with legs, hands, eyes, and ears. And there are a hundred reasons why you should work harder than ever before to make the most of this, the greatest of all your parts and powers.

Your mind learns things. That is its first task. As it learns, it uses its new knowledge so as to keep you well, guard you against dangers, help you to get along well with other people, do your daily work easily, and generally enjoy life in wholesome fashion. A few people are born rich and lucky—they get the good things of life without much effort; but most men and women have to strive and plan to get ahead and to live happily. They must learn much and make use of all they learn, and it is for them that this book has been written.

A few other fortunate people learn things with the same natural ease which we see in a musical prodigy who, at the age of ten, plays the violin like a master. This book will not help them, but it will help 999 readers out of every thousand—for the normal man is not born with the art of learning in his blood. He must master it by hard work. He must learn how to learn just as he had to learn how to walk, how to read, and how to write.

For thousands of years people have learned how to learn in a hit-and-miss way. They have studied all sorts of subjects except how to study! And that is one reason why the human race is not vastly richer and healthier and happier today. The untrained mind moves slowly and makes many mistakes. The trained mind races ahead lightly and gets far more fun out of its achievements than the untrained.

You will find this art of learning different from anything else you have ever studied. It is not at all like spelling or geography or history. Perhaps this novelty will add to its attractiveness.

When people talk about the art of learning, they probably have in mind the best ways and means of acquiring such information as the history of Holland, higher algebra, and American political practices. In a word, the sort of material which can be printed in a book and delivered in formal lectures. Now, this is a little unfortunate, from my point of view; for, you see, I must consider the art of learning from a much more comprehensive point of view.

The Special Arts of Learning.

The best way of learning anything must be, as I see it, an integral part of the complete art of learning. To fly an airplane, to build a dirigible, to become expert in designing suspension bridges, to carry on deep-sea diving, to sing soprano in grand opera, to perform acrobatic stunts in a circus, to conquer the intricacies of Roman Law, to make fancy confectioneries, to function as hostess in a fashionable night club, to make love, to break safes, to preach the gospel, to cure warts—these are only a few of the infinitude of human activities which must be learned and therefore must involve special arts of learning.

Because man himself remains essentially the same, while addressing himself to such diverse enterprises, we expect to find certain common elements in all tasks of learning. We also look for other elements which occur in large groups of activities but not in others. And, finally, we anticipate novel features in each special task. Learning to handle an automobile is not identical with learning to manage a motor boat. Indeed, you discover minute differences in the handling of two makes of cars—and a correspondingly slight difference in the manner of learning control. Thus the complete art of learning, like every other art, embraces all shades, levels, species, and degrees of muscular, emotional, and intellectual accomplishment. Having said that, we say in substance that it is one phase of the art of living—and by no means a minor one.

Live and Learn.

Here we come upon the profoundest aspect. "Live and learn." The old phrase strikes deep. As language is to thinking, so is learning to living. For, in some measure, all experience is one continuous learning, though the rate and quality of the latter may vary immensely. And it is hardly overshooting the fact to assert that, as a man learns, so he lives; and, as he lives, so he learns. A rich life is full of learning, a lean life empty of it. An evil life is busy with the learning of evil things, a good life packed with the acquiring of worthy skills and knowledge. While there can never be any moral obligation to be intelligent, there can be one to learn as much as we are capable of assimilating.

It is unfortunate that all of us, as a result of childhood experiences, have come to associate the term "learning" with school work. Both the content learned and the operation of acquiring are shot through with this narrow interpretation. Do we not call a man well educated when he has triumphed over the courses of high school and college? Yet, at the same time, do we not—in quite another mood—laugh at the young graduate on Commencement Day and declare that, now at last, he must go forth into the world and learn something? Thus we blandly contradict ourselves. And in the contradiction doth truth emerge. For a man who has learned only the content of a school course—be that the finest on earth—has but scratched the skin of Life and not yet drawn blood. As for his own maturity, he is, at that stage, hardly one-fifth of a man.

What has he still to learn? Let us glance at the grand divisions of the art.

The Grand Divisions of the Art.

The babe begins by learning to use his muscles in moving himself about and in handling things around him. Here are two distinct arts in embryo: first, the art of learning self-management on the lowest physical levels; and, secondly, the art of learning to manipulate physical objects.

The child, as he attains nervous maturity, next learns symbolic communication—which we usually term language. To do this, he must grasp subtle abstract relations and be able to generalize. This is a third and most peculiar special art. Nobody has ever fully mastered it, and grave are the confusions caused to all of us by our bungling with words.

At the same period of development, our young citizen begins to learn how to get along with people; and this involves skill in controlling his own's attitudes, remarks, and persistences. Finding that he cannot have his own way, he must give up reaching for the moon whenever he hungers for green cheese. He must become skillful in stooping to conquer and in winning his way through love and service, when blood and iron fail. And this is the art of social engineering, in its nuclear state. Nobody has ever bloomed to perfection in it: we are all still children with it. In its subjective phase, we might call it social mentality, but the term is clumsy. The skill sought here is the practical understanding of people and the deft handling of human relations. It is far removed from the other grand divisions of learning we have thus far listed.

Next comes the art of learning general abstract relations, such as those in mathematics and their applied forms in engineering. And, still further along the path of progress, we come upon the art of learning the techniques of scientific thinking in matters where fresh observation, statistical analysis, and rigidly supervised tests must be made. Last to be mentioned here, but by no means the last in reality, is the learning of special artistic techniques, in poetry, sculpture, painting, music, and so on. When we reach these, things begin to specialize to a degree which makes further cataloguing impracticable here.

The Relativity of the Art of Learning.

Would you master all of these arts? Impossible! Spare yourself inevitable discouragement, and stick to a few. Which of the arts is most important? Each age and culture answers that in its own manner. Thus, in the European epoch which began to die when Darwin came and is now about ready for lilies and dirge, Church and State dominated men's lives inordinately; and official education centered around the justification of those two mighty institutions. Men called themselves cultured only in so far as they knew the cults of religion, politics, and their attendant philosophies—not to mention their sophistic. All this involved immense learning in the ways of the authentic past. History, which was a patent-medicine blend of myth, apologetics, diplomatic lies, and incidental truth, was taught and taught to surfeit. Indeed, it still is over-taught;

and there are well-intentioned educators who sincerely believe that they can lay a sound basis for twentieth-century culture by drilling youths intensively in the history of Greece and Rome. Witness the project of Meikeljohn at the University of Wisconsin.

At the further extreme you come upon modern industrialists who, seeing nothing but autos, radio sets, miniature golf courses, and chewing gum, devoutly believe that the basis of the new culture must be fitness for the new factory system. Men must learn, above all, how to run lathes and punch time clocks and buy cars on the installment plan. And they must learn to think of all things in terms of production. Witness Henry Ford's intention to spend "perhaps as much as $100,000,000" on vocational schools and related institutions.

Pay your money and take your choice! It is not in order to discuss such philosophies of life here. I cite them merely by way of showing that what men crave to learn and what they deem most important in learning springs from their entire cultural outlook. It is a product of the human will as conditioned by the times.

What "Ought" You to Learn?

It seems to me that nine Americans out of ten feel confused as to what they "ought" to learn; and largely because of the deeper chaos in American culture. Old and new, fossil and embryo, exotic and autochthonous, all mingle in the miscalled melting pot of our as yet unborn civilization. How hard it is to see what is going and what is coming! Ten years hence some arts and crafts now held in high esteem will be as thoroughly extinct as the art of casting out devils and laying spells. Our present would-be legal system, the most evil jumble of all things American, will probably undergo drastic changes; likewise our political order, and no small part of our factory and store systems.

Each such change will force thousands of men to unlearn much and to learn strange novelties.

The Three Hardy Perennials.

It is not my present business to advise you what to learn. You must settle that problem for yourself. But may I not point to a general policy that strikes me as wise? The hardy perennials in the garden of knowledge will never be scathed by the swift alterations of the American scene. They depend on neither place nor time. They are geography, psychology, and mathematics, each in its broadest scope. Do not think of these in terms of the textbooks bearing their names. Most of those books give but a faint notion of their subjects; what more could they give, being adapted to the needs of young people?

Why do I pick this trio? It is the foundation of every genuine civilization. It is the basis of all progress and justice, of all health and happiness. Look at the human race as a whole; what is its situation, what are its problems, and how must it solve these? Man, a featherless biped, inhabits the surface of a tiny sphere which spins around one of the tiniest stars in the visible universe. His entire life is spent within one mile of the layer of dirt whence comes all his food. To this layer he is indissolubly bound. He must master its every peculiarity in order to be nourished, sheltered, clothed, and kept safe against beasts, insects, and pestilence.

He must also get along with himself and his fellows. This compels him to learn all he can about human nature at large and human nature in its individual manifestations, which are the ultimate psychic reality. On such an understanding, all group life, from the smallest family up to the League of Nations, must depend; and so too all institutions of social control, notably the law.

Finally, man must discover, in and through the horde of facts he observes about the world, all the individual prin-

ciples and interrelations. He must generalize, so that he
may compute. He must mark tendencies so that he may
forecast and foreguard. He must note causes and effects.
He must draw unmistakable inferences. This is the life of
reason. Its way of living is mathematical.

Geography.

Geography, in its fullness, embraces the entire science of
the earth on which we live; and, as we have good reason to
believe that, first, the earth will endure for considerable
years to come, and, secondly, we will have to spend most
of our lives on the surface of said earth, tilling the soil for
food and delving under the loams for ore, we cannot learn
too much about it. It is our entire physical environment,
the astrologers to the contrary notwithstanding.

Learn about the World, above All.

It is no longer necessary to exhort Americans to learn
about the world they live in; but it was, down to the days
of the World War. The younger generation has nearly as
keen an interest in knowing all the bypaths and sea lanes
of the globes as the intelligent young German and Briton.
Yet there is amazing ignorance abroad even now. Every
month or two I am shocked. Here's a recent upset.

I was talking over the Near Eastern situation with the
Sunday feature editor of a New York newspaper. Eventually we came to the Zionists and their clashes with the
Arabs. And this editor, whether you believe it or not, said
that he thought the Zionists ought to get out of Africa and
stay out. It took me some time and even more diplomacy
to break the news to him that Palestine was not in Africa.

A Columbia professor recently recounted his experience
in a Pennsylvania high school, where he was investigating
the fitness of certain courses for college preparatory work.
He observed signs of elementary ignorance, so gave a test

in the geography of the United States. An outline map with no names was distributed, and the students called upon to write in the names of the states, the largest cities, and a few major lakes and rivers. What chaos ensued! One youth placed New York City near Omaha. A girl placed California where Florida lies. The Mississippi ran all over the map; sometimes pouring into the Arctic, sometimes joining the St. Lawrence. Philadelphia was usually located within a hundred miles of its proper site; but there the ability of the high school students faded out.

How can a country peopled with such ignoramuses act successfully in international affairs? Is not our idiotic history in foreign relations in considerable measure the result of the ordinary citizen's blank mind in matters geographic? I am sure it is. And the rising generation shows its appreciation of the dangers of such ignorance by reading more than its parents ever did about the world at large. But it still has far to go, before it can equal the Germans or the upper-class British. In all the world they alone come close to knowing the sort of place the human race inhabits. And, in a fair competition for world trade or political influence, they can outstrip us.

Whoever wishes my opinion, then, as to geography will get strong words. Were I an educational despot, I'd command every American, young and old, who hasn't mastered the subject to work straight through the fascinating course which that distinguished geographer, J. Russell Smith, has prepared especially for this book. You will find it on page 375. It begins with the things which any boy who has only ten dollars or so to spend in the course of a year can buy and use; and it carries you up to the things which would best serve an adult who is able to spend much money for books and equipment. Nine-tenths of the material outlined is as entertaining as the best novel, if not more so.

Man Still Knows Little about His World.

The need of creative learning in geography is, in some respects, greater than ever before. As the world's population grows far up into the billions, room must be found for the crowded herd. There is still an immense pioneer fringe. Since the World War, hungry, homeless men have pressed on far into the north of Canada, in search of wheat lands. The Peace River district, away up alongside of Alaska, has been brought under the plough within the past decade. Down in Africa, the bread line batters its way into Rhodesia, driving out the animals and the black men, in the eternal quest for cheap farms. Nearly a million Chinese push northward into Manchuria and Mongolia every year, under the lash of famine. What can such pioneer countries yield? How should they be developed? Only long and careful study of their soils, locations, climates, and peoples will ever answer that question.

Again, the realm of the totally unknown remains far vaster than the schoolboy fancies. An area more than double the size of the United States has never been seen, much less studied, by any white man. In Arabia alone there are 400,000 square miles into which no Western explorer has ever penetrated. Both Americas are dotted with untracked spots; and, of course, the polar regions are hardly scratched as yet, but already we know enough about them to be convinced that they hold the secret of our own climate and farm prosperity. The next generation will see many keen minds at work on the part which Greenland and Antarctica play in filling the waters of the temperate zones with icebergs, in chilling the air, in giving direction to rains, and in influencing the rainfall of almost every land where the white man dwells, from raw Tasmania to the bleak fjords of Norway. Do you realize that we are living near the close of a great ice age? Do you know that, behind all the interplay of petty politics and the scheming of would-be big business, the winds and waters of the two polar regions influence this human race a hundredfold more powerfully than all governments, all philosophies, all religions, and all industrialists combined? If you doubt that, study geography for five years; then come back to this assertion!

Psychology.

Were these lines addressed to scientists alone, I should now speak, not of psychology, but of anthropology. For that is the most comprehensive word we have to describe the science of human nature. Strictly, the things the psychologist studies form only one grand division of anthropology; but as this fact is not commonly recognized, and as the anthropologists themselves incline to regard their own science as a study of social institutions, folkways, and language, it is better for us to stick to common usage here. Nevertheless, I would insist that the learner who aims to comprehend the broadest and deepest trends of mankind must study mankind in every major phase; and one of these phases, if not several, will be found in anthropology.

Psychology, in its usual sense and scope, hardly needs a press agent. It has been perhaps over-exploited of late, particularly by amateurs and promoters. Since the World War, men have seen a new light about this science. They are all suffering under a conviction of sin, the sin of ignorance about human nature. They suffer, too, under the feeling of the colossal practical importance of a deep understanding of human nature. Then too, they feel toward it as the earth: it is a fairly permanent affair, relatively absolute, as a paradoxologist might say. Man must deal with man as long as earth and race endure. Hence the art of learning about man abides as an immutable imperative.

Personal Psychology the Urgent Need.

Like geography, psychology embraces much more than you might gather from elementary textbooks. The subjects omitted from the latter are, indeed, of the highest practical value. Above all we must rate the study of personalities, for they are the living things with which we must deal. Ignorance here underlies misunderstandings, brutalities, and perverse policies everywhere else.

You may know by heart every rule of the game of poker and still be a poor player, because you fail to reckon with the personal methods and manners of your opponents. You may master etiquette, with its pat lines, bows, scrapings, gestures, and manipulation of knife, fork, and spoon, and yet make a poor impression on people you meet in society because you have never understood personal peculiarities and the way to deal with them.

You may study law until you know it by heart, from Blackstone to the Eighteenth Amendment, and yet never win an important case because you have not grasped the simple fact that cases are decided, not by Blackstone or by the Constitution, but by bipeds on the bench and bipeds in the jury box; each biped unlike all others in some respect which may prove decisive for you.

You may become the world's champion in the theory of government and may write the biggest and best tome on political science, yet go to Washington and help pass laws which nobody will obey—and all because you have never studied people closely enough to learn that, when all is said and done, you control the public only by controlling individuals, and individuals are controlled from within, never from without.

You may seek to remedy these defects in your upbringing by studying general biology and psychology. You may commit to memory William James and John Dewey. But when your head is packed with their facts, you may go right on blundering, just because what you have to deal with from day to day is not human nature but personalities. In all your walks and talks you will never meet human nature; you will meet only John Smith, the sauerkraut manufacturer from Flatbush, Susie Gall, the confectionery clerk, Dr. Dope, the specialist in children's diseases, and so on straight through the telephone directory.

The twentieth century is rediscovering the truth of all this, which Socrates clearly saw, and, in well-meant over-enthusiasm, exaggerated. The next generation will probably learn more about personality than the past thousand have, just as our generation has surpassed all predecessors in its study of geography and mathematics.

Mathematics.

As for mathematics, is it not the very cornerstone of our entire industrialism? Only the ill informed fail to perceive it as such. Just as psychology is the basis of self-control and social control, so is mathematics the basis of all thorough mastery of the physical environment. Our world, as now being fashioned anew, is shaped almost entirely by engineers. If you doubt that, prove it to yourself by writing off-hand a list of the hundred most important achievements of our age. Then check back on each. Fully eight out of every ten will prove to have arisen in the mind of some kind of engineer—or an untrained inventor who thinks in engineering terms. All these engineers reach their results mainly through mathematical computations, even though they do not think mathematically in the early stages of invention. In your home, at this very minute, the electric sweeper, the ice box, the linoleum on the floor, the paint on the walls, the water in the pipes, the cement on the cellar floor, the window glass, and the bricks in the walls are all the fruits of applied mathematics.

Our Civilization the First Based on Mathematics.

For at least 20,000 years civilizations and cultures have sprouted and withered to a dry shell of tradition. A thousand

and one adversities overtook them; but, underneath all of these, we find the common cause of disaster in man's inability to calculate. For it is calculation alone which enables us to overcome poverty, bad business, drought, and pestilence. In all the world there is not a science nor a technique of managing men or things which does not rest upon some kind of counting, multiplying, dividing, and classifying; but, until recent times, nobody had hit upon a system of numbers and numeration that could be used even for multiplying large numbers.

Did you know that the grossly overrated Athenians never achieved anything in any science, still less in engineering, mainly because they did not conceive of indicating numbers by positions along a line as we do? When our schoolboys learn that the number one may be used to stand for unity, ten, a hundred, a thousand, and so on, according to its position to the left of the decimal point, they thereby come into possession of a priceless heritage which Aristotle himself never enjoyed. No! Nor even that mathematical genius, Archimedes!

The result? Well, any eighth-grade boy today performs with utmost ease calculations which Pericles and all his galaxy could not have performed in ten years of brain-racking! No, not even if they had chanced upon positional values in numeration; for, by some freak of fate, the Greeks were still more incompetent in their mathematical thinking. They never could conceive of zero, in our modern sense as a symbol for nothing. Imagine their woes, then, in struggling to calculate without it! Some of our best mathematicians today regard such a task as almost impossible.

Our own great era could never have gained headway, had not an unknown Hindu and an unknown Arab found the art of positional symbolizing and the zero concept. It was in the thirteenth century that zero reached Europe. And by a wild coincidence—or was it something more?—that century was the turning point of Western civilization; the ancient barbarian culture and religion came to its peak then, and quickly lost ground. It had outlived its usefulness, for men could now calculate. And when they do, farewell to augurs, priests, soothsayers, astrologers, metaphysicians, and bad guessers!

As late as the fifteenth century, it is said, men had to travel from northern Europe to Italy in order to learn how to multiply. Is it to be wondered at that, since that time, as learning about mathematics has spread ever more widely, the Western World has leaped ahead of all other civilizations at lightning speed? Or that it is now progressing in its sciences and techniques faster than the keenest minds can trail it?

The man who knows not mathematics today is little brother to the cave man. He doesn't belong in our age. There isn't a single important modern business, science, or technique that is not firmly founded on mathematics. That's the greatest difference between our age and all preceding half-cultures.

All Knowledge of Human Nature Is Mathematical.

To what extent do you know yourself? Only in so far as you can observe correlation between some type of behavior and some causal factor or some concomitant variation in a sensation, feeling, attitude, or bodily condition of health or a necessary external condition of the behavior. Have you discovered that whenever you begin hard work less than thirty minutes after eating, you get a headache within two hours? That is the beginning of solid self-understanding. Could you extend this to the point of discovering the correlations, if any, between the time interval between eating and working and the ensuing circulation of the blood, you would therewith establish a psychological law of the highest importance. And its form would be mathematical. And no other form would yield true knowledge. At best you might get some vague feel of tendencies.

Two Modern Prophets.

I might tell stories about a hundred scientists who, by the skillful use of mathematics, have made predictions far more precise than ever old Isaiah dared, and have seen their forecasts come true. Lacking space here for such an epic, I must tell you one short and simple tale.

Suppose I were to give you the U. S. Census returns of 1920, now more than ten years out of date, and were to ask you to predict from these (and whatever else you happen to know) how many people will be living in our country in 1940. That would be a pretty stiff assignment, wouldn't it? And yet Raymond Pearl and Lowell Reed, both of Johns Hopkins, did the same thing and, thanks to mathematical knowledge, foretold events more accurately than any religious prophet.

In 1920, before the new census figures were published, these men took the 1910 Census returns and calculated probable changes year by year up to 1930. They found that in 1930 there would probably be 122.4 millions of American population. Ten years later, the U. S. Census counts heads and finds 122.7 millions!

But this feat is being matched over and over by statisticians in great corporations, such as the American Telephone & Telegraph Company. These mathematically-minded experts regularly predict changes in business within 2 per cent of complete accuracy, over long stretches of time. And nobody but masters of the laws of number ever do such amazing things. All others are just bad guessers.

All Knowledge of Events Is Mathematical.

Who knows the tides? Only he who grasps the sequences of high and low water in relation to sun and moon, to shore line and shift of winds, to ocean depths and whatever other factors influence the heave and settling of the seas. Who knows business? Only he who has discovered the relations between available supplies and current demands for commodities, the relations between earning power and buying power, the relations between human character and sound credits, and the relations between rates of producing goods and the rate at which people use these goods up. (This is why there are few business men of deep insight in all the world today; the intricacies of these relations exceed most men's grasp.)

So in every department of life. So with every learner. And the art of learning will avail you not at all unless you come to it with a mind attuned to ratios, proportions, sequences, groupings, masses, causes, and effects. I am not haranguing you to plunge into geometry and calculus, for few can advance into those ethereal dominions of high intellect. But there are many modes of mathematical observation of analysis much easier and not a whit less useful. For example, a host of important phenomena in psychology, business, finance, and engineering can be understood in terms of fairly simple arithmetic and algebra. Consider how many inquiries of the highest human value can be conducted with no mathesis more complicated than elementary statistics. Probably six out of every ten adults who have been able to graduate from good high schools can master such statistical principles and methods with no mental strain whatsoever. And that's quite a crowd—more than will ever dip into these pages!

Conquer the Fundamentals First!

All these remarks serve only to assist mature learners (of any age whatever) who are perplexed over the direction in which they can most advantageously study. When in doubt, seek the fundamentals. Be not content with frills. Spurn the kickshaws of pedantry. Always keep in mind that the mightiest achievements of the next hundred years will not occur in the domains of art, religion, philosophy, and the like, but in two and only two fields. One is the control of the physical environments, probably through the medium of advanced chemistry and physics. The other is the control of human nature, certainly through stupendous advances in mental hygiene, educational technique, and physiological chemistry—the latter by all odds most clearly predestined to accomplish miracles now past all mortal credulity. So why not learn the substances of things hoped for? Why not study the soul of the "great tomorrow?"

After all, whatever you may learn today you cannot use until tomorrow.

So much for facts, but there are many things besides facts which we must learn!

Learning Facts, Habits and Attitudes.

A man can learn three sorts of things: facts, habits, and attitudes. Facts must come first, for nobody can decide which habits and attitudes are sound unless he first gains some insight into the world, its principles, and its drift. Schools have, for untold centuries, concentrated chiefly upon fact teaching—and rightly! For men shape their habits, by and large, as adaptations to the world as they understand it. Knowledge is not virtue, as Socrates supposed; but it leads to a vast deal of virtuous behavior, just as a result of men's desire to get along. As for attitudes, it is still something of a problem as to how they can and should be taught.

The art of learning, then, may be subdivided in another dimension. There is the special art of learning facts, the art of learning habits, and the art of learning attitudes. Each art calls for its own peculiar method. A peculiar approach, a peculiar analysis, and a peculiar mode of practice. We must keep these clearly apart as we proceed.

We allot most space here to knowledge and attitudes solely because most readers of the book are interested chiefly in those arts. Do not infer from this that we belittle the learning of habits! Far from it! This will receive attention too, even though less than it deserves.

Many Arts, Many Ways of Learning.

The art of learning varies with the thing to be learned. There is one way of learning a language, and there is another way of learning how to handle a large telescope. The art is always conditioned by the things to be mastered. We might say, then, that there are almost as many arts of learning as there are things to be learned. But in practice we can group together under one class those which resemble one another in some striking way.

These resemblances are mostly of two kinds; first, in the material to be learned; and secondly, in the human activities invoked to deal with the material while learning it. Thus, learning Latin is very much like learning Greek, for both the substance of the languages and the learner's mental efforts to master them are pretty much alike. But learning Chinese is not at all like learning Latin, and no amount of practice in mastering Latin and cognate languages will help much in getting a firm grip upon those strange celestial pictographs. Again, to learn any language up to the point of being able to read it in its literary forms is one matter; and to learn to speak it in its colloquial is quite another. Distinct functions of speech, as well as of imagery, are called into play by the vernacular. A man may master the written form without ever being able to make much headway with the spoken form.

Transferring Skills in Learning.

Skill in one grand division of learning can be transferred to another only in so far as the things to be done in the two fields resemble each other. A man can master the Spanish language without thereby aiding himself to learn shorthand. This point has been frequently observed by educational psychologists in so far as it bears on school subjects. Now we must apply it to the larger arts of learning. What it means here we see exemplified in the lives of people around us every day. It means that a man can master the art of learning mathematics without thereby making an inch of progress in the art of learning self-control. Another can acquire new dexterities at an extraordinary rate and yet be a dolt in learning the simplest social relations.

Life makes profoundly different demands upon us. It presents us with a myriad diverse things to handle. So far as I can see, there are no common factors in these things— no essential resemblances. If they exist, it is somewhere beyond the range of the ordinary eye and mind. Hence for all practical purposes life falls into many different arts of learning, just as living itself is a collection of arts and not one art.

This forces me to break the ensuing study up into grand divisions.

The Two Major Arts of Learning: Learning the Old and Learning the New.

Every man learns in two ways. He picks up facts and principles and practices, first of all, by seeing, hearing, smelling, tasting, touching, manipulating, and contemplating. That is the way of direct experience. And we all agree that experience is the best teacher, albeit often the cruellest. Then again, man learns indirectly from his first hour of understanding. His mother tells him tales and issues warnings. His brothers and sisters convey messages to him. Older children reveal secrets of sex and society. Teachers give him books to absorb in which, translated into funny black marks, the things learned by generations long since vanished are precipitated in a thick sediment of lore.

It is ironic that, thanks to the press agents of the schools, the human race has been tricked into the belief that a man who learns certain things through these indirect channels is "educated" while one who has learned only by direct experience is "uneducated." I suspect that this absurdity has caused a vast deal of snobbery, of degree-hunting, of heartaches, and of perpetuated pedantry. And we all know of a certainty that it has skewed the perspective of millions of people in matters of learning. Book lore has been overrated, first-hand experience underesteemed—and the ancient warfare between the self-taught and the school-bred goes merrily onward.

When peace comes, both belligerents must concede much. The way of wisdom follows neither path alone. Just as we shall soon see in the case of intensive and extensive learning methods, so here: each technique and approach makes its own inalienable contribution to the larger art of learning. The master of the art learns wherever he can and however: the babble of fools may disclose wisdom to the wise, and the public library may add a flood to the ocean of his knowledge. There is no single direction of seeking; the road to truth runs east, west, north, south, up, and down. It also runs inside and outside, but I won't try to make that mystery clear just now.

Now, these two grand divisions of the art of learning embrace different sorts of things, and each leads to its own constellation of special techniques. You soon find that some things cannot be acquired through books, while others can be picked up effectively in no other way. Fully nine out of ten subjects, however, must be analyzed into their elements, and some of the latter learned directly while others are picked up indirectly, and, if my own experience is typical, as I believe it to be, the final art in each special case generally embodies a wide variety of learning methods. Now and then, you find an exception; to learn merely to speak a language, for example, you may effectively follow only one method, that of talking and listening to natives. But such subjects are rare.

Which method is best? The answer must come from the subject, first and foremost, and then from you, your interest, and your previous experience and special training. Books dealing with such problems usually address themselves to school teachers and their pupils. Educational psychologists have inevitably concentrated upon the child and his needs. The adult and the well trained mind find little in print to aid them in extending their learning to new fields. The finest techniques of teaching and learning appear in kindergarten and the elementary schools; next to that in the grammar grades. The matter covered in high school and college, being more complex, is harder to subjugate and also less well stabilized. So much of it is new, as compared to the three R's, and some of it changes every few years.

I mention all this mainly to put the learner on his guard against the pleasant supposition that he can acquire the latest, most intricate truths as easily as French grammar. Ancient subjects are easy. New topics require independent observations, original reflecting, experimental analyses— in a word, genuine scientific thinking. Memory and contemplation are required, above all, in learning the old, while fantasy, curiosity, ingenuity in inventing tests, and a singular open-mindedness must serve him who treads untrodden ways. He who studies old culture has a much easier time of it than he who faces the novel and the unknown.

Like every good textbook, this one must attack the problem of learning from its easiest angles first, and then advance cautiously into the thick of the fray. So we start with the techniques of learning old, well-organized matters.

There's No End to Learning.

The sea of knowledge is a big one; but it is only a small arm of the ocean of facts which booms forever just beyond the reefs that now hem in man, the learner. How big is the sea? Well, my morning paper tells me that in Chicago they offer courses to adults which, if taken by any one omnivorous learner, would keep him continuously busy for considerably longer than 250 years. Discouraging, isn't it? Especially when you think that home study and adult education courses cannot constitute more than a chemical trace of the present reservoir of human knowledge that can be tapped at any moment.

Later we are going to look at those gulfs and bays in the sea of truth which seem to lead mankind on to new worlds, and then you will glimpse a fresh vista of their endlessness.

BOOK II
YOU

YOU

The Will to Learn.

The will to learn is the beginning of all skill and knowledge. Do you truly want to conquer an art? If not, all the professors and libraries on earth cannot help you. The urge to acquire facts must come from within you.

It's Up to You.

You can lead a horse to water, but you can't make him drink. You can lead a man to school books, but you cannot make him think.

The best teacher in the world is, in the final show-down, at the mercy of his pupils. Unless they are disposed to learn what he offers them, he can teach them nothing. And a book like this one is worse off than a teacher; for it cannot even submit its advice and suggestions until after it has been bought (or borrowed).

It is futile to read these pages, if you lack a burning desire to learn something. I cannot inflame you. (Or, if I could, it would not be by way of literature.) And I shall not argue that you ought to have such a noble aspiration. Possibly you shouldn't. The world is full of people who would gain little by learning much. And they are by no means all knaves and fools. Many brilliant artists, in my opinion, serve themselves and the public best if they concentrate on self-expression. Study, especially when it deals with matters apart from the technique of self-expression, may easily benumb them or lead them into confusions which thwart their artistic impulses.

53

No! You must sincerely crave to master something before any printed word about learning can benefit you. And the more definite your wish, the less we can tell you, in a small book like this, of the best details of technique. We must stick to the broader principles here, for many men with many aspirations must be equally served. Would you learn calculus? There are some important matters about that which we cannot even mention here. Are you a physician eager to learn a specialty so that you can escape general practice? Again much of that art exceeds us; and thus with every other individual case.

Why Learn?

Why learn?

Ask yourself the question, before you launch upon a costly and arduous program.

For Practical Reasons?

Is it for strictly practical reasons? Do you seek a good job? Would you please your employer? Or, having a good job, do you aspire to a better one? Or, having as good a job as you wish, do you wish to improve your economic condition by saving more money, by investing what you save better, and by protecting yourself against possible illness and misfortunes?

If any of these interests move you, you should learn such things as:

1. A trade, craft, art, business, or profession.
2. Special efficiency methods in one of these lines which you have first mastered.
3. Methods of thrift and investment, as well as the intricate technique of insurance, so far as it affects you in your job and in your investments.

Or Social Reasons?

Perhaps nothing like this stirs you to study. You may be interested in improving your social status. This sometimes includes the art of improving your cultural background too. You may wish to get along with people better; or to be accepted socially by some who now do not know you or, knowing you, bar you from their circles. Or you may even have a keen desire to enjoy social affairs as a pastime, and, to that end, aim to cultivate acquaintances.

To attain such ends, you probably will study such things as:

1. Personal hygiene, which is of vast importance in social contacts.
2. Personal cosmetics, not in the narrow and rather dirty sense of bedaubing the face like a savage, but the fine, large Greek sense of personal orderliness, neatness, system, and presentability.
3. The psychology of personality, from the point of view of your own self-culture.
4. The art of conversation, which is not, as men so glibly say, a "lost art" but rather one which has never yet been found.
5. Some important forms of social play, perhaps card games such as bridge or outdoor games like golf.
6. Some serious social activities such as community welfare work, a charity, or politics.

Or for Fun?

These may fail to intrigue you. You may seek rather the richest possible development of your own private personality, not your social one. You may prefer to spend time and money upon some artistic urge or an intellectual one or, at the lowest level, an esthetic pursuit. And now you must learn such things as:

1. The art which specially appeals to you as a medium of self-expression, be it sculpture, poetry, painting, or fiction.
2. The science, history, language, philosophy, or other subject which appeals to your intellect most keenly.
3. The art of appreciation, in music, in travel, or in whatever else you set out to enjoy, as an esthete.
4. Some special technique within the arts and sciences just alluded to.
5. General information of an entertaining or illuminating sort.

Or as a Therapy?

A last category of motives remains. It is hard to characterize it, for it embraces remedial urges and the familiar

motives of escape. Perhaps your chief desire is to escape
a horrible boredom. Perhaps you would escape loneliness,
or some bitter experience. You may be a brooding introvert,
addicted to introspection and endless self-reproaches and
self-fears, and some psychiatrist has advised you strongly
to find a new interest outside of yourself. Or, finally, you
may tend to overdo some good activity at present and need
a counterbalance. You may be a too enthusiastic lawyer,
spending whole evenings at home reading cases, with the
result that you lose social contacts, make enemies, and
even get out of stride with the workaday world. You, no
less than the introvert, must have other interests which
widen your activities. Plainly, you must find something to
learn in the long list we have already mentioned.

There is a certain large sanity in the search for outside
interests which help you to forget yourself. The happiest
of all learners are probably those who go lost in their
favorite research.

Learning to Enjoy Things.

"What America needs," says a distinguished Frenchman,
"is more loafers and dreamers, if she is to be saved from
herself." Dr. David Riesman, of the University of Pennsylvania, who cited this line in a recent address at Yale,
supplemented it thus:

Supertension is a disease that has invaded the whole body politic of
American life and has its reflection in the tension under which every
American exists . . . Of the treatment for supertension in the mass,
a remedy may be found in time. Remedies in the offing are a different
standard, different ideals, a striving for contentment and a lessening
of competition in the chase for riches, the cultivating of a spirit of leisure,
making the luncheon hour in private and public a real rest hour, and
finally making sport not a passion conditioned on a desire to win but a
recreation pure and simple.

High blood pressure accompanies a low outlook on life
and happiness all too frequently. Our more intelligent

classes have accepted this truth wholeheartedly. This is why you seldom find a highly intelligent person among the parvenus. "Get rich quick" and "get wise slow" are twins.

Degrading an Art to a Religion.

What a singular perversion crops up in us Americans on the slightest provocation! We start something for fun, fling ourselves into it excitedly, and, first thing we know, we are taking it as seriously as the Panama Canal. Soon after, we become fanatics over it and fight bloody battles. Then all fun is gone, and only a pack of fools lingers on the scene, all sweaty and bruised.

Thus has it gone with golf, which of old was a gentlemen's amusement, but has become, thanks to our national perversion, a vulgar semi-religion full of professionalism and cheating. As Thomas Uzzell, himself an excellent player, recently confessed in *The North American Review*, he abandoned the game in disgust because it bred a bad spirit in himself and in many of the ex-gentlemen with whom he played. Not that we have not in our midst some people who preserve the wholesome fun of the game, but the trend is away from it. It has been the average business man, with his cheap standards of competition, who has fouled the green. To the befouling he has added a dash of pure poison by using the fairway as a place to sell his partner two crates of ladies' near-silk chemises.

Even men who perceive the stupidity of degrading fun to mere business and art to a fanaticism slip into the error while they plead. A sad spectacle of this sort is Murdock Pemberton, whose sprightly work on painting, called "Picture Book," starts out nobly and then changes its point of view almost imperceptibly.

Pemberton has the grandest idea ever: he believes that art is fun, that we should all dabble in it as a heavenly kind of play, and that the art of painting in particular is singularly well adapted to the spiritual needs of the man who seeks personal recreation. Among other advantages, painting can be carried on without fuss or ceremony or elaborate equipment.

"It's hard work and a lot of trouble to get to a golf course or to a place where you can ride a horse," says he. "You don't have to change your clothes, to paint a picture; and, until you try it, it's difficult to realize how much enjoyment there is in it."

Well said! And more power to your proselyting, sir, but why, oh why, didn't you stop right there?

Our enthusiast, quite unawares, undergoes a sad sea change between commas. Having most convincingly shown that many people could get much fun out of canvas, brushes, and paint tubes, Pemberton waxes serious, fanatical, and Rotarian. He argues that we ought to teach the public to appreciate the old masters; that there should be a government department to diffuse information and advice about painting in oils, so that any amateur might get free inspiration and cut rates on carmines. He wants an official statistician to gather facts about art and driers, said figures to be duly graphed and published.

Just a little further, good sir, and you will be asking that Congress enact a law compelling all youths between sixteen and twenty to work five hours a week in oils, and then the degradation of art into a State religion will be complete.

Never Take Any Play Seriously.

A few years ago a famous football coach in a large midwestern university signed an article in *Collier's Weekly* which argued that "any man who is a good loser in any sport is no good at all." And he proceeded to prove his point with grim earnestness by showing, among other things, that no game is worth playing unless the contestants do their utmost to win.

Probably some readers were taken in by this imbecility; and the alleged educational institution which pays the coach more than any of its professors must believe at least that his point of view is harmless, even though not wholly supportable. But those who study the problems of play understand that this grim earnestness is the last and lowest level of degeneration. It has corrupted American college sports. It has, as honest and penetrating sports writers like John Tunis have repeatedly shown, turned the Olympic games into dirty fraudulent enterprises.

No gentleman would allow a son of his to join a college football team ruled by a coach who practiced such a preachment. (Of course, few gentlemen's sons ever show the faintest interest in college football.) Only an ignorant father would encourage a son to attend a so-called school tolerating athletics which reek of the prize ring and professional baseball. Because of the degradation of a grand old game to a mere effort to win, football has lost its hold on undergraduates in all the good colleges. At Harvard the football team is a joke, and old graduates wail over the sad change. If only they could realize that the civilized world has moved on to better things!

The Cult of "Get Wise Quick."

Americans, eager to learn, allow their eagerness to conspire with our national zeal for instantaneous action and thereby prevent that calm and thoroughness on which the art of learning is founded. Will you believe me when I tell you that adults have come to my office asking me to teach them the art of writing in two or three months? And they were not fools. Every college swarms with impatient youths who sneer at the slow ways of study and chafe to zip through four years of work in as many months. We all seek short cuts. An excellent ambition, no doubt! And one, too, which can often be realized. But it has limits. And nowhere do they appear more clearly than in the domain of serious studies.

At bottom, the craving to "get wise quick" causes trouble by leading the sufferer to dabble at many things briefly. Instead of doing one thing at a time, and that well, the American youth—and his mother even more absurdly than he—goes in for golf, tennis, the history of religion, current fiction, aviation, radio, and heaven knows what not. He lacks time, if not energy, to master half of what he undertakes. So he reaches manhood half-baked.

Those "culture clubs" which move Europeans to rude laughter when they travel up and down our land represent this tendency at its silliest. They are infested with social climbers who seek to become intellectual climbers, because it is regarded as smart to be well informed. Women flock to the Thursday morning meetings, to listen to a well paid young lady who outlines the latest novels and plays, chats about their authors, and quotes the remarks of the newspaper critics concerning the works. The party then adjourns for bridge or golf. The only use to which these benighted women can put this shoddy veneer of culture is table chatter. When Dad brings home the new floorwalker to dinner, Ma can gas profoundly about Walpole's latest book and the trend in interior decoration in Poland. The floorwalker is impressed. It's all five-and-ten to him.

Now, the ghastly truth about all this is that, BY SPENDING ONLY A LITTLE MORE TIME AND BY APPLYING THE ART OF LEARNING WITH RIGOR, MOST OF THESE GET-WISE-QUICK DUPES COULD ACQUIRE SOLID AND ENDURING COMPREHENSION OF MANY SUBJECTS.

The Opposite Extreme: "Culture" in Its Bad Sense.

Among some serious Americans we find the complete opposite of this get-wise-quick tendency. It is, I suspect, a natural reaction against hurry and bustle and shallow dabbling. As such we may praise it. But unfortunately it usually trends toward learning nothing but old things which people of the past esteemed highly; toward buying paintings by the old masters and ancient pottery and rare books; toward the worship of ideas and the pursuit of practices in favor centuries ago. Among the rich, the same impulse bursts forth in the building of perfect copies of French chateaux in Westchester County and imitations of the Alhambra in Los Angeles. Among those of scholarly mind it expresses itself in the adoration of the Greek and Roman classics, in the minute study and interminable mooning over ancient poets, statesmen, and philosophers, always with profound conviction that these said and did the last, the truest, and the best thing. American buildings seem atrocious to such culture worshippers. The future can never equal the golden age of long ago.

This Culture Is the Noblest Infantilism.

It is hard to speak fairly of such culture. For the spirit of it, as understood by the people of the Old World, clashes with our own. And never can the American be reconciled with it. Perhaps I can make this clearest by a ponderous exegesis of those wonderful lines which Thomas Hardy wrote when he was invited to visit the United States.

> I shrink to seek a modern coast
> Whose riper times have yet to be;
> Where the new regions claim them free
> From that long drip of human tears
> Which people old in tragedy
> Have left upon the centuried years.

Now, why should that Old World philosopher-artist dread a new land thus? He implies the answer in the next lines:

> For, wonning in these ancient lands,
> Enchased and lettered as a tomb,
> And scored with print of perished hands

And chronicled with dates of doom,
Though my own Being bear no bloom
I trace the lives such scenes enshrine,
Give past exemplars present room,
And their experience count as mine.

In a word, Hardy lives in a dead past. And so does very-body else who preserves in himself the cultures of ancient Europe. How did that dead past come to him? What gives it such power over him? Only the fact that, as a little child, he beheld ruined castles, the shattered veterans of foreign wars, the great slabs of Roman roads beneath the village pave, hilltops whereon the Druids held their rites, and the wind-tortured seas over which a Spanish fool once sent his Armada. Feeding on the memories of barbarism from which the living horror has long since been extracted in the wine press of Time, the child tastes only beauty. He falls in love with the past and comes to count its experiences as his own. Its life becomes his.

As men so often conceive it, this is the essence of culture. It is the learning of the cult. The cult is whatever has been assiduously cultivated and institutionalized. The school is the chief center of perpetuating cults, and next to the school ranks the church. The moral standards and practices of good men long dead are there inculcated. So are doctrines about the State, the government, patriotism, art, and philosophy. When they were first evolved, those doctrines may have been the best. But times have changed, and man's insight has deepened greatly since then.

The man of culture, in this sense, is a beautifully pre-served child, when at his best. He thinks it is nobler to look at the big paintings of Rubens in the Louvre than to admire Winslow Homer or Rockwell Kent. He extols the scenery of Italy less for its intrinsic charm than for its reverberations of antiquity. He revels in old pottery, not for the sake of its color and lines but simply because it came from

Pompeii or Nineveh. He spends devout hours in a shabby old cathedral whose architecture is as awful as the Balaban and Katz motion picture houses, his eye blind to the monstrosities of sculpture and painting while his mind dreams worshipfully of the traditions embalmed in those same hideous statues and murals.

Because he does not live in the present, he delights in revery; for in revery his memory pictures flash most color-fully. His revery, moveover, is not creative. It does not say to him: "Well, where do we go from here?"—and then open up new roads of high adventure. Rather does it resound with echoes of footsteps, chant, and war cry of heroes doomed and done for.

Like Thomas Hardy, such a man of culture strives to make the experience of those heroes his own. But it simply cannot be done. He is like the Englishmen, twitted so neatly by the good Abbé Dimnet, who, "having trimmed their beards so as to look like Edward VII or George V, have never been themselves afterward." No man can make the experience of previous generations his own, except by reduc-ing himself to a living corpse. He may remain tolerably alive from the ears down, but he has committed suicide from the ears up. To adopt the thoughts and attitudes of the great thirteenth century in a world such as ours is as hopeless an enterprise as it would be if you and I were to try to adopt the outlook, the beliefs, and the daily practices of the men of the thirtieth century.

Culture of this antiquated breed stimulates reminiscent imagery but, in the same measure, paralyzes genuine learn-ing and thinking. Those who grow up under the spell of such become like the Bourbons, of whom it was said that "they never learn and they never forget." Having made ancient experience their own, as best they could, they have blinded themselves to their own day and place. So long as the spell remains unbroken, its victims contribute nothing to their own lives or to those of their fellows. They are the little brothers of the lotus eaters.

Get Ancient Culture Early, Then Get Over It!

Some gentle soul has probably wept over these cruel words. Does the art of learning as conceived by us Americans of the new age demand that we foreswear ancient history, the classics, love of country, and the enjoyment of old monuments? Are we shut of the Louvre that we may better live in the present? Is this a barbaric régime under whose sway the rising generation falls?

It is not easy to reply to such questions, without wandering far afield. (And heaven knows that I feel like an intellectual nomad already.) Perhaps the short cut lies through a curt summary of my view. The American learner of today is not advised to turn his back on all ancient things. He couldn't succeed at that if he tried, and it is much better that he face them and learn them with eyes to the front.

So, say I, let him learn the antiquities as early as possible, and with as much joy as he can squeeze from them. Let him learn them along with "Mother Goose" (which they largely resemble) and with Grimm's "Fairy Tales." Let him be taught their values and lack of such in the modern perspective. Let him learn to sense and appraise the economic and institutional forces behind great wars, migrations, invasions, and the slow decay of empire. Don't teach him merely the glory that was Rome's. Teach him rather the magnificent barbarism of those days and the inevitable collapse through ignorance, stupidity, superstition, folly, fraud, and—over and behind all these—the unseen changes of climate, the encroaching deserts, the havoc wrought upon greenery by goat and camels, erosion, pestilence, and the lesser blights.

Above all, be sure that he learns that, however useful the spirit and policy of Rome may have been at a certain

stage in the upwarding of barbarism, the time came when
mankind was ready to move further forward; and then
every force within the Empire arrayed itself against that
advance. Rome had to disappear utterly ere a real civilization in our modern sense could even sprout. Any why?
Simply because Rome's corner stone of rule and loyalty
and wealth was the complete subordination of man to State.
The individual in Rome existed for the sake of the Roman
State. He was no better than a private in an army. By and
of himself, he was nothing. Against this, all modern science
and morals rise up in revolt. It is well for us all that there is
not and cannot be any more Rome, not even if Mussolini
lives forever.

In this spirit, I say, let the young learner pick up such
of the past as seems worth while. Then, having absorbed
it, let him turn to the positive, creative learning of things
modern, real, and important. Roughly gaged, the years of
delving into ancient cultures ought to end well before
twenty-one, and whenever possible before eighteen.

What Shall You Study?

Most people who ask this question betray a schoolboy's
frame of mind. When young, they learned that the world
of knowledge is full of streets and stories. The babe enters
on the ground floor (if not through the basement). First
he turns to the right and walks up the three R's. Next he
comes out on the gents' furnishing floor, where he gets a
little geography, music, manners, and essay writing. Then
he ascends to the next higher level—and so on, in the best
Excelsior fashion, until he comes to the roof garden, where
all manner of subtle things are served. Having partaken
of these, to the extent his purse, appetite, and natural im-
munity permit, he has nothing to do higher up. Is it to be
marveled at that, after sitting there for a few years, he

leaps off the roof with a loud whoop and gets back to the pavement?

We are not going to condemn all schools and teachers for having fixed in young minds this scheme of a logical and inexorable progression of studies. There are many extenuating circumstances, and anyhow we aren't writing a book for teachers and school boards. Enough to declare that this notion goes all the way back to Plato and Aristotle, was picked up and refined by the Roman church, both in theology and in education, and received its finishing shine from those assiduous pedagogue-philosophers of Germany, about a century ago. In this perfect state it was imported to these United States, where, many years ago, John Dewey proceeded to demolish it to its original atoms of nonsense. Today no leading American educator holds it in its thoroughgoing Old World form.

What you learn next ought to be settled by yourself, in the light of what you most need, what you most enjoy, what you should undertake to improve your finances, your social status, your political worth, your health, your beauty, your brawn, and whatever else happens to concern you. You learn best when you study something you must soon be using for pleasure or for profit. But what will you next be needing? Heaven knows!

When I think back upon the sequence of things I had to learn, for one reason or another, the spectacle moves me to laughter. Such a dark, winding, crazy succession of events! Could anything be madder than most human careers, when judged by their lack of rational order? I began to learn Arabic —why? Because it was the next higher subject above what I had been learning? Because it represented an advance in my culture? Nonsense! Two and only two genuine motives came into play. The first and weaker motive was a more or less idle curiosity to study a language considerably harder than any yet attempted. I wondered whether this strange tongue would stump me. The second and far more potent motive grew out of a simple act: it was induced by my going swimming in the Detroit River, one scorching Fourth of July. Cold water penetrated my ear and brought on an excruciating attack of Eustachian tube inflammation, with temporary deafness. The doctors said I must spend my days in the driest climate possible, and that nothing else could improve my condition. I resolved to find a job in the North African consular service. And that's all!

Think of the changes in the careers of five hundred million men and women, as a result of the World War! What each of these had next to learn was determined by the start and the devious course of that great lunacy. Every generation is thus mauled and buffeted by circumstance. Over and above that, most active people change inwardly as they mature, and each change brings fresh wishes, to which the learning of the day and hour must conform.

I have no guidebooks to sell those who want to know what to do next. If you cannot settle that for yourself, you ought not be reading this book. But a few facts can be here reported which will aid you in choosing your next move. Above all I stress two considerations:

1. Every new study requires its own *background* of previous learning.
2. Every advance to such a new study must be made with intense *interest*.

In short, two serious blunders are ever possible. First, the learner may be intensely interested in a new subject but lack much of the background necessary for its comprehension. Secondly, he may have acquired the foundations but lack interest to advance; and if he pushes himself unwillingly into the next higher study simply because it is the one which logically follows, he will merely flagellate his spirit to no purpose.

Background Is Necessary.

No matter what you set out to learn, some background of experience and skill is needed for progress. And you must understand just what that is for each subject you undertake. This is a primary problem which must not be shirked. Every school attacks it whenever it sets up prerequisites for a given course.

Naturally we cannot list here every prerequisite of every important subject; that alone would fill to overflow a large book. The best way for you to find out what you must know before learning a subject you wish to take up is to look it up, either in the course announcement of some school which teaches it or in an elementary textbook.

Common sense will come to your aid here. It is plain that it would be wasteful of your time and energy to try to master cabinetmaking before, you had thoroughly learned the handling of a carpenter's simpler tools. On the other hand, common sense occasionally deceives you. Thus, for generations it led people to believe that the right way to learn to play the piano was to begin with five-finger exercises, conquer each individual key and each individual finger movement, and then advance to two hands and simple tunes, taking up the latter piecemeal. Now we know that such a method is bad: the best way is to plunge in and try to play music you enjoy, doing so with both hands from the very start. Likewise in the sequence of studies: it is more than doubtful whether one gains anything in the long run by studying Latin as a preliminary to French or Spanish. I am not discussing the study of Latin as a thing in itself, for the sake of understanding ancient Roman culture and history; I refer now only to the old, old argument that Latin is an excellent foundation for a later study of the languages derived from it.

Suppose that you have 500 hours to devote to the mastery of French. Which is the wiser course—to put all of

your time on French or to put, say, the first 200 hours on
Latin and the rest of the time on French? The answer is
clear: give French the full 500 hours. Latin is a clumsy,
even misleading, prelude to French; much that you learn
about it must be virtually unlearned or heavily qualified
when you turn to French.

On the other hand, a background of things French may
prove valuable. Knowing French history and literature
can give you a feeling for the language later, as well as a
smattering of its words and phrases. Travel in the country
is priceless, and acquaintance with French people even more
precious. In a sense, all France and her people are an integral part of the language, for the latter is their product
and their expression; and this marks them off from the
Romans, who had nothing to do with France as it is today.

Here is the core of the matter. Is the subject under consideration a living piece of another one? If so, then you
will probably do well to study it before you begin the main
one. If that cannot be managed, learn the two together.

Can You Specify Your Interest in Moving Onward?

It is much easier to be sure of your interest than of your
background. The feeling itself, the mere urge to look further, usually tells the story. But be on your guard against
allowing an interest in some minor phase of a subject to
sweep you out into the depths of heavy toil. How often this
occurs nobody knows; but I have seen it in a number of
students. A youth is genuinely interested in learning to
write well, so he commits himself to a long course in composition and later perhaps in journalism. He is unaware
that writing is only an insignificant part of the journalist's
labors. He lacks the urge to master the rest of the job and
sooner or later finds himself enmeshed in studies which
sour on him.

An Interest May Be a False Prophet.

An interest is, as Dewey says, "a sign and symptom of growing power, . . . a dawning capacity which prophesies the stage the learner is about to enter." But the diagnosis of the interest is fully as hard as the diagnosis of a strange disease. Of which power is it a symptom? Rehearse your own life, and you will probably come upon some past interest whose evolution will confirm my present argument.

Did you, at the innocent age of ten, love to bang the white keys on mother's piano? Did that indicate that you were endowed with the dawning capacity of a pianist? Alas, no! The whole business is much more complicated! Mother may be misled and spend her savings on your musical education, to her own bitter disillusionment. Years later she may realize that your baby tinklings were merely a dawning capacity to manipulate your fingers, or to evoke responses out of mechanical things in general. The piano being the only mechanical thing around the house, you naturally spilled your energies and love upon it. Had there been an old automobile in your back yard, you would have turned away from the piano. Many little girls are doing that very thing today. The piano is passing, thanks to Henry Ford.

Give Every Interest a Fair Try-out.

Do not misapply this fact. It does not mean that you should distrust your interests. Never refrain from learning something merely because you doubt whether you have it in you to follow through. Every interest is worth testing and trying as far as it lives in you. Abandon it only when it itself dies. There is no telling to what it may lead. Here is the place to tell strange tales about the pleasant labyrinths of mystery and surprise through which an interest, at first seemingly casual and thin, has led men.

Ambition Must Fit the Learner.

No matter what your larger life ambition may be, it must lead you to learning. To become the world's most silvery orator, you must learn oratory. To shine as a stock broker, you must learn many things beyond the ticker symbols. To become a saint, you must learn a vast deal of psychology, over and above your creed—and so on. Hence the art of learning is the very corner stone of all important ambitions. Through it men may realize themselves most effectively, with many pleasant short cuts.

Plainly, too, skill in learning will measure to a nicety the fitness of an ambition. A boy who aspires to master twenty foreign languages can readily determine for himself whether this is a foolish wish or not. Let him observe the ease and accuracy with which he learns the first language. Would he become a Marathon runner? Let him do a little running that tests his limbs and wind. Every thoughtful man puts himself through such try-outs in a hit-and-miss fashion. It is the aim of vocational psychologists to reduce the haphazard in the measuring; and, though little progress has thus far been made, all indications point to an eventual triumph.

One Thing Leads to Another.

The smooth transition from an esthetic interest to a religious one has never been better illustrated than in the career of the Rev. Barton Berger, one of the most efficient, progressive, diplomatic, and brilliantly successful of the American clergy. Many years ago he was a typical business man in every respect save his fondness for beautiful buildings. As he rose in the ranks of commerce, he finally became general agent in Europe for a large corporation. Now he enjoyed more wealth and leisure than ever before; so he spent his free time in the observation and study of Old World architecture. Hardly a week-end passed without a visit to some palace, tower, country estate, or cathedral.

Little by little, Berger focused on churches, chiefly because in them he found more to enjoy than in any other type of design. According to his own statement, the profound impression which the great cathedrals made upon him broadened and deepened into a religious feeling. Not that he underwent anything like an ordinary conversion—rather that he came to believe in the supreme worth of everything that centered in this strange, rich beauty of flying buttresses, spires, and fairy arches.

To himself he put it thus: "There must be something to religion, to have produced all this loveliness and to be so marvelously expressed by it." With this new thought as a basis, he became more directly interested in religion itself. He studied its history and its heroes. At length he reached a momentous decision. He would become a church builder himself, and to this end he would first fit himself for the ministry.

He resigned his lucrative post, went to a theological seminary, and in due course of time became a minister. This was not the goal, though. It was only the first step toward his true objective. He now set out to find a parish where he might build a church that would realize his dream. That meant a parish of people both rich and cultured. Not an easy thing to find in America, where culture is as scarce among churchmen as cash is plentiful. Berger persisted, however, and, having means of his own, he was able to continue his search for many years.

Finally he found his opportunity, and ever since, while nominally a man of God, he is in reality an inspired architect. He knows more about the details of church building than any professional architect in our country—this is admitted by the architects themselves, who freely seek his advice and aid. He has no interest in church affairs, as these are commonly conducted in American parishes, and he does not hesitate to let his parishioners understand this. They have the good sense to leave him alone with his vision. Assistants attend to the strawberry ice cream festivals, marriages, and other family quarrels. Berger spends his days studying architecture and applying his lore to his own edifice and to those of less fortunate parishes all over the land.

Interest Cannot Be Forced.

Said Mr. Dooley: "It doesn't matter what you teach a boy, Hennessy, so long as he doesn't like it."

Said one of my high school teachers to me, away back in the dawn of the un-Christian Era: "I know you don't like geometry. And I know you are stupid in it. None the less, you must study it in order to develop character."

How many Americans support these ideas even today? I fear many million do. Our required courses in school and college smack of tyranny. And yet every man of experience knows that young people must learn many things. How lead them to the task? Let teachers find the answer! Our concern is with the reader who wishes to acquire the art of learning. To him we need say only a word: learn whatever interests you, but bear in mind that you can pick up new interests by browsing around and by occasionally allowing somebody to urge a strange task upon you. Force yourself now and then in an experimental mood. See what happens, for instance, if you take up an incomprehensible treatise on "The History of Erosion in Mesopotamia." You have never visited Mesopotamia. You have never eroded. You dislike history. What a fascinating experiment is psychology, then! Torment and tease yourself a little. Chain yourself to a chair and order the cook to serve you no food until you have mastered the first twenty pages. Who knows what may result?

All these remarks serve to point one moral. You cannot trust your present interests *utterly* as guides to what will interest you tomorrow. If, then, you tend to stick to the

good old rut of past interests, try forcing yourself. That's
not half so bad as being forced by somebody else.

Your Abilities.

Do you know your abilities? Do you understand thoroughly just what you can do and what you cannot?

If so, then you are a man in a million. For nothing is
rarer than such self-knowledge.

When most men assert that they know what they can do,
they mean that they know what they have been well trained
to do. But training is never a fair measure of ability. What
a person is trained to do is always a matter of accident and
never the result of a comprehensive insight into his possibilities. I venture to say that, since the human race began,
not one member of it has ever found himself in this strict
sense. And I add that when the new civilization reaches
the point at which any man who so desires may find himself
by visiting laboratories and experts, the social order will
be transformed.

To discuss man's abilities at length calls for several
volumes beyond our present one. We must approach the
vast problem from the learner's angle. For is it not plain
that nobody ought to study a subject unless he either is
interested in discovering his ability or lack of it along that
line or has already assured himself that he possesses the
requisite ability?

What abilities are needed for the chief subjects to be
learned? Where can you find out about them? Who will
undertake to assist you in measuring your own? Every
vocational psychologist of good standing can tell you a good
deal about the demands made on the learner of almost any
common handicraft, trade, or business, but, unfortunately,
few can contribute much to your enlightenment if you seek
to gage your powers in the higher pursuits. Here and there
a solitary investigator has advanced considerably ahead of

his fellows. Thus, Carl Seashore has devoted his life to an analysis of the traits required in a musical career. Thus, too, Edward Strong has spent several years seeking the typical interests of men in many walks of life, on the assumption that the natural spread of interests probably reveals indirectly the requisite abilities. (The assumption seems to be well founded.) Thus, also, Donald Laird's researches in industrial psychology have led him into matters of individual measurement and job analysis.

I cannot know your personal problems here. Hence I cannot recommend the best psychologist for your own needs. But I can say that if you seek light as to your abilities you can surely receive help by writing to the chief psychologist in the nearest large university and outlining your problem. He can at least refer you to the best specialist in the vicinity.

They may also be consulted with reference to your general intelligence, which, luckily, is much more readily measured than your special abilities. In some respects, it is more important to find out where you stand intellectually than where you rank in the traits which make good doctors and lawyers, for your personal satisfaction in studying frequently depends upon your power to grasp, rather than upon your skill in performance. Even in the professions, distinction assumes great practical significance. Thus, in law some students never can become able court attorneys; they lack the peculiar abilities involved in cajoling juries and outwitting judges—yet they understand the distinctions, rulings, and principles of law thoroughly. So they become office lawyers, spending their days mainly in study of records and statutes. Likewise in medicine. How many learners here have been brilliant in their books and laboratories but almost total failures in practice! Some fail with patients through lack of agreeable personality, others because of some slight clumsiness in minor operations, and still others by reason of worries and fears over diagnosis and treatment. Does this eliminate them from a medical career? Not at all! It merely serves to guide them into the right one, which may be that of a laboratory research worker, a consultant whose clients are other specialists, a writer of medical textbooks, or what not.

In brief, many of us set out to learn for a career and discover, midway in it, that we suffer under limitations which block our progress to the particular work we originally envisaged. If the limitations are not purely intellectual, however, we can readjust so that we find closely related outlets for our interests and our energies. Why, then, not find out as soon as possible our intellectual level?

READ WITH CARE!

1. Between 1919 and 1927, 4,000,000 persons gave up farming; 19,000,000 acres ceased to be cultivated; 76,000 farms went out of existence as farms.

2. Production in agriculture between 1919 and 1927 increased 25 per cent.

3. A farmer with a tractor can plow from four to eight times as many acres daily as can a farmer with a two-horse team.

4. It is not unusual today to find one farm worker handling 300 acres of wheat alone.

5. A Pennsylvania school teacher made the following comment about farms in her neighborhood: "I have visited most of the farms in the township within range of my school. Fully half of the housewives I have met are distinctly subnormal in their intelligence. Many of them are complete morons, while half a dozen are true feebleminded types. The shocking thing, though, is that many of these inferior creatures are the wives of the solid, hard-working and competent small farmers. What will their children be? Just peasants, men with hoes and women with mops."

The Four Levels of Learning.

Four levels of learning may easily be distinguished. They are:

1. Preventive learning.
2. Remedial learning.
3. Expansive learning.
4. Creative learning.

Preventive Learning.

Preventive learning is the act of informing oneself in order to avoid some grave evil, such as poverty, personal disgrace, or boredom. Virtually all elementary school work is, at bottom, of this sort. The public has come to understand the perils of gross ignorance, as well as the price which society must pay for it in incompetence, immorality, and crime. To reduce these curses to a minimum, the State takes over the task of forcing a minimal amount of study upon every child.

Remedial Learning.

Remedial learning has been largely overlooked. It aims to correct an existing incompetence. The child of immigrant parents hears their language at home and another in school. He makes errors in his English which, on analysis, prove to be transfers from the home speech to the new one. So he must pursue a special study which will correct his mistakes. Schools in factory towns filled with aliens encounter this problem and create courses to cope with it. Most of the high-grade private correspondence courses in ordinary subjects are aimed at the same defect. So are many of the better books on etiquette, which are studied hardest by men and women who, having started life in humble circumstances, find themselves prosperous and able to move in higher circles of society, could they only unlearn the coarse manners of their childhood.

Expansive Learning.

Expansive learning aims to enlarge a man's horizon, vision, and insight through mastery of subjects hitherto beyond him. The motive is not to avoid poverty or the mishaps of crass ignorance, but rather to digest and enjoy the fruits of modern civilization to the utmost. The eager learner, whether in school or out, who pursues the arts and sciences to their limits is usually of this expansive variety.

Creative Learning.

Creative learning carries us over into another realm. Now the learner is not satisfied to acquire what others have amassed before him. He strikes out for himself. He would discover facts and principles by himself, for himself; or, in other instances, he would create something, as a result of first learning a new technique. Now we are advanced into the fields of artistic creation and scientific discovery and invention. These are the highest plateaus of human achievement. The things learned and the methods of learning them differ profoundly from those of the three lower levels. Indeed, it is exceedingly hard to depict them here, even in part, for they involve subtleties which go far beyond the scope of this book.

On which level do you now wish to learn something? Make your answer clear as crystal to yourself. It will determine your whole policy.

EXERCISE

How Well Do You Know the United States?

Study carefully the map on the next page. Note the state boundaries, chief rivers, mountains, lakes, and cities. Later we shall discuss these.

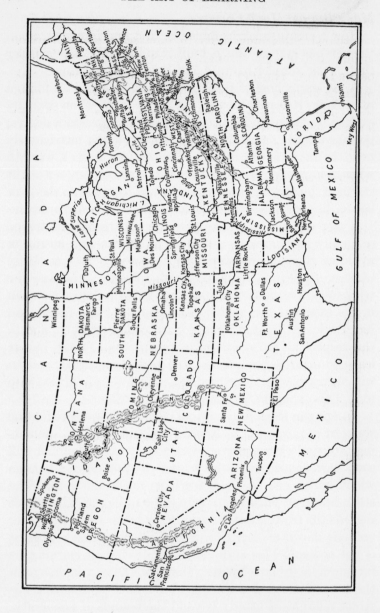

Many Brains, Many Learners.

How a creature learns depends, first and foremost, upon the nervous system that is built into his body. The simpler that is, the simpler his rate and quality of learning.

A rat learns how to reach food, even though it is hidden in a maze. It learns how to get to its mate when sexually excited. It learns to identify traps and, to a certain degree, poisoned food, particularly when it is placed suspiciously near the rat hole or runway. It also learns to seek warmth when winter approaches; the first cool September night starts it burrowing to gnaw a path into barn, shed, or house. Beyond that, the creature isn't able to learn much.

A dog can be taught to perform all manner of tricks, originally as a price for getting food or else as a means of avoiding punishment. But only a few seconds can elapse between the stimulus and the dog's response; otherwise the trick fails, for the canine has a woefully limited time span in his memory. He readily learns to recognize friend and foe. He learns to stand guard until called off duty, and in this respect his perseveration is remarkable. Finally he can learn to utter barks, whines, and growls on signal; and he will attack people according to a plan carefully drilled into him. This exhausts his range of assimilation.

An ape can learn to use a tool of the simplest sort for the simplest of purposes. As Koehler has shown in his fascinating study of chimpanzees, even a very young animal will soon learn to pick up a stick in order to pull down a banana which hangs just too high for it to reach and grasp. The stick, however, must be in plain sight while the chimpanzee regards the fruit; if out of vision, it is never used. The older animals, however, learn to go and fetch the stick when it is out of sight. This is the upper limit of their learning, as far as anybody now knows. That apes have a language in the human sense of a system of symbols representing abstract relations is utterly beyond the bounds of possibility.

But it is possible that they have a fairly elaborate set of signals, each linked with an emotion and attitude, that are instantly recognized by the hearers as indicating danger, food, sheer surprise, and the like.

A human imbecile is below the chimpanzee in some respects, notably the more important, while an idiot is even lower than a rat, for he cannot seek his own food, cannot shun danger, and can neither dress nor feed himself. The true idiot can learn absolutely nothing.

At the border line between idiocy and imbecility we sometimes find a tiny flash of primitive learning. The creature understands a few simple commands of the asylum keepers, can handle knife and fork, and manages to learn how to put on a few clothes.

The lower type of imbecile can learn only five or ten genuine words. He can learn to handle a broom and to sweep a room. He may be able to bathe himself and brush his hair. One step further up the human scale we find imbeciles with vocabularies of a few hundred words, which they love to use over and over. Here the crudest exhibitionist appears, as in the amusing case, C. K., in the records of Dr. Martin W. Barr. This gentleman, when meeting a stranger, always pulls the same line: "If I don't kiss you, I will," whereat he laughs uproariously. He sings sweetly (many singers are subnormal mentally, alas!) but demands loud and prolonged applause. Once, when taking part in a school tableau, he stood on the stage shouting: "It's me. I'm here. Clap! Clap! Why don't you clap?"[1] He thoroughly mastered housework and took immense pride in it. But in five years of school work he was unable to learn anything.

A moron can learn a good deal. He can learn simple tunes and play them on harmonica or piano. He may master arithmetic up to the point of fractions. He may absorb a

[1] "Types of Mental Defectives," Barr & Maloney, 1920, p. 38.

smattering of facts about history and geography, though he will never grasp the significance of masses of facts. Simple machines may excite him and lead him to master their operation. Mechanical dishwashers and laundry equipment fall well within his powers. He can learn to draw, perhaps, and may even master words and grammar enough to write an intelligible letter, but he usually forgets spelling and rules of rhetoric quickly and has to relearn them. His span of retention is brief in all things save the elemental muscular learning. Now and then we even find a moron who becomes highly skilled in some motor dexterity such as cabinetmaking, playing the violin, or handling guns in the U. S. Navy. Some fine common sailors and marines are morons. Theirs not to reason why, theirs but to do and die. Intellectually, a very light brigade!

The average adult soars far above all these. He can learn without a severe strain all of the subjects up to the end of the typical grammar school, but positively cannot succeed in the first year of a good high school. It is the more abstract subjects which balk him soonest—mathematics above all, and then the niceties of language. He usually learns acts of manual skill pretty well, and he learns the social standards too. He can become a first-class carpenter or mason, but not a surveyor nor a public accountant.

A fairly superior man gets through algebra swimmingly. He may, however, be thwarted when he reaches calculus, at least under prevalent methods of teaching this subject. He can learn history and European languages related to his own, but he will probably be confused and discouraged if asked to master an Asiatic language or the intricacies of a non-European culture. He can master, in short order, such activities as typewriting and telegraphy. If need arose, he could become a master printer or an electrician. But his preferences run in other directions. He learns to read fast, grasping all that he reads, and he enjoys solid books and serious conversation. Finance and banking generally seem easy to him.

When we rise to the rare plateaus of genius, what a bewildering species of learner we find there! Is there a better specimen to parade here than the immortal Ben Franklin? What he learned is reflected clearly by his range of active interests and the enterprises which he undertook and carried through to success.

This Ulysses of modern science and citizenship, was deeply interested in all aspects of physics. His experiments in this field are excelled only by his general theories and by his ingenious practical applications of new principles. He invented the lightning rod, the electric detonator of explosives, the wood-burning stove, the smoke-consuming furnace, the copying press, double spectacles, a laundry mangle (which George Washington saw demonstrated), and fully fifty other things. Each of these, you must bear in mind, represents a fresh direction of interest.

He reorganized the entire city of Philadelphia. He started the first fire insurance company in America. He wrote popular songs. He played the harp, the guitar, and the violin. He was intensely curious about the weather and its laws, made several noteworthy discoveries about the direction of storms and prevailing winds, and was the chief instigator of the United States Weather Bureau. He was considered the finest swimmer of his day and also taught the art. He conceived and launched the first circulating library in the world. His passion for public education was fiery, and he founded the University of Pennsylvania. He became America's first political economist. He proposed a daylight-saving system. He tried to reform the alphabet, but found this harder than putting over the American Revolution. He instituted our postal system and became the first Postmaster General. He mastered the printing business so well that he was able to retire, at the age of forty-two, with a comfortable fortune. And, as if all this were not enough, he wrote scores of pamphlets and his marvelous autobiography.

Such a genius could, it seems, learn anything he liked; and he liked to learn and apply almost every variety of human skill, wisdom, and attitudes. The differences between his brains and the rat's are all but infinite in number. Between him and the rat appear ten thousand grades and shades of learner. Among these it is only the upper varieties to whom these pages are addressed, for to study the art of learning requires a superior ability in learning.

Not every reader will extract the same benefits from our discussion. What each brings to the reading determines his response to each sentence. I have tried to broaden the exercises so as to give free play to all such individual variations. The book will succeed if it stimulates you to study your own problems of learning in a new light. And its highest triumph will be your discovery of your own special, hitherto unappreciated aptitudes and limitations as a learner.

Learners of the Herd and Solitary Scholars.

Some study best alone, others in a group, so there will always be a demand for two radically different methods of learning, and for corresponding equipments. We anticipate an enormous increase in home study during the next generation. By that I do not mean merely an extending of the so-called home-study courses offered by the larger universities. I mean rather private study conducted quite apart from institutional supervision. That trend is natural: education hitherto has been shaped for the masses, first and foremost, with the result that stereotyped courses doled out paragraph-wise to immense assemblages of learners have been perfected and popularized at the expense of the costly and difficult, small, select class under an instructor able to devote personal attention to each learner.

The pendulum swings back. Prosperity accelerates it. So too does the superior learner who thinks best away from the crowd. So too does the learner, superior or otherwise, who cannot attend fixed lectures but wants some guidance for private study. The idle rich, the ambitious poor, and the outcast of the herd thus conspire to restore the lost art of personal learning.

The Four Learners.

The average man learns in many ways at once. There are four varieties of exceptional people, however, whose nervous systems are specially adapted to particular ways and singularly poor in others. These varieties are the eye learner, the ear learner, the throat-and-tongue learner, and the manipulative learner.

The Eye Learner.

The eye learner is a clearly marked type about whom there is never much doubt. His absolute visual memory identifies him. Reading a book, he literally sees the printed pages with such vividness that the impression lingers as a photograph in his brain. Now and then we find this ability exaggerated to the point of freakishness, as in the career of Frank Paxton, which I have reported elsewhere.[1] This youth retains every visual impression in complete form for an indefinitely long time. In public exhibitions he memorizes whole pages of newspapers, lists of strange names and foreign words, merely by looking once at them. No more effort is involved here than in the recording of light on a photographic plate. The two processes are identical, of course.

Many eminent botanists, physicians, and zoologists owe no small part of their scientific attainments to this same

[1] See "The Psychology of Achievement," p. 445*ff*.

gift. Some of my Columbia colleagues in those departments
fall only a little behind Paxton in their camera-like eye
work. Painters and sculptors, obviously, lean heavily upon
this same function. And it is the very foundation of
Toscanini's genius as a symphony orchestra conductor.

Ear Learners.

Ear learners, on the other hand, are found most often
among linguists and philologians, so far as my own observations testify. The most amazing case of this which I can
adduce is that of a young German orientalist whom I taught
English while in Berlin. He came to me while we were both
reading Arabic under Sachau, at the University. Sachau had
recommended him for a curatorship in the British Museum,
and the authorities of the institution had invited him to
London. Though already a master of ten or twelve languages, he had never bothered with English; it lay too far
afield. Now he must learn in a hurry! But I must teach him
in his own way.

He prescribed the way, to a hair, and I obeyed. Every
afternoon we would walk in the Thiergarten for two hours
or so. I would talk English in a random conversational way,
touching exclusively upon topics which had appeared in
the morning papers. He merely listened. After an hour of this,
he would ask me in German what various sounds I had
uttered meant. He did not pick out single words, as a rule;
he heard long phrases, even paragraphs, as units. This
alone was proof of an amazing ear. Then he would give me
a list of English words or a reading passage, and I would
explain it or correct his pronunciation as he struggled with
it. The next afternoon he would rattle off the words letter
perfect before I started the day's conversation. Thus in
about six weeks he learned to speak English with considerable ease.

Throat-and-tongue Learners.

Throat-and-tongue learners are common. So common indeed that John B. Watson is led to believe that everybody must belong to this type. This suggests strongly that he is of the type himself. Certainly the powerful and prolonged drill we all endure while learning to speak our mother tongue, in our first years, enlarges and perfects this mechanism to its limit. Probably thousands of people who are indifferently endowed for speech become predominantly throat-and-tongue learners and thinkers, through this necessity. Anybody who commits long poems to memory with great ease is almost certainly of this species. So are all great talkers. So are most people who prefer to read aloud.

The Manipulative Learner.

The manipulative learner is also common. He is likely to be the youth who dislikes books, is impatient of lectures, but wild over tools, instruments, machinery, or acts of dexterity such as dancing, acrobatics, and feats of brawn. A brilliant pianist, a virtuoso on the violin, and a surgeon all possess this variety of perception and response, usually linked up with other kinds. Many a young man who is dropped from school early in life later makes good in work calling for nimble hands or legs. There seems to be no connection whatsoever between this trait and the intellectual abilities which go to produce a scholar.

Which Kind Are You?

Now, what does all this mean to you, the learner? Simply this: Before you commit yourself irrevocably to a prolonged program of study, measure yourself. Does your eye tend to dominate the rest of you? Or does your ear? Or are you an average person? The answer may make a great difference in your plans. For some things cannot be learned through the eye, and others are barred to the ear. You know, of course, that a person who has no ear for music is foolish in persisting to master music. But do you realize that one who lacks the ease of hand and foot required for fancy dancing is equally foolish to spend years and dollars trying to become a graceful dancer? Or that a person who is markedly deficient in ear learning and in throat-and-tongue learning has no business aspiring to conquer foreign languages on a grand scale? Here as in industry, the job determines the worker, not the worker the job. Each task of learning has its own set of requirements in the learner. There may be fifteen or twenty-seven requirements; if you can fulfill eleven or nineteen of them, you may rise to mediocre accomplishment, but no higher. Is it worth while? Answer that for yourself.

Discover Your Special Abilities.

Many subjects demand nothing more than a little skill of many sorts—these the average learner can make his own. But let him beware of the specialties! They will only bring him to grief! Even more important is it for the exceptional learner to shun fields far removed from his special abilities. School records teem with tragedies of misplaced geniuses who, but for the necessity or ill-witted choice of studying subjects beyond them, might have risen to dizzy heights. We also find a pleasanter picture in the comic cases of geniuses whom schoolmasters deemed fools for that very reason.

Charles Darwin, for instance, was, by his own statement, "singularly incapable of mastering any language." In the English schools of his day, this frailty was almost synonymous with imbecility; for how the quality English did worship Greek and Latin and French! Young Darwin's school teachers all regarded him as a "most ordinary boy." His father joined in this opinion and went so far as to rate his offspring well below the common standard of intelligence.

Linnaeus, the founder of systematic botany, so discouraged the high school principal under whom he toiled that the worthy personally advised the youth's father to bring him up as a cobbler. "He is utterly unfit to make progress in any learned profession," quoth he.

Henrik Ibsen received at the high school in Christiania the lowest grades which admitted of graduation. His class marks in Norwegian composition were mediocre, too. Yet he became the greatest dramatist of modern times.

Pierre Curie, who, with his wife, was destined to discover radium in later years, was pronounced completely stupid by his school teachers. In despair his parents removed him from the institution and put him under a private tutor who was to temper the winds of wisdom to the bald lamb.

And so it goes! What was wrong in these cases? The young learners had not found themselves. But what does that mean? Simply that each lacked something which was necessary for learning the kind of subjects taught in the schools. Darwin's poor language sense surely rooted in some inferiority of ear, tongue, or throat, or the brain centers linked to these. His dominant learning function was linked to his eye. He was one of the most amazing observers who ever looked upon Nature and read her secrets in a myriad manifestations. In other instances, the limitation is more perhaps obscure; but it must have been there and observable at the time it caused trouble.

EXERCISE

How clearly can you visualize the following situation? How does the problem present itself to you? If it baffles you, just what is the mystery? Can you solve it easily, with long effort, or not at all?

Two balls are placed against a smooth wall which is parallel to another smooth wall opposite it in a room having a smooth and level floor. Both balls are set in motion at exactly the same instant and with exactly the same velocity; and neither is accelerated nor retarded during its passage across the floor. Both balls are, furthermore, impelled along a course at right angles to the wall that serves as the starting point; and they therefore move toward the opposite wall so that, upon reaching it, the path of their motion will also be at right angles to that latter wall.

One ball arrives at the second wall, which is the goal, in one-half of the time required by the other ball to arrive there.

Describe precisely how this is possible.

If you see all this easily and quickly, you are probably more eye-minded than the average man.

If you cannot understand it at all, you will almost certainly do well to avoid studies which require much eye-imagination.

EXERCISE

Here is a test which will show you the rate at which you can learn to improve your manual dexterity.

Every day practice drawing twelve circles of the same size on a sheet of paper, drawing six from right to left, and six from left to right. You will learn many astonishing things about how easily you can improve your manual skill by regular drill.

Then practice drawing a line three inches long as straight as possible. In no case should you go back and repeat or redraw either circles or lines.

Keep the papers you use, and after thirty days compare the first drawings with the last.

If you find that you improve much and get pleasure from such work, set for yourself several harder tasks in drawing. For instance, draw four straight lines, making the second twice the length of the first, the third three times the length of the second, and the fourth four times the length of the third. Try each such exercise at least fifty times.

EXERCISE

How well have you learned distances and dimensions? Hold up your hands and, with the index fingers, measure off in the space before you sixteen inches.

How sure do you feel that you have come close to that distance?

Now bring your fingers down to a desk top or a wall where you can mark off the space. Then measure it with a ruler.

How large was your error?

Repeat this sort of test once a day for fifty days. Use a different length for each day's test. Range from six inches up to three feet. Jump up and down this scale, doing nineteen inches one day, seven the next, thirty-one the next and so on.

Keep a record of the size of your error. At the end of the series of tests, inspect the errors.

Have you steadily improved? If not, can you guess what has hindered you?

Test yourself likewise in estimating distances. Practice on the dimensions of the rooms in your home and office. Then attack outdoor distances, selecting always those which you can easily measure. As a rule it is hard to work on distances greater than 100 feet; and, of course, it is still harder to use this test with heights, as you can rarely measure these.

EXERCISE

Read this passage carefully, for later on we shall ask you questions about various aspects taken up in the selection.

The most significant aspect of the attitude of Great Britain toward her colonies is the fact that in so widely recognizing their autonomy, she is binding them to her even more closely with powerful ties of sentiment. And so it is that she is entering upon one of the greatest experiments in government which have ever taken place.

It has been said that this change of attitude was caused by the American Revolution. This is only partly true. At that time the British Empire was developing into the stage where the foundations of the sovereignty of the Parliament of Great Britain and its right to legislate for the entire British Empire were being laid. At the time of the Revolution, the Parliament sought to legislate for the American colonies by taxing them and otherwise regulating their business and political affairs, when the colonies desired autonomy above all else. Thus the legislative and governmental changes in Great Britain were important factors in causing the American Revolution. It is true, however, that the fact that Great Britain today grants to her colonies autonomy over their own affairs is in a large sense the foundation of the Empire.

Great Britain's dominions today have passed through many stages of development: from unorganized settlements to crown colonies, then to self-governing dominions, finally to nations, autonomously regulated, equal in general status to one another, and to the mother country, living under the same King, and yet entirely independent in the management of all of their domestic and foreign affairs.

It is true that the Parliament of Great Britain still retains a theoretical legal sovereignty. But this power is never exercised over the dominions except with their consent.

In their management of their own foreign affairs, the dominions have shown their most marked development. Formerly the British Empire was considered as a unit in all questions of international policy. Now, however, the dominions are rapidly becoming integral units. They signed the peace treaty separately and independently. In the Assembly of the League of Nations they have separate seats. And in addition to being eligible to membership in the Council of the League of Nations, they may make separate treaties and appoint their own diplomatic representatives in foreign countries.

Any attempt at binding the Empire together by means of a central political organization or by a written constitution has always been and will continue to be an impossibility. Great Britain clearly recognizes the wisdom of granting autonomy to her dominions, and her greatest strength lies, paradoxically enough, in the weakness of the legal bonds which unite the parts of the whole.

You will find a fairly complete description of the traits which count most in achievement presented in my recent book, "The Psychology of Achievement," New York, 1930. Study especially Book II on Energy and Book III on Interest. Then try to discover your own fifty most important characteristics as shown in the Personality Charts at the back of the volume.

As virtually every type of achievement is based on a special sort of learning ability, the chart will throw much light on your aptitudes as a learner.

If you have ever held a job long enough to discover your fitness and unfitness for it, analyze yourself with reference to it.

What was hardest for you to learn about it? What was easiest? What did you dislike most in the work? What did you enjoy?

BOOK III

TRAINING YOURSELF

TRAINING YOURSELF

Handicaps and Obstacles.

Man's inertia in the face of hard study surpasses the belief of anybody who has not tried to teach. Dean D. E. Carpenter, of the International Correspondence Schools, in a report to his salesman in 1929, said:

> The ordinary human being has a lot of mental inertia to overcome; many persons are mentally lazy. There is an important part in the educational program for the student to play. He must exert himself mentally; he must study. Our part is to coax, cajole, encourage, persuade, induce, or compel him to study and to see that he profits by what he studies. Last year we mailed 413,528 letters to students *with the sole purpose of securing lessons from them.* Encouragement letters, we call them, and they are filled with all the inspiration to study and improve that we can command. These letters cost us probably more than $22,500 last year . . .

Mind you! These were not letters dealing with lessons or with payments or anything but the encouraging of dilatory students. And here is the place, perhaps, for me to betray a hideous secret of the correspondence school business. Among those of us who have followed it intimately, it is well recognized that its promoters would never make a dollar, were it not for the faint-hearted, the dull, the overworked, the misguided, and the supremely lazy subscribers to courses who begin with fanfares and fade out in a few weeks. Those who never finish the courses are the sole source of dividends. What a comment on human nature!

What, now, are the causes of this? They fall into a few large classes:

1. Inferior intelligence.
2. Inferior training.
3. Lack of energy or dexterity.
4. Emotional instability.
5. A fixed harmful attitude.
6. Wrong choice of studies.

Of course, some people suffer from two or more of these handicaps and obstacles. For them the art of learning will prove hard indeed. But it need not prove impossible, provided only they select the right studies. It is foolish, of course, for a man who has "no head for figures" to pore for years over higher mathematics. Even though he makes progress up to a certain point, he will still be paying too high a price for it—unless he studies purely for fun.

But suppose he chooses subjects within his potential abilities and training. What can he do to overcome the handicaps and obstacles that afflict him? This is a personal question whose answer depends on a thorough understanding of the personality involved, so no generalization I can frame will serve anybody's purpose. None the less, it is useful to point out certain aspects of each impediment to learning; for the learner may then apply these to his own case, often with quick profit.

The Unintelligent Learner.

Serious indeed is the lack of high intelligence, but not at all fatal. Happily there are interesting and valuable things to be learned by people of all levels of intelligence above the very lowest. Some of the happiest students I know, bar none, are simple folks of limited attainments and aptitudes who have been lucky enough to find work and play well within their capacities. I have in mind one old codger who had a long and jolly life sweetly flavored with pottering about a blacksmith shop, tinkering with all sorts of machines and contraptions which the neighbors fetched in for him. A horseshoer by trade, and an excellent one too, he had the great good luck to be kicked by a recalcitrant Percheron one hot Saturday morning, and thereafter he had to take life somewhat more easily. He undertook the lighter work around the shop, and there he found himself as never before.

That was years ago. Today he nears his end, cheery as any cricket that has found its hearth. They had put him to work doing odds and ends of repair jobs, mending hammers, smoothing down grindstones, and all that. He ran into new problems every day or two. He studied each and was led over into the arts of welding, brazing, stamping. milling, and finally precision machinery work. In this he could not advance far, for the blacksmith shop lacked the necessary equipment; but he found quite enough to do, as it was. I think it fair to guess that, as our trade schools count jobs, he can manage at least ten or a dozen. And it has given him the tingle of all-around success, to which, I suspect, is added a dash of superiority, for all sorts of workingmen bring him things to do which they cannot do themselves.

The Motor-minded Man Is Different, Not Inferior.

As schoolmasters measure intelligence, this old fellow is something of a dolt. But isn't there something wrong with the academic yardstick? Yes, indeed! We have tended to exaggerate the superiority of the learner who uses his eyes to read and his ear to record dear teacher's remarks. Book learning has been glorified ever since the age of Pericles. And some singular merit has been attributed to the individual who can take and recall extensive notes on a lecture. Many people, however, learn important things well through other mechanisms, especially by way of the larger muscles and the throat. They appear stupid when tested in reading and listening, but, if given a chance to learn in some way which uses the open channels of their nervous system, they turn out to be brilliant. It is not the same brilliance as that of the book scholar, but it is genuine nevertheless.

Some children who have been rated as feebleminded turn out to be mentally normal as soon as they are taken out of the conventional school and put to work learning things through their muscles. Instead of learning to spell by reading the words, they must trace the letters over and over with their fingers and speak the words aloud at the same time. Once the association is thus established, it is exactly as good as the commoner sort that arises between eye impression and meaning.

Amazing cases of progress in learning have been reported, perhaps none more striking than that of the young man who, at the age of twenty-one, had been rejected twice for admission to Leland Stanford University. He was put into the new clinic using the methods perfected by Grace Fernald and B. W. De Busk. Eleven weeks he studied there, and then passed the Stanford entrance examination. During his first year in college he received five grades of A, the highest possible score!

Find Your Own Type of Intelligence; Then Learn Accordingly.
The advice to the learner who reads these pages is now obvious. If you have the slightest reason for thinking that your intelligence has been handicapping you in learning, check up on it. The best way to do this is to put yourself in the hands of a competent psychologist for some simple tests which will take little time and cost you, at most, a trifling sum. Unless you live miles from a large city, you can be put in touch with a scientist in short order. Almost every state in the Union now has several able psychologists.

Should it turn out that you are of an extreme motor type, you must promptly give up reading and listening as the *primary* method of learning. This does not mean that you abandon all books, of course. It means rather that you must subordinate them to talking, writing, making things, and going through various other motions suited to the subject at hand.

Poor Training.

Learners are hampered by several varieties of poor training. It is vital to discover, as early as possible, which kind has cramped your own style. Do not imagine for a moment that mere lack of training is the worst misfortune here. Far from it! For many adults this is a great piece of good luck. It enables them to come at a new subject with clear mind and a set of muscles that have not been warped and bent to some wrong practice. Every teacher knows that an unspoiled mind and body are the easiest of all things to train. His troubles start when he has to overcome, at the outset, years of miseducation.

The Three Worst Forms of Training.

This handicap assumes any one or more of the three following forms:

1. A bad method of learning mastered only too well.
2. The wrong subjects mastered only too well.
3. Misinformation acquired only too well.

Let me cite myself as a horrible specimen of the first handicap.

The Wrong Method.

I learned to typewrite in 1894. The one-finger and two-eye technique was faithfully followed, of course, as there were no teachers within miles of my back room. Painfully picking out each letter, I slowly sped up. From one finger, I advanced to two, from two to four; but I never went beyond this except on rare occasions, and then the results were not so good. Nor have I ever been able to type by the touch system. I am so thoroughly dependent upon the linking of eye to finger that, just this week, I tried my ability at typing without looking at the keys; and the product was something more fearful than wonderful. Nor can I revive in visual memory as much as one-quarter of the keyboard. Ask me to imagine where the letter "1" is, and I fail miserably. All of which proves how poor this method of learning by the unit letter and working with the single finger is. Any modern learner drilled in the touch system can outspeed me easily. In spite of this, I type fast and with considerable accuracy; but the labor back of this efficiency is fully five times greater than it should have been, with proper training.

On three occasions I resolved to learn typing afresh by the touch system—and thrice I failed ignominiously. Struggle as I would, something messed me up inside. My progress was simply abominable—down around moron level. And I found that the old habits were far too strong to be cast off except by efforts prodigious and out of all proportion to the prospective benefits. So I must go on wasting time and energy.

The Wrong Subject.

Mastery of the wrong subject causes trouble mainly as a result of one's shifting interests and work. A youth sets out to be a stone mason, finds himself unhappy in the work, and turns to cabinetmaking. In the new trade he bungles much because he is heavy-handed. When we analyze the varieties of manual labor, it appears that there are at least three elemental kinds; in the first, the worker operates the entire arm, in unison with large body movements; in the second, he uses chiefly the forearm, wrist, and palm; and in the third, he uses wrist and fingertips. The first is usually the heaviest rough work like that of the ditch digger and roustabout. The second includes many skilled types, among them most of the labor of a stone mason. The third is the most delicate, most dexterous, and least strenuous; it occurs in the work of a linotype operator, a loom worker, and, of course, a cabinetmaker. Now, the entire manner of manipulating arm, hand, and finger in the course of picking up and placing stones in a masonry wall differs from that of handling thin veneers and working with fine chisels and planes. In watching a mason who has undertaken fine tool work I have observed his surprising clumsiness even with the cruder tools; and, on closer inspection, it is plainly traceable to the way he persists in moving the entire arm after the stone mason's fashion.

You see this same clumsiness sometimes in people who having learned to handle the violin well, turn to the piano; in a subtler form it crops out when a pianist learns the pipe organ. The whole technique of touch differs from that of his original instrument, hence he must unlearn before he can learn. Even more delicate is the change of skill required of a parlor singer who aspires to the concert stage. The acoustics of the large auditorium impose severe demands now; and in these difficult alterations in the handling of diaphragm and larynx are involved. Thus we might go on and on, citing hundreds of cases.

Prefer Studies Closely Related to the Old.

All this bears upon your choice of studies, does it not? In so far as it is feasible, make it a rule to learn new things, especially new activities, to which you can transfer old skill. Don't jump off on a tangent to a new task which taxes eye, ear, hand, and memory in strange ways that clash with the habits of all these. If you have learned the violin and wish to extend your pleasures, consider the other stringed instruments first—say, the cello. If you have learned carpentering, take up cabinetmaking next. If you have conquered French, try Spanish or Italian.

Naturally, this advice must be qualified to fit your true needs. Perhaps you seek something wholly different by way of sheer variety. All right, but do not expect great success! If it comes, that marks you as an unusual person.

Misinformation the Least Serious Handicap.

I need not dwell on the evils of misinformation. As I write these lines, my newspaper tells me that the great prophet-evangelist, Voliva, Lord of Zion City, is going on a trip which men of other faiths call "around the world." Voliva laughs at this phrase, for he knows the earth is flat like a saucer, with the North Pole squarely in the middle of the saucer. For many years he has defended this doctrine against all comers. He tells the reporters now that his ship will merely sail around the rim of the terrestrial saucer. Will he be convinced of his error as he watches the compass and makes observations on the way? Probably not. To unlearn his misinformation will be all but impossible. Why so? Because, first of all, it is highly emotionalized, for it is a part of his religion and a necessary support of his ecclesiastical authority over his freakish followers. Then too, it is so tightly interwoven with many other beliefs that the latter must all be swept away in the unlearning process.

Few of us, luckily, are so desperately throttled by fictions as Voliva. Only the extreme sentimentalist is as badly off, for he too has charged his information with emotions and cannot approach contrary facts with an open mind. When we come to look at the emotional factors in learning, we shall have more to say about this.

Lack of Energy or Dexterity.

Every job calls for its own peculiar amount and pattern of energy. The watchmaker must have exceptional eyes and delicate fingers, the boilermaker must have tough ears to resist the hideous thunder of riveting machines, the dentist must be able to stand erect all day without lowering the exquisite touch of his tools. Some varieties of work which, to the outside observer, call for little effort are the most strenuous; thus the daily routine of a minister, thus, too, the grind of a grammar school teacher. To give piano recitals such as professionals offer, more muscular work must be performed than in blacksmithing. So, if you would learn a craft, art, sport, or what not, be sure to check up on your own energies first!

Long before such vocational oddities became known to me, I discovered in myself parallel handicaps in learning various exercises, sports, games, and labor. As a boy I was never able to chin myself on a horizontal bar more than two or three times; nor could I climb a rope, hand over hand. The muscles most heavily strained in such upward movements seem constitutionally feeble. Years later, when playing tennis, I found that it was these which stood in the way of my ever playing a consistent game. For half an hour or thereabouts I could put up a creditable game, but every overhand swing of the racket exhausted me, though I would continue fresh and snappy in all the other strokes. Soon I would lose every game I served, and that was the inglorious end. At times I found myself unable even to swing the racket idle, before the first set was over.

The longer I watch learners, the more vivid grows the perception of their struggles with their own energies. More and more sonorously rings the truth sounded by Sherwood Anderson in these words:

. . . The whole question of whether any American workman can go through the long apprenticeship which good craftsmanship requires— whether or not he can manage to make a living while keeping a part of his nerve for creative work—is largely a matter of physical stamina.

This whole range of phenomena is too vast to discuss at length here. I have gone into it at some length in "The

Psychology of Achievement,"[1] and most of the points there investigated have a certain relevance to learning. Especially do they throw light on hitherto neglected problems in adult education.

[1] New York, 1930. All of Book II.

Self-analysis for Learners

To see yourself clearly as a learner, fill out the following self-analysis form as accurately as you can.

1. I know the following subjects very well:

2. I can do the following things with great skill:

3. Of all the subjects I have ever studied, the following have been the hardest for me:

4. Of these hard subjects, I have learned least about the following:

5. Of all the acts of skill I have ever tried to learn, the following have been the hardest for me to master:

6. Of these difficult acts of skill, I have made the least progress with the following:

7. I believe, on reflection, that the causes of poor learning in each case mentioned above (in Paragraphs 4 and 6) have been as follows:
    The subject   •   Cause of poor learning

8. My natural method of studying a new subject seems to be about as follows:

9. I have broken the following bad habits of reading, study, and thinking:

10. My present interests lead me toward the following new subjects:

11. My physical energy usually shows the following characteristics at the various times of day:

a. before 7 A.M...

b. just after breakfast;..

   c. toward noon;...

   d. just after lunch;...

   e. mid-afternoon;...

   f. around sunset;..

   g. in the early evening;.......................................

   h. late at night..

12. I learn most readily when I
   a. listen to somebody expounding the subject;
   b. read the subject myself;
   c. discuss the subject informally with somebody;
   d. write my own ideas on the subject;
   e. try to apply what I learn to some practical situation.
   f. commit the subject to memory.

Clearing the Mental Decks for Action.

You wish to learn something and have four hours tomorrow afternoon to devote to the task? Then arrange your schedule so that your mind will be unoccupied with serious affairs throughout the hours immediately preceding the study period.

If you must be thinking about some important matter then, arrange your schedule so that this topic be as far removed from the topic to be studied as is possible. That is to say, if you intend to work on the history of French literature during those four hours, avoid thinking about anything connected with the history of other literatures just before then. Avoid all history, in fact. Avoid studying French. Let the subject be something which is no wise bears upon either France or literature. Let it be algebra or bee keeping or chiropody.

In some learners the harm done by thinking about related matters just before learning new facts is slight, in other learners it is serious. In all cases there are two ill effects. Less is learned in the given study period, and more errors crop up in what the student thinks he has learned well.

Now suppose that you have learned something today and must use the new information tomorrow at four o'clock. Our advice must be still sterner. Under no conditions engage in serious mental effort dealing with more or less related subjects just before four o'clock. Keep your mind free and clear as long as possible before then. If you do not, the things you think about are sure to blur and block the things you must recall at four o'clock.

Many college students discover this psychic law for themselves. They sleep or else lie around and do nothing in the hours immediately preceding a stiff examination. Or, if they tend to think about other matters while lying around idle, they check that tendency by doing something trivial, such as playing checkers or indulging in horseplay.

Now for the third case. What if you have just been studying hard on some difficult subject and wish to retain every detail of it? Then beware of turning directly from it to some closely related subject. Should you violate this rule, your memory will not be blurred so badly as it would be if you reversed this sequence and attended to the related subject *before* taking up the important study. None the less, the harm done will be considerable.

The ideal is total relaxation after learning. Drop all books. Turn from your desk. Forsake your library. Loaf. Day-dream. Saw wood. Stroll up the lane. Chat with children. Do anything to escape into a serene and indolent state, for there is some sort of an after-process like soaking in or photographic developing during which the results of learning become fixed, ordered, and linked up with one's whole concourse of experiences. While that is going on, the mind must be at rest.

How long that rest should be depends upon the man, the subject, the place, the time, and a few million other circumstances. Let each learner discover it for himself. Perhaps my own experience may be suggestive, though you must not imitate it unless you find that it fits your own nature.

For more than thirty years I have made it a rule to study and do other intellectual work as early as possible in the morning. Whenever I can get under way before seven, I do so. Eight o'clock is late. Nine is fatal. For me, those first hours of the day are worth three or four times as much as any later than one in the afternoon. And I think the chief reason is that my mind is entirely clear and free from all distractions then. To be sure, I also happen to be so constituted that I am wide awake, the very instant I open my eyes; were I slow to rouse, I might not be so enthusiastic about the merits of dawn.

I have also followed the general practice of never studying anything serious after five in the afternoon. Now and then I have been forced to violate this rule; but always I return to its observance. So far as I can observe, I have not fallen far behind by honoring the nine-hour day. Apparently the soaking up process runs on vigorously through the six or seven hours of complete relaxation between day's end and bedtime.

During the nine-hour day, as a rule, intensive study naturally breaks up into many intense spurts with intervals of total mental relaxation. The spurts are never longer than forty minutes. The intervals vary, according to the subject, from five to fifteen minutes. Invariably I either walk about or snatch at some strenuous physical exercise then. When at home, I usually go outdoors.

An unusual variety of minor interests has helped me considerably in making the most of such time as is devoted to the major interests. For, as we saw a moment ago, the learning process is not seriously impaired by one's turning to subjects far removed from the study topic, after the study period. A game of chess at the end of forty minutes devoted to psychology doubtless blurs the latter a trifle, but not more than a trifle. At least three times daily I shift to some subject far from either psychology or journalism. I am sure that the habit enables me to soak up my work in these two fields much better than if I, in a desire to comprehend all of their areas and ranges, turned from psychology to neurology and psychiatry, or from journalism to the book trade. For, remember, it is the cognate subject that blurs your learning most.

Warming up to the Problem.

Warming up to your problem is by no means the same as solving it. It is exactly like warming up for a football game. Some players rehearse a few signals. Others run around a little. Others sit perfectly still. Others listen to the cheering from the bleachers. Others converse on topics far removed. There is no rule of procedure here, and he is a bad teacher who assures you to the contrary—likewise in tackling an intellectual problem.

Here are some real cases. One young engineer I know simply has to stand up at a drafting table and fiddle around with compasses and slide rules before he can get under way with an important and difficult problem in designing. He cannot begin sitting down, hands idle. A mathematician has to turn his back on the real work and chatter aimlessly about motion pictures and the local slanders of college gossip. Then, suddenly, his mind begins to function smoothly. A third man, still more eminent, walks miles all alone, scarcely seeing anything or anybody. How he has escaped motor trucks and an early death is beyond my wildest conjecture. Many thinkers potter at drawing inane designs on scraps of paper. Others lapse into daydreams for a while. Others have to sleep on their problem before it clears up. One chemist I used to know told me that he had to omit at least one meal.

Beware, then, of the would-be teacher who gives you a neat formula for thinking. No matter what it is, the formula is wrong. Genuine, fruitful thinking always grows out of your own personality. You approach the work from your own intimate angle, and no man can reveal that to you. There is no telling which of the billion channels in your brain will serve you best. Your entire past figures heavily here. Little habits may clog one route, while some preposterously trivial native ability may open another passage wide and deep. You may, for instance, have been tall when twelve; and you may have been cramped in the school seat while you were studying American history. Stiff legs and aching back may have turned the tales of Paul Revere and Ben Franklin into nightmares. So, ever since those days, you must stretch your legs and stand up, in order to use your head at its best. Of such tremendous trifles is the art of learning composed!

The trick is to find your own best way of reflecting. Your body posture, the light in the room, the noises outside, the size of type in the book you are reading, the pen point you are using, the color and texture of your scratch paper, and a myriad other items ought all be inspected carefully. Many will turn out to be insignificant. A few may influence you profoundly. You will laugh at some and curse others.

Don't Coddle Yourself!

Some experts in the art of learning advise you to seek the most favorable conditions for study. Always seek a quiet room. Fix your desk, chair, papers, and everything else so that you are as comfortable as possible. One authority even recommends that you relax completely by smoking your favorite pipe or cigarette. Most others make fun of that doctrine, but they encourage you to make every physical and psychic detail right.

If you qualify this advice properly, it is all right. But it is all wrong unless you do so. For, first of all, the learner must learn the art of concentrating; and he can never do that if he makes concentrating easy. He might as well try to learn boxing by using only pillows as gloves and never allowing his trainer to hit him hard.

So we draw a distinction. IN THE YEARS WHEN YOU ARE PERFECTING YOUR SKILL AS A LEARNER, NEVER CODDLE YOURSELF. ON THE CONTRARY, LEARN HOW TO STUDY, READ, AND PRACTICE UNDER THE MOST UNFAVORABLE CONDITIONS.

ONCE YOU HAVE ESTABLISHED THESE HABITS, REVERSE THE RULE. NOW FAVOR YOURSELF.

Go at this great task in an orderly and determined fashion. Start at the bottom and work up. May I suggest a program for your first year of self-discipline? Here it is. I have tried most of it myself and have seen others use it to high advantage.

1. Pick up your morning newspaper. Say to yourself: "I shall turn to page five and read only the second column there. I am not going to see even the headlines of the other columns." Repeat this every day for six months. You will surely improve your eye control and your power of narrow attention.

2. Next something harder! Try to concentrate on every alternate headline of the first page of your newspaper. Do your best to avoid reading the intervening headlines. You will never succeed wholly at this, I warn you. Nobody can. But you will be able to miss certain headlines now and then.

3. If you enjoy music, put on a phonograph record and play it while you study something fairly difficult. When the tune is ended, recite to yourself aloud what you have been studying. Perhaps you will attain here the same curious concentration which I did, many years ago; I forced myself to blot out sounds to such a degree that I became virtually deaf to them.

4. Now put on a phonograph record of some interesting talk. Study while it runs on. This will prove much harder. The words distract you far more than melody can. Persist in this exercise. It will drill you more intensively than any other single one. Do your utmost, for a year at least, to conquer the impulse to listen to the speech. Of course, you must not repeat the same record often; for that would make concentration on your study quite simple.

5. While all these exercises are being carried out, persuade a friend to talk to you or read aloud something interesting, while you keep your mind on your study. This is much harder than the phonograph test. The personality of the talker intrudes upon you.

6. Whenever you feel confident of your growing concentration, advance to the higher level of skill, which is involved in rapid shifts of attention. Select four widely different things to attend to. For instance, choose a new novel, a stiff article on industrial chemistry, a long poem, and a few problems in mathematics of moderate difficulty. Spread all four out before you on your desk. Have paper and pencil ready for the mathematics problems. Place a watch or clock in plain view, then begin. Concentrate for two minutes on each subject in turn. Go the rounds, say three or four times. Then stop. Now recite to yourself the gist of each individual subject, without glancing at the printed pages or at your mathematical solutions.

It won't be easy, I promise you! But persistence will bring a new ability, in time. And how useful it will prove!

7. During all these severe undertakings, practice at ear-concentration too. That is to say, take your newspaper and glance through it as naturally as possible, while somebody talks to you or reads a lesson to you from the subject of your study. Without looking away from the newspaper, endeavor to attend dominantly to the spoken words.

8. Next try to attend selectively to each of three persons, all of whom are talking to you at the same time. Instruct the speakers as to their duties here: each one is to read aloud to you a passage from some book or article dealing with the subject you are studying. All of these passages must be strange to you, of course. The readers are to speak at about the same rate and pitch and loudness. Break the tests up into one-minute periods. In the first period, attend to the first reader, in the second to the next one, and so on. Stand about ten feet away from the readers.

Whenever you are in a large gathering where many persons are talking at once, practice listening to one at a time in this same manner. Shift every half-minute or so. It will tax your powers—and that's a good thing.

9. If you become interested in this new intellectual ability, carry it still further along any line that appeals to you. For instance, you may practice at talking to somebody on some topic you have lately studied, while somebody else talks away at you. Not very hard for most of us! But still worth doing, simply because it involves a slightly different form of concentration. Or again, you may drill yourself to attend to your own thoughts inwardly, while various distractions surround you. I find this invaluable. When I am forced to attend stupid dinner parties or teas, I use most of my time there thinking about things of solid worth; and not all the chatter and clatter of inanity disturbs me much. People say I seem to be having a good time. Well, I am. But not as they imagine!

The Best Work Hardest.

To anybody except a person who suffers from an anti-Puritan complex it must be self-evident that those learners who expend the most time and effort on their subjects usually progress fastest. But would anybody have guessed that the hardest workers show up superior to all others, even when much of the work they do falls outside of those subjects? Yet this has been clearly shown by Roy N. Anderson, at Teachers' College, in a study made in 1930.

Among the students of that institution Anderson found that those who work forty-three or more hours weekly, either at their studies or in some remunerative outside job, win higher grades than those who put in, all told, only twenty-three hours. It is, says he emphatically, not an indication of any higher intelligence in the heavy workers. Rather does it seem to show that the heavy workers are engaged in outside work which teaches them something about related subjects carried in college; and then too, those who work hardest outside of college sign up for fewer courses in college and thus concentrate more effectively on them.

This may well be. But, over and above Anderson's cautious observations, cannot any observer see that volume of work means high energy, persistence of effort, freedom from load, and therefore ideal factors for any kind of learning?

Don't Fool Yourself with Daydreams!

Some people fondly fancy that they are thinking whenever vague images float through their minds. When they see a man sunk in revery, they say: "Ah! There's a deep thinker!" Ask them their notion of a great scientist, and they are likely to describe a gentleman sitting very still, chin on a hand, eyes fixed on the horizon—a caricature of Rodin's famous and sadly misleading statue, "The Thinker."

Now this notion is itself a mere conventionalized image, largely the product of ignorance in poets and artists and all common users of language. You can visit almost any large insane asylum and find inmates who remain sunken in vacuous broodings which never lead to the feeblest act of thinking, in the true sense. They might readily have posed for Rodin's statue. Conversely, you may observe and quiz men who have contributed priceless thoughts to science; and you will surely find, among them, many who declare that they don't know what those images are; and many others who, as they think, never attend to their topics after the manner of the daydreamer, but rather busy themselves with retorts and flames and galvanometers in fashion most objective.

Here then we have a perfect proof that thinking is not merely a stream of images. Many who have images never reach any conclusions that have validity; and, on the other hand, many who reach brilliant conclusions never daydream and are unaware of all images. This should explode, once and for all, the error that the quality of a man's thinking is in any wise to be gauged by his images.

One of the most interesting and, in some respects, ablest intellectual men I know has, in the course of sixty years, learned astonishingly little—simply because he cannot resist the joys of revery. Hour in, hour out, he loves to sit around musing over nothing in particular. Has he no strong interests? Oh, yes! Several. And these he pursues zealously up to the point at which hard work sets in. Then, perhaps seven times out of ten, he succumbs to the lure of daydreams.

Work Every Day!

And now we are headed for a quarrel! Many readers will dissent from the preachment of the next few paragraphs. But I stand my ground none the less.

Work a little every day at your subject. I mean that you should work 365 days a year at it, except during leap years. Then put in 366 days. I am not commanding you to devote any particular length of time for each day's task. All I urge is that you never drop the job for so much as twenty-four hours, except when too sick to hold up your head or when caught in some crisis. Otherwise stick to your enterprise as you adhere to your three meals a day!

Why be so drastic? Isn't this a bit fanatical? Perhaps a little. But let me present my argument for the measure.

The aim of ideal learning is to convert the subject matter into a reflex, or something as nearly like a reflex as possible. Automatic, unconscious recalling, judging, feeling, and doing is the obvious goal; for only as we draw near to it do we reap the huge rewards of learning, namely the economy of effort that true mastery brings. To him who has learned well, all things are as easy as breathing.

Keeping Everlastingly at It.

But how accomplish this? By steady pounding. Any rest longer than twenty-four hours is downright injurious. Something fades, a tie weakens, a link in the chain of memories cracks. I do not hesitate for a moment to declare that the two most serious weaknesses in the American public schools system are, first, the Saturday and Sunday holiday and, secondly, the long summer vacation. Breaks like these in the learning process destroy almost as much as teachers have laboriously built up during the week or term. Every teacher knows this only too well.

How dull the pupils are on Monday mornings! How much duller are they when they return to school in the fall after ten or more weeks of escape from class subjects! Little morons would shine as brightly as these during the opening fortnight of the year. Nor are college students much better, except in their general attitude toward study. And the curse of idleness extends even to adult workers, whose "Monday morning slump" is notorious. They spoil goods, they get caught in machines, they sell badly, they slow down at every job, and part of the decline, though not all of it, is traceable to nothing more than the mere stopping for forty-eight hours.

Let me quote once again the over-cited confession of Paderewski concerning his own skill at the piano.

If I omit my practicing for one day, I know the difference. If I miss it for two days, the critics know it. And if for three days, the audience knows it.

The law holds with peculiar force, I believe, in habits of high dexterity, such as Paderewski's playing, and in linguistic achievements, such as the mastery of a language radically different from one's native tongue. This explains the tremendous advantage of learning a language by living among the natives. You cannot escape it for even twelve hours at a stretch, except by sleeping too long of nights. It is ever with you, flaunting itself on billboards, yelling at you through the rusty throats of street peddlers, coaxing you to give ear as it trickles from the lips of waiters, salesmen, and fair ladies. By the same token, we explain also the higher dexterity of the professional, as contrasted to the amateur (and still more strikingly to the dilettante), in the performance of difficult feats, be they acrobatic or artistic. The professional must earn his bread and butter by going through the severe routine of giving his show and "doing his stuff" on schedule. The professional is not superior to the amateur in his abilities. He outstrips his easygoing rival only by unrelenting drill.

Theory and Practice.

Here too we come upon one of the deepest differences between the so-called academic mind and the practical mind. A brilliant man elects to devote his life to a study of, let us say, finance. He pursues the subject as an amateur—that is, just for love of it. He seeks neither wealth nor fame, simply insight. He accepts a college professorship and lectures three times a week to undergraduates, for about thirty-two weeks of the year. He puts in perhaps four days a week, all told, on some aspect of his subject. During the summer he goes off to the seashore and has a joyful vacation. How does his grasp of finance compare with that of a man of equal brilliance who takes a job in a bank and works on financial problems every hour of the day for six days a week? The sheer repetition and continuity of his performance deepens the reflexity of his knowledge, his motor responses, and his attitudes toward men and affairs. He deals with these fast and surely, while his academic brother speculates timidly, gropes, messes about with generalities, and all too often arrives at conclusions which fail to reckon with concrete factors.

The evils of long breaks in learning are least apparent at the very beginning of a course of study; for then it is that you make the fastest progress, relative to the total amount to be learned. Those evils become flagrant as you approach the finish and wrestle with the utmost niceties of complete knowledge and smooth dexterity; for there men always advance most slowly toward their goal of mastery.

We all recognize this fact when we say that anybody can learn to play a passable game of billiards but only a marvel can become expert in eighteen-inch balk line; or that any nimble youth can pick up the rudiments of tennis in a few weeks so as to have a bully good time, while nothing short of years of practice, every day of each month, will make a Tilden or a Cochet. Of course, if you study a subject simply to get fun out of it, you need not take my present exhortation seriously to heart. Most learners, however, toil under some stronger impulsion than fun. This is true of the best amateurs no less than of all professionals who work for a living.

Bobby Jones and Harold Vanderbilt.

At this moment, the two best known amateurs who deserve all the fame they have won are Bobby Jones, in golf, and Harold Vanderbilt, the skipper who beat Sir Thomas Lipton's Shamrock V. Both demonstrate my argument. Could you know the hours each has spent practicing the niceties of his hobby, you would not marvel much at his display of skill. Vanderbilt has literally lived at the helm from childhood. It is more than likely that he has handled a sailing vessel of some sort fully five hours for every one hour so spent by Ted Heard, the skipper of Shamrock V, who is said to receive the highest salary in his profession. Bobby Jones has doubtless been able to devote far more time to the refining of his strokes than most professionals can; for it is the lot of the usual professional to spend most of his day teaching dubs, advising fat brokers as to their clubs and sins of putting, and repairing shattered midirons.

It is practice that makes perfect. Nothing else brings to top performance whatever abilities lie dormant in the learner. And practice follows the sun. Any break is a setback.

The Wise Learner Eats and Sleeps Well.

If you want to slow down, grow dull, develop inaccurate observations, and draw illogical conclusions, go on a stern diet! Reduce the amount of sugar to, say, half of the stomach's desire. Cut your daily intake of calories from 3,000 or thereabout to 2,000 or fewer. That will bring you down toward the moron grade so fast that you may feel like the stick of a burned-out sky rocket, on its way back to earth.

This is no mere bogie. It has been demonstrated fully. For many years we have known that the poorest pupils in the public schools are the undernourished. School lunches have raised the achievement level of tens of thousands of sad little youngsters who have been compelled to rush off to school with hardly a bite to eat. An empty stomach makes an empty head. Nature ordains that we care for the necessities of existence before we indulge in the regal luxury of learning.

Laboratory experiments on adults have lately been made by Donald Laird, at Colgate University, all confirming the experiences of school teachers. Women who go on a diet to reduce their weight become clumsy, bungle in their common judgments, and work much more slowly than before they undertook to meddle with their bodies. To this let me add personal testimony. I find it impossible to do any intellectual work, even of a trivial sort, on an empty stomach. And many people tell me they behave likewise. I make absurd errors in adding columns of figures and in hitting the keys of my typewriter. The drop in skill is nearly as great as that caused by smoking.

There are all sorts of eating habits, and he would be a crank who laid down rules about them to fit all men. What I have said applies to the rank and file of humanity. But no doubt, here and there in the world, you can find a few rare specimens who study best when underfed. Have there not been great ascetic scholars? Probably such need little food; hence they are not denying themselves at all but rather striking the correct life balance even as do others who eat thrice as much.

Among distinguished intellectuals what an astonishing number of lusty trenchermen appear! Hark back to the great Thomas Aquinas, philosopher, theologian, fat giant, and mighty consumer of protein and vitamines, not to mention wine. Trace the lineage of the gourmands and gluttons from him to our day. How many vigorous minds crop out there! Nobody has done a clean job of enumeration here; I speak therefore simply on general impressions drawn from many biographies. But I am on safer ground in saying that not only are undernourished and badly fed scholars rare but, when they do learn much, they warp much and give back a distorted view of life.

As for sleep, we tread on the shaky ground that overlays a volcano of controversy. To thresh through all the evidence about the importance of sleep is impossible now. The conclusion I have reached, however, is that, while individuals vary amazingly in the way they sleep and the length of time they must sleep, each one seems to have a certain narrow range beyond which he cannot pass without disturbing some of his functions. And too little sleep is far more serious than too much.

That Scarlet Woman, Lady Nicotine.

If you wish to learn easily and fast, beware of that sweet-scented strumpet, Lady Nicotine! We do not advocate that she be wholly banned from good society. Many there be who need her—and some who need her every hour. But we speak here of the ambitious learner, and in no wavering phase nor timid word. Proof is at hand that, for the vast majority of men and women, every ounce of tobacco smoked retards and confuses their intellectual work to a degree easily measured in the laboratory.

Indeed, it has been so measured, and by highly competent, disinterested physicians and psychologists. Probably

you have never heard about the researches of the committee
of scientists, under the presidency of Dr. Alexander Lam-
bert. Many of the leaders in physiology, neurology, psychology, genetics, economics and social science served on
that committee. Carefully controlled laboratory tests and
statistical surveys were made; and several important
monographs published. The two which concern us here
are M. V. O'Shea's sizable book, entitled "Tobacco and
Mental Efficiency" (1923) and a general committee summary of clinical data, entitled "Tobacco and Physical
Efficiency" (1927).

The newspapers and magazines have seen to it that
few Americans found a fair chance to learn the findings of
these works. For the entire periodical press is terrified at the
thought of losing their tobacco advertisements as a result
of printing anything even faintly adverse to nicotine.
I shall sum up a few of the proved facts bearing on the art
of learning. As no tobacconist is likely to open these pages,
they may escape the wrath of the poisoners.

The mental efficiency of telegraphers sinks rapidly as
the amount of smoking increases. This is most conspicuous
toward the end of the day's work, as we might well expect.
The heavy smokers cannot hold the pace. They make more
mistakes in receiving and sending messages, and they also
slow down. Put on the pressure, and they fail, while the
non-smokers and light smokers speed up.

The large majority of young men who have been tested
concentrate upon reading matter and work problems more
poorly during and soon after smoking. Moderate and heavy
smokers among college students are, on the broad average,
about 10 per cent less efficient than non-smokers in all
types of mental work. The greatest loss of ability seems to
be in mental imagery, which plays such an important part
in much thinking. (To some, like Dimnet, imagery seems
the very core of thinking; hence all such should note well
this fact!) In some students it has been found that the

smoker is 22 per cent below the non-smoker in this lively trait.

The slumps in perception and association are also marked. Oddly enough, the greatest losses in ability occurred in cigarette smokers, not in pipe and cigar smokers.

Smokers cannot commit things to memory nearly so well as non-smokers. Nor do they show up nearly so well in any behavior which calls for nice coordinations, such as in drafting, playing the violin or piano, free composition in drawing, or literary essays. They cannot, of course, maintain the speed of the non-smokers in any type of work, mental or physical. Now and then, a freak bobs up who can smoke ten cigars and then win a hundred-yard dash; but we may ignore him here.

All this explains the striking observation made in many colleges that, as J. R. Earp puts it in his study of English university students:

> Although the number of smokers and non-smokers in the college (which he investigated) is practically the same, yet out of 23 students dismissed last year for low scholarship, no less than 21 were smokers. As one ascends the scale of scholarship, the proportion of non-smokers grows steadily greater. And, in general, those who smoke much have lower scholarships than those who smoke little.[1]

This squares with my own observations during twenty-five years of college professors and students alike. With only a few exceptions—so few as to be meaningless in any statistical survey—the most brilliant have been either non-smokers or very light smokers; and, when light smokers, rarely cigarette smokers but most often pipe smokers who burn up three or four pipe loads a day, rarely more. A careful check-up on my own mental efficiency as a heavy smoker convinced me in a jiffy that tobacco is the most expensive luxury in the world. A dollar's worth of it invariably reduced my working ability by fully one-third; and

[1] See *The Lancet*, London, 1925, vol. 218, Part I, p. 213.

that was the same as losing one-third of my waking hours. Not being pleased at this partial suicide, I quit all forms of tobacco sharply; with no tapering off or other coddling habits. I just stopped one day and never again touched the weed. The good effects were colossal.

I read faster and more accurately. I retained more of what I read. I typed much faster and with fewer errors. I lectured more fluently and with no trace of a mild exhaustion which had formerly appeared now and then after two or three hours of public speaking. But perhaps the most striking improvement was one which few people appreciate. I found that I shifted from one task to another far more nimbly; hence I could work on a wider variety of topics in the course of an ordinary day.

During the last two years of heavy smoking, my velocity of writing newspaper copy was declining, not greatly but enough to give me pause. It was a distinctly unpleasant effort to finish, in decent form, more than 1,000 words. Within six months after foreswearing nicotine, I found it almost too easy to maintain an average of 2,000 words daily; and not long thereafter I improved to the degree of 3,000 words. To be sure I never had cause to write as much as that every day for any long stretch; but, whenever it has been necessary, I have had no trouble in holding the pace, which, modesty compels me to relate, is very slow as compared to writers like Dr. Henry Smith Williams, who, by dictating instead of typing, readily turns out 10,000 words a day of book copy so polished that hardly any subsequent revising is called for. Need I add that Dr. Williams never smokes?

Lindbergh, Hearst, Vanderbilt.

Remember, please! I am not arguing that no man ever accomplished much while smoking. We are concerned here solely with the act of learning and the direct application of what has been learned. News reporting is a fair sample of the practical work I refer to; so is aviation and any behavior calling for high dexterity during the learning and its first use. After the learner has mastered his subject, he may continue to use it while smoking considerably, just as General Grant devoured miles of black cigars during his campaigns. This does not contradict what has here been said, for using habits already perfected is a far simpler process than establishing those habits. Then too, the stimulus to use them differs vastly from the stimulus to learn; usually it is ten times stronger and more visible. Nevertheless, does it not follow that he who learns best is most likely to do things best afterward? And that he is also likely to continue all those incidental habits of self-discipline which aided him while learning? I think so. This doubtless explains, at least in part, why men who have been amazingly keen learners of difficult techniques have refrained from smoking, while learning, and have gone on tobaccoless afterward, when the prime necessity for so doing was over. I cite here such striking models as Lindbergh, Hearst, and Harold Vanderbilt. No three men could differ more widely in every respect save the one point I now discuss. Each excels in a peculiar field of skill and knowledge: Lindbergh in flying, Hearst in newspaper management, and Vanderbilt in yachting. The first two seem to be constitutionally uninterested in nicotine. Vanderbilt is not, and to that degree is a better exemplar for us, particularly in his self-control during the four months preceding the America Cup races, when he swore off of all tobacco, even cigarettes, in order to become keener at the helm.

I wish that some amiable fanatic would finance a disinterested investigation of the smoking habits of eminent men during their years of intensive learning. We know, of course, that surprisingly many great personalities like Edison and Ford never smoke. But I suspect we would discover that many who took up the weed after they became successful and famous had abstained from it through the critical years of conquering. In some classes this is self-evident: no great boxer, wrestler, runner, or other athlete smokes while training, save an occasional freak of nature. But most of them resume the weed after they have won the highest laurels and have nothing left to do except to sign articles for the newspaper syndicates. Doesn't this hold true in other fields? Let some eager truth seeker find the answer!

Let me repeat, I am concerned here only with the art of learning. Far be it from me to dissuade anybody from his favorite "coffin nail" or pipe on broad hygienic principles. I believe that millions of people truly need to be slightly narcotized in order to endure the world (and themselves), just as I believe that millions of Asiatics are much better off when steeped in opium than when clear-headed. Few men can face reality, least of all in China and India. As for our own land, that dullness of wit which smoking almost always induces prevents excessive competition for the more lucrative and honorable positions in business and society. The gentle poison thus takes the edge off our industrialism, especially for the weaker spirits. Thousands of men whose abilities are mediocre or slightly better become content with their lot, as a result of tobacco. Their faintly narcotized brains do not crave work. They take things easily. Smokers are surely better natured than non-smokers, as a rule. They are less inquisitive, less ambitious, and less thorough than they themselves would be, if they did not smoke. Why should any reformer break in upon such happy doldrums?

But what if a young man truly desires to master something? Then my advice in unequivocal. If that is your aim, then train for the Great Race! And, first of all, cut out all narcotics, weed and wet alike, at least until you have gained your goal. What you do after the Great Race is not my present affair at all. I pose now as a trainer, and you as a contestant in a Marathon. To conserve your wind and wit, I order an uncontaminated nervous system.

EXERCISE
THESE FACTS DESERVE YOUR ATTENTION

It is estimated that people spend about $100,000,000 a year on drugs. Headache powders are particularly harmful if used indiscriminately and without medical advice, for they tend to obscure the causes of the headache, which may range from brain tumor, Bright's disease, high blood pressure, and anaemia, through many other diseases and physical defects. Many people use purgatives and laxatives unintelligently, and they do real injury to their systems through the bad habit. Even the value of mineral waters is greatly exaggerated, and often these do as much harm to the body as do patent medicines. Tea and coffee do have a definite drug effect on the body, but their use in moderation seldom does immediate harm to most people. Over indulgence in tea and coffee, however, unquestionably has bad effects and may cause serious disturbance in the circulation and the nervous system, especially over a long period of years.

Overlearning.

It is useless to learn something up to the point at which you can perform its operations for a little while after study is ended but not for longer. Students who cram for examination are merely wasting their own time and lives. They learn for an hour and then forget. The game isn't worth the candle. As well not have learned at all and gone fishing! Even if no fish were caught, the time would be more profitably spent.

People often say: "Oh, yes, I learned French once. But that was years ago! I can't read a line of it now." We have come to accept that meaning of the verb. We permit its use as indicating as little as a moment's mastery. So we shall have to adopt, for the moment at least, another expression to describe genuine mastery—and that is overlearning. It is a poor word, forced upon us by popular misuse of the shorter and nobler term.

You have not mastered a subject until your habits have become as quick and as automatic as reflexes. You have not mastered that same subject until those reflex-like habits have struck root so deeply that, a year or more after you have ceased studying in the formal sense, these operate with ease, grace, and precision. How acquire this ability?

The rule is straightforward and inflexible.

AFTER YOU HAVE LEARNED YOUR LESSON UP TO THE POINT OF BEING ABLE TO REPEAT IT SMOOTHLY, CONTINUE TO DRILL YOURSELF IN IT JUST AS IF YOU HAD NOT YET COMMITTED IT TO MEMORY. ACCORDING TO THE DIFFICULTY OF THE SUBJECT, KEEP THIS UP FOR A FEW WEEKS OR A FEW MONTHS.

Let me illustrate this from my own experience. The hardest material I ever undertook to learn was the vocabulary of the Arabic philosophers who translated Aristotle and Plato into their own tongue. The terms had absolutely no connection with any words I had previously learned. Many of them were inaccurate translations of the Greek, hence confusing. There was nothing to do but grind them in by brute force.

To this ignoble end, I wrote each word on a small square of paper and its translation, in either Greek or Latin, on the back. I bundled the papers in lots of twenty-five with rubber bands and made a rule to carry at least two bundles about with me at all times. I would practice at these as I rode on train and street car, while I was waiting to meet somebody, in between classes, at meal time, and on every other occasion when nothing more pressing was at hand.

I kept this up for about two years. The result was that the basic vocabulary was beaten into my nervous system very well indeed. But there were several hundred words to which I had devoted little time, and they never stuck right. The others stayed by me for several years; down to the time when I put aside the entire subject of Oriental philosophy and determined to forget it because it was worthless. Today I probably could not recall offhand more than a dozen of those technical terms.

Follow Your Heart.

Work your brain in sincere imitation of your heart. Do you know how your heart works? After every contraction of its mighty muscles, they rest. In no other way could they hold the tremendous pace which every healthy heart must for seventy years or more.

Probably every organ of the body works more or less in the same manner. Each one can do work only when it has the fuel for it; and the blood furnishes that fuel, which is pumped in many mighty spurts from the heart to the seat of activities. Let the fuel supply drop ever so little, and the organ must slow down. Dizziness and fainting spells are often caused by a tiny shortage of blood somewhere in the brain while the latter is being driven to work. It is even likely that some profound constitutional stupidities such as we behold in morons are caused by a lack of fuel channels into the large brain, or by a poor quality of blood.

Be that as it may, we know for a certainty that the brain cannot work continuously, even for a few minutes. No function of thinking is continuous. The very basis of all mental work, of course, is the act of attending to something; but this cannot be prolonged beyond one or two seconds. To me, the parallel between the work-and-rest cycle of the heart and that of the act of attending seems highly significant. I wish some psychologist would make a careful study of it. I suspect he would find more than one important correlation between the rate and vigor of the two processes.

The keenest, most fruitful intellectual work is done in many short spurts, between which a state of complete rest is attained. The length of each spurt varies from man to man; but I doubt whether anybody, save a few odd characters, ever concentrates for longer than ten or fifteen minutes at a stretch. They may think otherwise, but they are overlooking the brief relaxations.

EXERCISES

Describe the four lions in the path of learning!

What do you remember about the effects of headache powders, purgatives and laxatives, mineral waters, tea, and coffee on the organism?

State, in outline form, my argument against smoking while learning.

What are the chief advantages of learning a little every day?

Study your own work cycles with care. Tackle some task involving considerable study. Check up on yourself with a watch. Write the record of your periods of intense effort and rest. Do you discover anything about your work habits?

One Thing at a Time!

One thing at a time! One idea mastered by itself! One unit operation practiced to the point of your executing it smoothly! That is a basic rule of learning.

Many of you can recall the anguish of certain studies in school. Could you turn back to the pages you pored over then and recall the precise manners of the classroom, you would almost certainly find that the teacher—possibly under orders from a stupid school board committee—had chopped up your lessons into lengths very much as a small boy chops up a big angleworm for bait. The ends of the angle worm wriggle off, each in its own direction; and the middle pieces perish. A career is ended. So too with you and those hacked morsels of truth.

"Tomorrow, children, you are to read forty lines of Evangeline, starting at the top of page 43."

"The next lesson will be the next four theorems about isosceles triangles."

Of such was your schooling, in no small measure, many years ago. And that was what made Jack a dull boy.

If now, being grown to adult estate, you seek to learn things for yourself, shun that anglewormy method as the plague. It defeats itself. Each lesson must be a single unit of thought. It must make a point clearly, then stop. To be sure, this point relates to some larger whole; but that's another story.

But what if the books you read do not break up into neat units thus? Well, that's a pity, but you can still make progress. Seek out the essential features yourself. Do so by skimming over the entire book, catching a rough bird's-eye view of its whole treatment, all its outstanding propositions, and the larger relations among them. Then come back and study each proposition by itself. You are doing work which the author ought to have done for you. Except in very complex subjects, however, you can probably do it.

To help yourself in this difficult task, draw back for a long running start. I mean that you should orient yourself in the larger subject by first looking it up in the encyclopaedias and in lightly written popular works. There you invariably find the chief points clearly put. After learning them, you can attack badly written textbooks with profit.

Review Early and Often!

Go over and over the ground you have lately covered. Do not be satisfied with an occasional backward glance. The review serves several deep purposes which young learners especially are prone to miss. Each survey brings out something missed or unduly minimized previously. It also reinforces the habit formation and advances you toward the point at which you know and use the new material in a reflex manner, with no conscious effort.

It is impossible to lay down hard-and-fast rules as to the frequency of reviewing. The ideal is to approach one review daily, even though it is brief. In some complicated subjects, the daily review may fail to show results simply because the single day's lesson lacks logical unity. None the less, repeat and repeat and repeat, even though you are not aware of the benefits at the moment.

Scarcely anybody reads the important books of his favorite subject often enough. Some great works deserve to be reviewed thoroughly from cover to cover at least once a year for twenty years. The stiffer the content, the more urgent is frequent review.

Learning to Read.

Reading plays a larger part in learning than adults usually think. We have become dulled to this seemingly simple performance, through years of habit. Still worse, most of us have lost proficiency since school days. The typical American reads more slowly and less accurately than he used to when in grammar school. Even high school students read more poorly than they did two years before entering the ninth grade. And great has been the perturbation of teachers over this phenomenon.

How well can you read? Don't guess! Measure yourself. Here are the standards of speed and accuracy.

1. The usual run of first-page stories in your daily newspaper should be read by a well trained adult at the average rate of at least five words per second.

2. Serious material containing details which do not call for study but rather for close attention, say such as would be found in a solid magazine article, should be read at the rate of four words per second.

3. Fairly difficult articles dealing with matters about which you know little, but in words with which you are familiar, should be read at the rate of around three words per second.

4. Technical subjects using words strange to you may require almost any time, according to their difficulty; it is hard to set up a standard of attainment here.

The art of reading is head man in our show. He who is not master of the first of the three R's is lost. If you are a skillful reader, however, you have learned the most important single factor in learning, for in undertaking any intellectual problem, you must read, understand, and make a part of your intellectual equipment thousands of pages of printed matter. What, then, should you know about the technique of reading?

There are three kinds of reading in which you must acquire expert skill. You must first know how to study, which involves slow, careful reading of strange text. Next, you must be able to read at medium speed in order to seize the general content of books and articles of interest and importance. And finally, you should be able to skim, in order to hit the high spots of material whose content is neither difficult nor important enough for you to cover with care. We do not here discuss the question of reading for pleasure alone, for that is a special problem in aesthetics, and unrelated to the art of learning.

We cannot undertake to teach you here how to increase your reading speed. We must assume that you have at least average skill in reading and comprehending discussions of subjects almost wholly new to you at a rate of about 6,000 words per hour. You should read slightly less difficult material with thorough understanding at a rate of about 10,000 words per hour. The competent reader usually speeds up to about 14,000 words an hour in reading serious books and articles of only moderate difficulty.

Test your own rates in reading. How long by the clock does it take you to read 1,000 words of each of these three grades of reading matter—from the simple to the highly technical? In each case, after you have completed the passage, write down the *essential* facts which you recall. If your reading rates come close to those which we have indicated above, and if, at the same time, you recall with fair accuracy at least half of the subject matter, average and regular drill should quickly improve you. If, on the other hand, you read much more slowly than does the competent reader, or if, reading at a fair rate of speed, you find yourself sadly deficient in accurately recalling the substance of what you have read, you should drill yourself in reading for several months.

The way to read fast is to read fast.

That sounds silly, doesn't it? But it isn't. The trick is to force yourself up to your top speed, not once but repeatedly. For some time, of course, you will lose some of the important points; and you may even conclude that you are spoiling your mind and eye. But rarely is that true. You are merely going through the throes of wrecking a bad habit and building up a new one.

Be ruthless and methodical in your ruthlessness. Measure your speed every day or two. Aim to break your own record at least every week for some months. Keep your series of records posted in a conspicuous place, to remind you that a great contest is on.

The fundamentals have been taken up in a separate volume.[1] You should improve your skill by studying that book with care and doing the exercises regularly. Before you do that, you may begin with the following ten rules:

1. Never read when tired.

2. Read in a good position. Most people read best when sitting fairly erect, with the head slightly inclined.

3. The light should come from behind and slightly above your shoulder in such a way that the type on the page before you is evenly illumined.

4. Hold the book or magazine at your own best reading distance.

5. Read phrases and sentences. Do NOT read word by word.

6. Do not move your lips as you read.

7. Don't read when likely to be distracted by interruptions.

8. READ FOR RELATIVE IMPORTANCES. Select what you want to read. Discard everything else. You need not read every chapter of every book which is recommended to you. And in only the most technical and solid of reading matter do you need to read every word of copy.

9. When you have finished a difficult passage, think through its important points. Are there any other related points which are implied but not discussed in the text? Have you read other books or articles bearing on the same problems? Do you agree with the main contentions? Think the thing through—and drop it.

10. When you come back to further study, look through the chapters last read and refresh your memory on their important points.

The learner differs from the average reader in one important point. His purpose is to master his subject as he goes along. His aim is to discover various aspects of a particular problem. The way he reads, therefore, is determined by this purpose. His reading speed, of course, will vary according to the difficulty of the subject matter. He cannot set his own pace. This must depend entirely on the difficulty of the material whose content he wishes to master.

¹ PITKIN, W. B., "The Art of Rapid Reading," McGraw-Hill Book Company, Inc., New York, 1929.

EXERCISES

Here is a news item about the value of silent reading. Before you begin it, place one finger on your lips and two other fingers of the same hand on your laryngx. Do not press hard; just let the fingers rest lightly in position. They are to register any movements you may make while reading.

Now read rapidly.

When you have finished, turn away from the passage and jot down the main points in it, as far as you recall them.

Did you move lips or throat while reading? If so, set out to conquer this harmful habit at once. Read a little every day with fingers on the ill trained organs of speech. Try hard to keep the latter quiet. It may prove hard. But, unless you have the bad luck to be an extreme type of throat-thinker, you will make progress and speed up your literary adventures.

SCHOOLS TO STRESS READING IN SILENCE

New Syllabus for Elementary Grades Prescribes Tests for Text-Perusing Skill.

CALLED AID IN ALL STUDIES

Revised Course Supplements Oral Method to Add to Proficiency in Learning and Pleasure.

Emphasis on the importance of silent reading, diagnostic testing with a view to remedying specific defects and the procedures in teaching skill in reading for recreation and for study are the outstanding features of a new reading course to be introduced in elementary schools throughout the city next semester.

The revised course is one of the many new curricula prepared during the last few years with a view to improving and modernizing instruction in the public schools. Arithmetic and science courses already have been revised.

The new outline describes different practices in teaching oral and silent reading. Training in oral reading alone does not lead to efficient reading, the syllabus declares, and for that reason "definite training in silent reading should begin in the first grade." Again and again the syllabus emphasizes silent reading as the basis of all later study.

Oral Reading Easier to Teach.

It is pointed out that scientific studies have shown that radical changes in pupils' attitude toward the two types of reading appear in the fourth or fifth grade. "It is here that independent silent reading begins to take on marked significance as a separate aspect of mental life," the syllabus quotes a monograph on the subject as declaring.

The syllabus warns instructors that silent reading is not so easy to teach as oral reading and calls for "resourcefulness in arousing various responses to test the child's comprehension of the material read." Responses may be tested by requiring responses to directions or questions in regard to material read. The answers may be vocal or, as in some of the specially prepared examinations, written or pictorial. The children may be asked to correlate a word with a picture by underlining or otherwise indicating a crucial term.

Such testing belongs to the early stages of reading practice. Other ways of judging comprehension in silent reading are given by the syllabus, as follows:

"Dramatization—the performance should be the child's own interpretation as far as possible. Puppet shows and pantomime may also be employed.

"Graphic illustration—pictures to illustrate characters in the story and diagrams to explain events may be drawn by the child.

"Reproduction—the child may reproduce the subject-matter in his own words."

Reading Related to Other Work.

Special stress is laid on the supplying of sets of books for individual work, but teachers are asked to make an effort to give comprehension tests after the completion of each work. Classes are to have a library hour when children may select their own books and "a library table or shelf for the child's use should form part of the equipment of each classroom." In addition, home reading is to be encouraged, although the "basal" reader is to be kept in school and used only under supervision.

"The new course," said Superintendent William J. O'Shea in a circular describing the syllabus sent yesterday to all principals, "prescribes oral reading in all grades, but requires a predominance of it only in the first three years, an equal division of time between oral and silent reading in the fourth year, and a predominance of silent reading thereafter. In the seventh and eighth years silent reading should receive the major emphasis, but oral reading should not be neglected.

"The basis of nearly all study is the ability to read silently, because it is largely through silent reading that knowledge is acquired. Silent reading in school is important, then, not only as a part of the required work in reading, but as a means of obtaining information in every subject. Even in arithmetic, failure may be due to weakness in silent reading, which may result in inability to understand the facts given and the nature of the problem which is to be solved.

"One of the best ways to improve the ability to study arithmetic is to lead pupils to read the problem carefully and analyze it into its elements, so that they may understand clearly what is given and what is required before they do any of the computation."[1]

[1] From the *New York Times*.

Broad Learning Is Invaluable.

Of late it has become the fashion to decry the old-style liberal education and to stress only those studies which aid the learner to earn more money. The vocational school has been ousting all other kinds at a great rate. Grave the injuries which will result, if this practice runs riot. The most useful things in this world have no special connection with any job. Yet, paradoxically, they do butter your bread. They give you your bearings in the whole domain of life; they enable you to see the forest in spite of the trees—and that is your best guidance to your own best way of life, which naturally includes your own best job.

A truly liberal education has one and only one aim; it frees the learner from superstitions, from prejudices, from the cramped thoughts and habits of the home and neighborhood in which his early notions have been formed; and, constructively, it aids him in developing new habits which vent his own fullest personality in the environment at hand. When, therefore, I speak of a subject in the following pages as useless, I mean, above all, that it lacks power to emancipate as well as to develop the learner. For example, I shall have occasion to oppose the "cultural study" of French, German, and other modern languages; and I shall call them sterile and useless. This must not be taken to mean that I advise you to shun such studies if your aim is merely pleasure. Nor would I even warn you against them if you are keenly inquisitive about them. Curiosity should never be thwarted. All I say, in such cases, is that you will have to live and learn; that, after you have spent precious months toiling over alien grammars and mouthing phrases which you will never use in any real conversation, you may —if you are keenly thoughtful—at least learn the emptiness of your efforts. And that is something!

The Great God Trash!

Who will have the hardest time with the art of learning? He who formed the habit of reading endless trash between the ages of ten and sixteen. His vocabulary will be thin and inexact. He will expect to be entertained in every paragraph. He will find slow study irksome to the point of agony; and, having a foggy perspective in serious matters, he will find it hard to grasp the drift and significance of his reading and observations.

To such a learner my best advice is: Work doubly hard to overcome your unfortunate handicap of bad home training. And count your victory as correspondingly greater! While learning, expect difficulties beyond those which luckier men must surmount. Do not be discouraged if, for example, you must spend much more time on each exercise in observing, analyzing, reading, and reporting than is indicated in the text of this book.

Unless you have money to waste, buy no cheap novels, no cheap magazines, no tabloid newspapers. What little you possess that can wisely be devoted to the art of learning ought to be spent for substantial books and periodicals. In seeking the best, keep in mind one inexorable fact: the truly significant books for the learner are almost never to be found among best sellers or on the lists of book clubs. Be assured that almost any book that is bought by a quarter-million or more people cannot teach you anything. It has won its immense sales because it pleases readers, either by offering them an escape from realities or by flattering them hugely (such flattery being a disguised escape from one's own private reality!).

It is from less popular books that you will learn most. And, obviously, from text books, about which we have not been speaking thus far. Probably not more than one such in every ten offers an adult much; nor should we expect otherwise, seeing that they have been prepared for the young. Scientific and technical volumes yield you much more; but these, alas, are too often written with leaden words and ink of mud. Slovenly English, bad arranging of topics, excess of trivial references, and many tempests in the teapots of pedantry make them dull reading. With such you must put up until something better appears.

EXERCISE

In the following passage you will find two kinds of information: facts dealing with the prevailing conditions of health in the United States, and facts about the business conditions of the country in the late summer of 1930. Ignore the latter. Read only the evidence having to do with the health conditions of the United States.

Whether or not the increased tariffs have played an important part in the fall in revenue in the United States from July 1 to August 19, 1930, is not certain. The fact remains, however, that customs receipts during that period have fallen from about $85,000,000 to around $45,000,000, or $40,000,000 less than the receipts for the same period in 1929. This country loses annually more than $3,000,000,000 from preventable disease and death, of which more than half is among persons gainfully employed. Every year 42,000,000 workers lose 350,000,000 days from illness and accidents, and 28,000 die from industrial accidents. The general downward trend in production, however, shows a single exception in the case of cigarette production, which rose to nearly 12,000,000,000 during July, 1930, as compared with about 10,700,000,000 in the same month of 1929. Half a million workers die each year. At least 250,000 of them could be saved by adequate medical supervision, regular medical examination and community hygiene. But, of course, experts will disagree, and the responsibility of the tariff for the general decline in business will be a moot question for some time.

NOW TURN THE PAGE

What do you recall from this passage about:

a. The annual loss in the United States from preventable disease and death.

b. The number of workers losing days from illness and accidents.

c. The value in lives of adequate medical examination, supervision, and general hygiene.

d. The number of workers dying each year.

How accurately have you remembered the figures in this passage? Probably only moderately so. If you have remembered half of those dealing with the health of the United States, you have done well.

Learning to Listen.

If you take notes while listening to a lecture, you will probably recall no more of the speaker's remarks than if you had simply listened. There is just one condition under which your notes would help considerably: had you been drilled in taking well organized notes, you might surpass your best record as a simple listener. Seasoned newspaper reporters usually have thus trained themselves; and yet it is significant that few of them ever do jot down memoranda in the midst of an interview or lecture, except where it is vital to record a statement verbatim.

EXERCISE

Persuade a friend to read aloud to you the following account of intelligence tests. Do not interrupt him unless it be to hear more clearly. He should not repeat any of the passage. But be sure that he enunciates well and reads rather slowly.

As soon as he has finished reading, have him take pencil and paper. Then do you report to him by word of mouth as much as you can of what he read. He is to jot down all you say, item by item. Later you are to compare the amount and accuracy of your report with one which you base on reading instead of listening. From this and other similar tests you will be able to form a pretty clear idea as to whether you learn better through the eye than through the ear, or possibly, best of all, by use of speech.

INTELLIGENCE TEST HAS LIMITED SCOPE

With Its Aid Generalizations Can Be Made Regarding Groups, but Not Always for Individuals.

OF VALUE IN THE SCHOOL

But Qualities Needed for Contact With the Outside World Cannot Be Easily Measured by IQ's.

This is the second of two articles appraising the intelligence tests twenty years after their introduction into America. Last week Dr. Watson discussed the evidence that the tests are a reliable measure of an inborn capacity. This week he discusses the relation of that capacity to success in school and after-life.

By GOODWIN WATSON,
Associate Professor of Education, Teachers College, Columbia

How seriously should intelligence test scores be taken in guiding the life of a child? Does the IQ give a fair and full index of the worth of an individual to society? Most of the harm that has arisen in connection with the use of intelligence tests seems to have grown out of misunderstandings of the answer to these questions. Even scientifically trained psychologists have not always been careful to emphasize the distinction between a relationship which holds with great masses of data, and that which exists in a particular case.

Only in extreme cases can individual predictions of a far-reaching nature safely be made. A child born feeble-minded can be recognized within the first year or two of life and it can be ventured that he will never pass college entrance examinations and will probably never be elected to Congress. He may, however, as the best institutions have shown, be trained to earn his own living at useful tasks. A child with an IQ of 150 may have trouble with school work but it is unlikely, and the trouble is likely to be of an unusual sort.

Where the Tests Fall Down.

When the intelligence test score of an ordinary person is known that does not tell very much about him. Even in school work, where intelligence would seem to be more useful than anywhere else, the relationship is far from close. Spelling ability is very slightly related to intelligence. Handwriting shows almost no relationship. Exceptions are numerous even in the more "intellectual" subjects. If pupils are grouped by intelligence test scores into three sections, one bright, one average, and one dull, and if all three sections are given the same reading test, some of the dull section will prove better readers than some of the bright section. If the test be given in arithmetic, in language or science or history, the same result will be found.

Many other factors enter in to determine who succeeds in school. In one junior high school, 56 per cent of the failures had IQ's below 90, but it must be noted that nearly half of the failures came from a group normal or better in intelligence. A mid-western university carried on its customary process of sending home after Christmas those freshmen who were proving hopeless failures. To their dismay they later discovered that the average intelligence rating of students sent home was slightly higher than that of the students who were "making good." In an eastern college for men, a recent study showed that 64 per cent of the failures during sophomore year were made by men above the campus average in intelligence.

Outside the Classroom.

Once outside the classroom the significance of an intelligence test score becomes much more doubtful. Tests in other fields have shown that an individual varies in his abilities. Some things he does well. Others he does poorly. The truth of the matter is that individual intelligence test scores do not predict any other known ability of the individual with an accuracy that is 50 per cent better than chance. Though we know in general that in the following abilities 1,000 children of high intelligence would excel on the average 1,000 children of low intelligence, we might about as well base our guess as to a particular child's achievement in them on a lottery number, or the length of his big toe, as on his IQ. Personal happiness; popularity with classmates; speed and accuracy of simple learning tasks; mechanical ability; ability to discriminate between good and bad music; ability to sing or play a musical instrument; ability to recognize artistic merit; ability to draw or paint; handwriting speed or quality; cooperativeness, helpfulness; physique, health, athletic ability; persistence; self-control; breadth and variety of play interests; cheerfulness; dependability; speed of decision; self-confidence; ability to keep out of insane asylum during later years, and ability to keep out of prison during later years.

The list is not exhaustive. The point, however, may be clear. Whatever may be true about people in large numbers, individual IQ's cannot be taken too seriously. In the past many school systems (including that of the New York City schools at present) employed psychologists who did little but give intelligence tests. The opposite tendency is exemplified by the new "Psychological Consultation Centre" at Speyer Hall of Teachers College, which is centring especial attention upon discovering the specific abilities possessed by each individual.

Value in Generalizations.

In answering the general question, "What good are the intelligence tests?" we have so far emphasized only the answer that they are not much good for sizing up a total personality. That is a far from adequate reply. If we turn from predictions about specific persons to generalizations about groups of human beings, we come upon the major contributions of this movement in the last dozen years. We have learned that intelligence is distributed in much the same fashion that height is. There are a few very short persons, an equal number of very tall persons, with a completely continuous scale of heights in between. The largest number would be found near the average. In spite of some journalistic assumptions, we are not a nation of morons with a sprinkling of good minds at the top of the scale. About 1 per cent of the population is so mentally deficient as to need lifelong institutional care. About the same proportion will be found possessing IQs in that superior class of 140 and above. Half of the population can be expected to have IQs in the normal range, between 90 and 110.

We have learned, too, that while individual exceptions need to be made, certain vocations, in general, require more intelligence than others. In the army draft groups, the barbers had more intelligence than the farm laborers, the bricklayers more than the barbers, the brakemen more than the bricklayers, the auto-mechanics more than the brakemen, the shipping clerks more than the auto-mechanics, the bookkeepers more than the shipping clerks, the dentists more than the bookkeepers, and the engineering officers and chaplains more than the dentists. Yet this hierarchy is not, of course, absolute. There are certainly some happy and efficient farm laborers who excel in intelligence, some engineers and ministers who are likewise happy and getting along reasonably well. The more general statement would be that men of high intelligence can succeed at almost any occupation for which they have the taste and other specialized abilities, whereas men of low intelligence are much less likely to succeed in the more complex and higher-level jobs.

Differences in Races.

Differences in intelligence among races have been the subject of many investigations and more arguments. No large groups of any race or nationality has been found to fall entirely above or below the average of any other act. There are, however, differences in averages which seem fairly well established. Yet it must be remembered that the individuals of each race vary widely, some surpassing, others inferior to, the average of other groups. Jewish children in most studies have a higher average intelligence than Anglo-Saxons. Chinese and Japanese children in this country usually equal or excel the Anglo-Saxons, on the average. Among those of English, French, German and Scandinavian extraction no clear differences appear. Average scores of Italians, Poles, Greeks and other South Europeans in the United States are usually somewhat lower. Negroes, Indians and Mexicans, tested in large numbers, have on the average scored consistently below the Anglo-Saxons.

In interpreting these differences it is well to remember that environmental and cultural and language handicaps may need to be taken into account. Again let it be said that there are some of every group, some Negroes, some Indians, some Mexicans, who make higher scores than the average white Nordic or the average Jew. There should be few more ineffective methods for selecting able citizens than the method of admitting immigrants by nationality rather than by personal qualities.

Men and Women

One of the useful results of intelligence tests has been the undermining of a common superstition to the effect that men are intellectually superior to women. During childhood, at least, no such differences can be found. The slightly superior average test scores of boys in some tests given in the high school years is usually accounted for in terms of selection. Stupid boys are more likely to drop out and go to work than are stupid girls, who get on better in school as a rule than do boys of similar intelligence. The boys may also have some advantage on tests containing arithmetical and scientific elements.

Of extraordinary value is the aid given by intelligence testing to the shattering of the popular notion that hard study of useless subjects is especially likely to develop the mind. This month, I suppose, fully 2,000,000 high school boys and girls in the United States will be misled into supposing that, while algebra or geometry or Latin may not appeal to them and may not have any direct use in their careers, nevertheless these subjects will have special value in improving their mental faculties. Dr. E. L. Thorndike has given intelligence tests to some 11,000 high school pupils at the beginning and again at the end of the school year. His results confirm the other psychological findings. General intelligence develops quite as well in the pupil who is busy in a laboratory, enjoying literature, producing plays, learning accounting, practicing typewriting or household arts, as it does in a pupil with a classical curriculum. Serious questions about the value of much that is included in the curriculum of high schools and colleges are arising from this observation.[1]

[1] From *The New York Times*, by permission.

EXERCISE

Read the following statements with care.

1. Henry Beckwith usually pays about eight or ten dollars for a pair of shoes. But when shoes cost fifteen dollars a pair, he balks and refuses to buy.

2. Tom Alexander tells his family that he can afford to buy them a Ford car this month. But he says that if they will wait a year or two, he can certainly afford a much more expensive and comfortable automobile. He cannot, however, buy both. There is no car in the family, and they unanimously vote to have the Ford now.

3. Sylvia Smollett, eighteen years old, is going to her first formal party. She has an evening dress, but no jewelry. Her mother gives her fifteen dollars to buy whatever accessories she wishes. She sees at a jewelry store a beautiful pin of fine quality costing exactly fifteen dollars. But at a department store she discovers that she can buy a bracelet, a necklace, and a flower to wear on her shoulder. None of these accessories is of very good quality. Their total cost is fifteen dollars. She hesitates not a moment, and buys the necklace, bracelet, and flower without delay.

4. People who consume the same amount of goods do not necessarily get the same satisfactions from them.

5. The poor man weighs the satisfactions he gets from spending a dollar with far greater care than does the rich man.

EXERCISE

What is the most significant aspect of Great Britain's attitude toward her dominions today?

When and where did you last read something on this subject?

Amassing Facts.

The cabbage is by no means a modern vegetable. It was well known to Hippocrates, who ascribed to it sundry medical values. Pythagoras also mentions it.

A tree growing in moist soil makes a better lightning conductor than one in dry soil, and one that has much rotten wood in it attracts the bolts more than one that is sound throughout. Oaks are struck by lightning more often than any other species.

If a lame man crosses the path of a Scotch fisherman, the latter will not put out to sea for days. Around the Firth of Forth there also flourishes the superstition that a barefoot woman with flat feet brings bad luck, if seen on a sailing day.

All languages must first have been baby talk, for all people are babies before they are adults; and they always start talking when very young. This may explain the enormous variety of language forms among savages, who lack written traditions and hence remodel their speech with each succeeding generation.

How would you like to have a mind that carried around thousands of tag ends like the little facts you have just been reading in the last four paragraphs? I think it would be fun, provided that you could do one of two things with them: use them lightly in conversation, or else understand their significances. But it would be a nuisance to retain such a clutter without use or understanding. I am sorry for people who, in spite of themselves, go through life burdened with such futile memories. Those whom I have known are failures or semi-failures, largely because of their camera-like brains.

Years ago, down in Park Row, I used to know an old man who remembered almost everything his eyes ever lighted upon. His conversation resembled the opening paragraphs of this chapter, only it was still wilder, because he often tried to connect facts which simply wouldn't connect; and you, the listener, would rack your brain for the invisible nexus. The old fellow was sure he was a great linguist. He jabbered along in a sort of Spanish, German, Italian, Russian, Polish, Portugese, and English broth of words which, in truth, were no language at all. He had picked up phrases in the many lands he had visited and echoed them without the faintest grasp of their finer shades of pronunciation or meaning.

He also looked upon himself as a scholar of rank. The hours he had spent in the public libraries won him his diplomas. And what had he done there? He had looked up the answers to letters from inquisitive correspondents. For he was earning ten dollars a week conducting an "Asked and Answered" column of a newspaper. And in that function he had risen to the peak of his abilities, without a doubt.

Here we see a variety of imperfect (or perhaps retarded) development. The brain itself probably grew only to the memory level; those immense systems of associative fibers which are the channels through which experience links up with experience seem never to have developed. So the art of learning stops with its first stage.

No normal man need suffer thus. He has the native ability to organize and interpret much of what he picks up.

Among the thousands of tourists who visit Honululu every year, there bob up with unfailing regularity several score who try to exchange their American money for Hawaiian currency, believing the islands to be a foreign land.

I have met many New Englanders who declare that all Canadians speak French. Innumerable Americans address letters to Newfoundland "Newfoundland, Canada." Not a few business men who have been clever enough to make money read their newspapers so dully that, when asked about current news, they make absurd replies. One man says that Alekhine is the world's champion bicyclist. Another tells me that William Jennings Bryan died in jail, whither he had been sent for contempt of court. A third writes in a letter: "The Italian cabinet is sending the lyre back to a gold basis." You can continue the list out of your own experience as long as you like, I dare say.

How are such blunders possible? The perpetrators have never been genuinely interested in the subjects. That explains nine out of every ten. Each item has merely floated past, like a mote in the sunbeam; it has attracted barely enough attention to adhere lightly to the magnet of remembrances. It lacks context and usefulness; hence it has not been checked up, analyzed, and rehearsed.

The By-no-means Minor Art of Observing Things.

For every blind man on this earth there must be a hundred half-blind creatures whose frailty no oculist can detect, even with his finest instruments. The blind have no eyes to use, but these half-blind have excellent retinas and sound optic nerves which are rarely pressed into service. Such people stand amazed at the feats of Sherlock Holmes, who, entering a room, tells you after a glance or two that the man who made the divan there was a Methodist whose mother suffered from arthritis during her thirty-ninth year. And yet, in contrast to the daily observations of many scientists, most of Holmes' exploits are commonplace.

Meet Tillie.

While writing the last pages of this book, I ran into Tillie again. I hadn't seen her for more than a year, which was quite the usual thing, for Tillie is a globe-trotter. Here she bobbed up, in the Pennsylvania Station, hemmed in with porters and bags, not to mention her mother and the three poor cousins, just in from Australia. Thrice around the world, four or five times to Africa, and nobody knows how many times to little old Europe, Tillie feels, with no more humility than is necessary, that she knows the world. Gray and wrinkled at last, she still looks out upon the fleeting continents and the seven times seventy seas with the eyes of a babe.

What has she learned about this globe? Well, she can tell you where to get the hottest *bouillabaisse* in Marseilles. To a decimal she can tell you the correct tip to a dragoman. Which country has second-class trains fit for Americans, she knows with astrophysical precision. She can walk all alone on a moonless night from her hotel in Singapore out to the gardens, then along the docks and back again without ever asking the way. And she can pronounce nearly all of the words on an Italian menu, telling you pretty nearly what each dish contains.

Yet, so far as I can testify, Tillie has never learned anything about the world and its people beyond these sniffs of information. She has never once glimpsed the connection between any two items, never reacted to the ten thousand trends of the human race which have been occurring before her unseeing eyes. If Tillie hadn't inherited several millions and a high society name, she would be called a moron, and put to washing dishes in a sailors' lodging house. As it is, she is said to have a charmingly fresh, unspoiled eye for far places.

I know newspaper men and dusty bureaucrats who, in their offices long immured, have learned more about the internal politics of China than a million Tillies could acquire in as many generations. I know correspondents who fill their magazine pages with penetrating articles about affairs of State in France and Germany, and have not seen one-tenth as many towns, cathedrals, zoos, and cabarets in those lands as our Tillie. Not a few of the world's greatest

experts on geography have never looked upon most of the
lands they understand so well. Some of the deepest students
of history are in the same plight. So we infer that there is
much more to the art of learning than merely staring at
things.

Your Point of View and Its Perspective.

When you are not trying to observe anything in particular, you will almost certainly observe nothing. Or, at best, you will note a chaos of items which, just because they are a chaos, will not stick in your memory and will never serve any purpose.

You must take some point of view in order to learn even the simplest matters. For it is the point of view which brings the latter into perspective. It reveals some items as important and near, others as trivial and remote. It discloses channels of approach, techniques, and appraisals.

Haven't you known somebody who, in the presence of something new, instantly says: "I wonder how much that cost?" There is a clear perspective, not one that we can praise but one that gives its owner a valuable point of view for learning all sorts of things. Everything on earth can be seen as a thing for sale at a certain price. An economist or a miser might be able to learn even highly technical matters by consistently taking such a position.

Haven't you known somebody else who, when shown a dress or a rug or a rare book or a sunset or a theory of astronomy, irrepressibly exclaims: "Well, what use is that to me?" Here is the highly organized perspective of the narrowly practical mind. Let us beware of extolling it too highly; but let us be fair and admit that it aids learning tremendously simply because it relates all experiences in the tight web of human interest.

Do you instinctively take such a point of view? If so, what is it? You don't know? Then you must find out!

Stop! Look around you. Fix your gaze on any object within easy vision. How much can you observe? If it connects in some way with other things, observe them also.

As you look, think about whatever you see. As soon as your mind wanders from the object in view, make a note of whatever arose in your imagination; then come back to the observed thing promptly.

Assume various points of view. Consider the object in its physical structure. Think of the methods of its manufacture and see if the visible form bears any mark of those. Reflect on its uses; do they appear to the eye in any way? Study it from the point of view of its material, its cost, its origin, its artistic qualities, and its precise color and form.

Keep this up for about five minutes. Do it just once every day for one hundred days. Select a different object to observe on every day.

On the hundredth day, sum up your experiences. Have you improved in your powers of observation?

If so, in which ways is the improvement most conspicuous?

If you have not improved, can you guess why?

Classify the hundred objects you have observed.

Do you detect anything significant in the selections you have been making?

Do the selections reveal something about yourself?

An acquaintance of mine looked at a young woman with whom he had been talking and said, "You just had a *very* sarcastic and horrid thought, didn't you?"

The young lady blushed mightily, but, being for the most part honest, admitted to her frailty with a mixture of embarrassment, bewilderment, and admiration for the magician who could so successfully read a secret and evil thought. And then, getting up her courage, she asked, somewhat timidly, "B-b-b-ut *how* did you know?"

Said the observing gentleman, "By the look of your lower lid indeed. Your eyes, you see, are normally well-shaped and curved. Each time you make a sarcastic comment— either audible or unexpressed—your lower lid straightens slightly and your eyes narrow and become smaller."

We learn much about human nature by simple observation. But how few form the habit of watching the common

behavior of men and women! It's a pity, for no small amount
of worldly wisdom comes through this channel. It is one
of the inlets to the great sea of psychology—and one, I
may add, which trained psychologists ignore unduly,
just as some novelists favor too warmly. As psychology
is one of the three basic subjects of useful learning, you
should look upon the art of watching people as a worthy
pastime.

EXERCISES

At the end of this sentence, stop reading and write down the number of different sounds and noises you hear. Practice listening to and identifying various sounds two or three times a day. You will be surprised at the speed with which your auditory keenness improves.

How well can you smell? I know a man who is so sensitive to smell that he often has to leave the room when some of his more pungent friends are about! The ordinary nose would find these same companions quite innocuous. Test yourself right now, for example. What, if anything, can you smell? Try identifying the odors of various kinds of foods in any restaurant. You may make trouble for yourself, but this is one way to train yourself to be a good bloodhound.

Try watching your friends, should their mere conversation become a little dull. "Each little wrinkle has a meaning all its own," and you'll have a lot of fun in addition to learning much if you will observe changing expressions on faces that, to the unobservant one, seem vacant and unrevealing.

Keep notes throughout all these observations. Do not burden your memory.

The next time you go for an automobile ride, observe the landmarks on the road you take. See if you can recall them in order. Probably you can't. Anyway, if you have a chance, see whether you can later cover the same route with the aid of your memory and observation of schoolhouses and cemeteries and red-barns-by-a-hayfield. If the ride is long enough, this is real work, and it's real training too.

At the end of this sentence, close your eyes for about thirty seconds; then turn to the next page.

Now write the answers to the following questions without looking up from the book:

1. What color are the walls of the room where you are now sitting?
2. How many pictures are there on the walls? What kinds?
3. How many chairs?
4. Where is the electric light button?
5. What shape are the electric bulbs?
6. Is there anything in the room out of its proper place?
7. If there is a carpet or linoleum on the floor, do you recall its pattern?
8. Describe in some detail what can be seen from the windows.
9. About how long and wide is the room?
10. Of what material is the doorknob made?
11. Are there any other outstanding details which are peculiar to this room?

Now look around you and check your answers with what you now observe.

Do not think that, because you have missed much, you are a poor observer. The best observers always misses much. We shall discuss this matter.

Your Learning Rate.

Don't expect to learn all things equally fast. And do not expect to hold the same rate of learning from the outset to the finish of a new subject. Such false hopes will only lead to unpleasant disillusionment, sooner or later.

In general, the more complex a subject or practice is, the more slowly it can be mastered. A man can learn to operate a typewriter very well in about eight weeks, without giving much time daily to the study. But he cannot learn to play a good game of golf in that time. Still less easily can he become a successful speller of many English words.

Why so? Simply because typewriting consists of a few score of movements and no more. Drill yourself thoroughly in these, and you are a proficient typist. But in golf there are almost as many distinct ways of hitting the ball as there are positions in which the ball may lie; and, of course, there are thousands of distinct conditions of distance, wind, clarity of vision, and so on, all of which influence the golfer's every least move. There you have the marvelous thing about golf: no two strokes are ever quite the same, no two games even remotely alike. And that's why a man spends twenty years at the great game and still remains an amateur, even though he wins four and twenty tournament cups.

Oddly enough, spelling is a little like golf, at least in our language. Students simply cannot speed up their rate of learning new words, even through months of practice. And why not? Surely because each word has to be learned by itself. We lack neat, fixed rules of spelling. So let me warn you that, if you aspire to improve your spelling faster, this book is not likely to aid you much.

You Learn Fastest at First.

As for being able to hold an even acceleration in learning, that can never be done. All learning advances fastest at first. Then come periods during which little or no progress appears. There may even be, at least in appearance, a loss of what seems to have been thoroughly learned. Afterward we advance in quick spurts followed by long stretches of little or no improvement. Gradually the spurts taper off. Each one lifts us less and less. The span between spurts lengthens. And at length we attain our maximum.

The Bleak Plateau.

Many a learner grows discouraged when he enters upon the first long stretch in which little or no progress seems to occur. Be on your guard against the mood. It may spoil things for you. You fear lest you have reached your limit? But that is nonsense. Keep in mind that such slowing down is normal and, for reasons still unclear to psychologists, a necessary stage of assimilation.

Teachers know that the journey across these bleak plateaus must often be enlivened. The weary marcher must be cheered on his way, even coddled a little now and then. He who marches alone must spur himself on.

In creative learning, men advance fastest by stopping dead now and then. I do not mean merely that they rest. They turn away from the subject, dismiss it, and busy themselves with anything else that happens to intrigue them. Most scientists testify that they have to drop their studies in this manner at intervals. They reach a point at which progress becomes impossible until they are able to withdraw, relax, and later come back from a fresh angle; then a new prospective reveals things previously hidden.

When you come out upon one of those wide, chill plateaus of learning, be sure to practice this art of dropping the problem! It is vital to larger success.

EXERCISE

The next time you see a good motion picture, try to report the main sequence of its episodes and best photographic effects. Do this about one hour after you have left the theatre. Take no notes during the performance, of course.

Analyze your report. What did you omit from it? Did you succeed in catching the gist of the story? Did some feature overshadow the plot and confuse you a little?

Eye-minded people generally favor the movies more than ear-minded people. Does this suggest anything about yourself?

EXERCISE

Read the following passage at least twice with the utmost care. Then underline the sentence which, in your opinion, sets forth the most important point in the entire passage.

Then mark with an X in the margin the least important sentence.

At the close of the Civil War the victorious North had a puzzling question on its hands. What would be the status of the southern states. What would be done to the rebels? Many demanded that they be punished. Were they not conquered territory? Had they not revoked their rights as states by seceding? Had they not become an independent country and then been overthrown? And if they had, what right did they have to be aught but provinces governed as the rest of the country saw fit? But wiser men realized that the North had fought them on the theory that no state could leave the union; that they were still states or the northern cause was wrong. As Lincoln said, it was now the duty of the nation to withdraw federal troops as soon as order was restored and set the states functioning once more as they had before the strife. Lincoln proposed to pardon and restore lost property, except lost slaves, to every Confederate on the condition that he take an oath of loyalty to the union. He added that when, in any of the Confederate states, a body of voters the size of one-tenth of the total vote of the state in 1860 swore allegiance to the union, that state would be readmitted as a state government.

Had Lincoln lived to complete his plan in his own way the Reconstruction of the South might have been a different story than it was.

Measure Your Curiosity.

Man differs from man in native inquisitiveness. One child takes everything for granted and goes through life serenely and with magnificent ignorance. Another child pokes into every dark corner, observes every stray cat, wonders how people know the moon isn't made of green cheese, asks his mother where the roundness of a soap bubble goes after the bubble bursts, lies awake half of a night trying to count the Pleiades, runs away from home for a week-end in the hope of reaching the rainbow's end, struggles to understand every foreigner he overhears speaking alien words, and thus on and on until—with luck and years—he comes to know an amazing mass of things.

Plainly the inquisitive youth has a better chance of growing up as a skilled learner. So it is important that you discover the breadth and depth of your own curiosity as soon as possible. Alas, we have no patent machine for measuring this trait. So the best I can suggest is painfully simple. First of all, write down in black and white a list of the things about which you are especially curious. This may be an hour's work, or it may take a year. All depends on your personality. Next keep a record of the number and variety of news items which you read straight through in your newspaper. This, to be sure, reveals more than mere curiosity; but it will throw some indirect light on the range of the latter.

After some practice along these lines, go on to the more reliable measurement. Open a good encyclopaedia at random. Read the topics there discussed. Which—if any— arouse your curiosity to the point of reading into the text? Jot down those which do so move you. Repeat this perhaps 500 times in the course of a few months. Then look over the list. Is it long or short? Are the topics more or less alike? Or do they scatter widely?

Which of the following statements excite your curiosity?
All are true.

The poor quality of thread nowadays is the result of
the Federal Reserve banking law.

We are still living in the Glacial Period. ⊹

Water often runs uphill and rises above its source.

Our country was founded by traitors.

In San Diego, California, the sun does not shine for
nearly one-third of every year. ⊰

Most of the money in our country is spent by women.

Half a loaf is sometimes worse than none.

William Benjamin Bertels, formerly of Dallas, Texas,
began learning history and studying autobiographies at the
age of eighty. At the same age he committed entire chapters of the bible to memory.

A large New York City corporation trains its salesmen
from start to finish in about two months.

Before men learned to till the soil, the natural resources
of the entire world sufficed to support not more than 30,000,-
000 people.

BOOK IV

EMOTIONS AND ATTITUDES

EMOTIONS AND ATTITUDES

Learning Good Attitudes.

One grand division of the art of learning is concerned with the acquiring of good attitudes. Here we distinguish between the learning of attitudes toward things in the world about us, such as the attitudes of good citizenship, loyalty, and so on, and learning attitudes toward the learning process itself. This is not the place to discuss the former. But the latter are, I dare say, as important as anything mentioned in this book; and, so far as I know, nobody has ever catalogued and analyzed them.

Now, attitudes link intimately with emotions. Indeed some psychologists believe, with a good show of evidence, that the two are one and the same thing. An attitude is an act in embryo. It is the inner set of nerve and muscle which occurs when, for instance, the runner in a race "gets ready and gets set." As soon as he goes, he no longer takes an attitude; he is doing the thing he set out to do.

Thus every act of will develops as an attitude. Some emotional tone merges with this attitude. And by the one, you may know the other. So let us look at the learner and see what attitudes he may take toward the subjects he sets out to learn. Which attitudes interfere with learning? Which help it? Which tend to go with certain kinds of subjects?

Learning Isn't Purely Intellectual.

One of the gravest errors in school teaching has been founded upon the erroneous assumption that he who learns is merely using his intellect. The modern teacher has begun

183

to rid himself and his classroom of this sorry blunder. He has learned, from his own experience if not from psychologists, that the driving force in the learner is rarely his sheer intelligence but rather some emotional attitude, now toward the subject matter, now toward the teacher, now toward the benefits to be derived from mastering the subject. The mind is the auto motor, but it takes the fuel of feeling to drive the old bus along the Parnassus Parkway.

The first thing to learn here is that no single emotion is enough to facilitate every stage of the process. A few combinations do it. Best of all is a fusion of three:

1. Lively enthusiasm over the subject and its worthwhileness.
2. Firm self-confidence in your ability to learn it through and through.
3. Openminded compliance not only with the teacher and the author of the textbook but with the propositions to be learned.

Any emotional attitude in which any one of these three favorable factors is wholly lacking prevents effective learning, or at least slows it down seriously. The student who comes to his books without a trace of enthusiasm finds everything eluding him. If, being enthusiastic, he hasn't a shred of confidence in his mental powers, he is doomed. And if, while enthusiastic and self-confident, he comes to the task prejudiced against the teacher or filled with pre-convictions concerning the subject, of which he truly knows little, or is swollen with egotism and boasts that nobody can teach him anything, he will win a large solid cardboard dunce cap. Of these harmful states we shall soon be speaking at some length. Look now at the compliant attitude, which is the very soul and fire of superior learning.

The Compliant Attitude: Openmindedness.

The learner's motto must be: "Stop! Look! And Listen!" He must apply this drastically to every fiber of his being. He must, for the moment, slow down every voluntary process which distracts him from the thing to be learned.

This usually means that he must sit still at certain stages (but not all) and must facilitate keen listening and observing. Even if he is learning how to dance he must do this while watching his teacher go through the steps.

In the act of observing he must keep his mind wide open to every impression, fact, allegation, principle, and motion. The more freely he can receive, the better. Let the thing to be learned dominate! Never try to dominate it! This rule must be learned early so that compliance becomes a wholly unconscious habit. A little later, I shall offer some suggestions for self-drill along these lines. Meanwhile, please learn to distinguish openmindedness from the submissive attitude.

Submissiveness Is a Poor Substitute.

In its Simon-pure form the submissive attitude leads one to surrender sweetly to the will of somebody else, without thought and with no feeling save pleasant meekness. "Not my will but thine be done" is the submissive man's motto—and herein lies the danger when he turns learner. It is possible to surrender so utterly that you cannot think for yourself about what you have been studying. This is especially true in those cases, all too common, of people who strive to please their teacher. The teacher who encourages this will seldom look upon any rich fruits of his labor. The teacher's pet is usually just such a sweet and loving little soul far more interested in winning the teacher's love than in conquering the subject. And, I fear, few teacher's pets rise to great heights in later years—though the U. S. Census is discreetly silent on this point.

Good Students Are Naturally Compliant.

The higher we go in school the greater the percentage of naturally compliant, openminded students we find. The stubborn, the egotists, and the constitutional bigots are weeded out relentlessly, not by fiat but through their own incompetence. When we reach the senior classes of any well managed university we find nearly all men and women conspicuously openminded and delightfully easy to teach. This is one of the chief explanations of the oft recorded superiority of college graduates in business and industry.

Connie Mack Testifies.

Connie Mack, the Grand Old Man of American baseball, received the Philadelphia Award of 1929 for the worthiest acts of citizenship. Edward Bok, who founded the prize award, told Mack that nobody deserved the $10,000 and the gold medal more. For fifty years Mack has stood forth as the champion of clean sports. Through all the recent scandals and exposures of dishonesty among professional baseball players, Mack has fought the knaves.

When he first became manager of a ball team, many years ago, he set out to develop the world's finest nine. He sought men everywhere. He put all candidates through gruelling tests. And he finally reached a significant decision. As far as possible, he would take on college students or graduates.

"They are," said Mack, "easier to teach and more amenable to discipline."

Thus it happened that the first very great in-field of the Athletics, which Mack was managing, was composed almost exclusively of college men. Ever since that day, nearly twenty years ago, college men have been favored by other managers as well as by Mack—and simply because they could learn!

An uneducated man who has not formed habits of system and has never taken the attitude of a student makes poor raw material for baseball geniuses like Connie Mack. Professional baseball is full of subtle and complex tricks and techniques. It must be mastered just as engineering or medicine, by intensive drill. The poor learner has no chance there.

The Power of Enthusiasm.

Isn't it a waste of time to palaver about the power of enthusiasm? Doesn't everybody discover, early in life, that this particular tingle mysteriously tunes us in on whatever the cosmos has to offer? Next to openmindedness, it vivifies the act of learning most of all, and it may do so in either or both of two ways. It may be the enthusiasm of the teacher for the subject, or it may be the learner's own enthusiasm for it. In the first instance, the teacher's emotion is infectious, now through sheer mannerism, now through a knack of ballyhooing the subject with the blatant side-show barker's art. As I look back upon my own past, I find that half a dozen turning points were determined entirely by somebody's enthusiasm. Here is the tale of the most remarkable.

A Night of Wonder.

These lines are written in memory of a man whom I saw only once, and that hour some forty years gone. In the dark I saw him, never clearly enough to perceive his lineaments sharply. And what he said impressed me so deeply that he himself has long since vanished behind the aura of his words.

There came to Detroit, then a civilized town of infinite serenity, an open-air show with fireworks, presenting "Lalla Rookh": admission, fifty cents. I lacked the price but yearned to see. So, knowing the vicinage well, I sought out a tall tree on the north side of the Boulevard, near Fourteenth Street; and, many hours before the exhibition began behind the ten-foot fence, I lurked in the offing. Dusk fell. I climbed but not successfully, for the tree was of mighty girth.

There was nothing to do but fetch a ladder. So, chagrined at my lack of foresight, I sped after one. It was dark when

I returned to the tree. The lights twinkled inside the grounds, and a band was playing brassily. I leaned the ladder against the trunk and began the ascent to Parnassus.

"And where might ye be goin', young man?"

I looked behind me and saw a policeman. His badge shone evilly in the dark. His face I saw only as a whitish blur. The one thing I saw most clearly was my doom. I would not see "Lalla Rookh," after all.

The bluecoat marked my mood.

"Ye arrunt permitted to peep over the fince." said he in a kindly Irish. "But if ye'll sit here, I'll tell ye the whole story while the rockets pop."

As there was nothing better to do, I sat down. And this plain cop began to recite "Lalla Rookh" to me. Now and then he would pause to tell details of the story, or to explain a line. As the music and fireworks proceeded beyond the big fence, he would tell me just what was going on in the story, point for point, bang for bang, pinwheel for pinwheel.

Thus he went on until the show was over. It was very dark by then. The only lights in sight were atop those funny tall steel towers which then dotted the town. All were far, far away. I was about to go, bewildered by the torrent of poetry the man had poured forth and vaguely delighted with his exhibition, which, even then, I sensed to be quite as wonderful as the fireworks themselves.

"Ah!" said he softly. "But there's another poem that puts 'Lalla Rookh' to shame, it does. Would you hear part of it, lad?"

"Yes." I must have seemed eager. For I recall his chuckle. He began, in a voice wholly strange, as if under a spell.

> In Xanadu did Kubla Khan
> A stately pleasure dome decree:
> Where Alph, the sacred river, ran
> Through caverns measureless to man
> Down to a sunless sea.

Sometime later—how much later there's no telling, for time ceased that night—I walked home. Somehow I got into bed. Through the hours of sleep I heard the sacred river running. Forty years gone, and still it runs, "meandering with a mazy motion."

How lucky a small boy I, that I had no half dollar to get through the gate that night! Had I gone in, I would have had a brief hour's childish pleasure, with the gaping herd. Barred from that tinsel paradise, I fell in with a great spirit. He trod a dusty beat from the old Twelfth Street Police Station and back again, yet he walked in beauty, like the night. And in that night he made me learn more than a year of school ever gave me.

I cheapen that great experience when I add, as I must for pedantic purpose, that the unknown cop stands forth as one of the few great spirits who led me into the art of learning. Those hours were like a religious conversion, a mystic's flash of intuition, or a scientist's sudden illumination of a vexed problem. Thenceforth I assumed a new attitude toward great verse and men who knew it. I read innumerable poems in the following years, ending up with Dante's "Divine Comedy," which, though never more than one-tenth understood, affected me profoundly, and, I fear, rather unwholesomely.

By the time I went to high school, there was nothing of consequence left for me to read in the literature courses. I had gained, from the unknown and half-seen Irish policeman, some strange insight and feeling which reduced classroom recitals to an empty drone.

To become a great learner, one must have a great teacher. A perfect university is a student on one end of a log and Mark Hopkins on the other. Well, if that's true, then I became a great learner of lovely language when a cop chased me out of a tree.

The Teacher Outshines the Taught.

And now we come to the most significant aspect of that experience. I read "Lalla Rookh" among the first poems after that night of wonder. And, I grieve to say, the lines failed to impress me as they had when they fell from the Irish policeman's lips. Indeed, they rang like a leaden bell at times. How then had I been so moved and inwardly illumined? It was beyond my powers of comprehension then. But now I know that the personality of the minstrel revealed to his young listener, not "Lalla Rookh" at all, or even the matchless "Kubla Khan," but the power of beauty and the precious art of learning loveliness.

In short, the teacher taught an attitude toward life and all the things of life—and not by trying to teach it, but wholly as an unconscious by-product of his exhibiting his intense love of poetry and his amazing skill as a learner of poetry. He taught that greater things than jingles can be learned, even by small boys. But the small boys must fall under the spell of the right magician, if they would get that!

The Playful Learner.

"To be playful and serious at the same time is possible," says Dewey, "and it defines the ideal mental condition." When he adds that "mental play is openmindedness," he touches one of the most fruitful thoughts in the whole art of learning.

Play assumes many forms. The meanings we attach to the word itself reveal our understanding of the common element in those forms, as well as their deep differences. The openmindedness which every voracious learner possesses is more than bovine passivity. It involves a sort of free play which, in turn, may be either of two kinds; first, a sprightly fantasy and darting perception, and, secondly, a freedom from prejudice or fixed belief—that on the intellectual side. On the motor side, the two forms reappear in behavior: the first sort leads to aimless romping, fingering, manipulating, and experimenting with objects; and the second sort leads to the purposeful devisings of the scientist and inventor.

The playful learner, you see, is not to be confused with the learner who cannot take his tasks seriously, nor with him who learns only to enjoy esthetically. Playfulness is a method of learning; it is not an avoidance of the work. It is much more than pleasant perceptions, horseplay, and buffoonery. It is a diabolically ingenious technique of gaining knowledge. Lucky the man who catches onto the trick!

Aimless Browsing.

The simplest- and, in a sense, the lowest-form of playful learning is aimless browsing. It should be carried on in a more liberal spirit and with more adventurous dash than the browsing of cows and goats. As you watch a cow meandering about her pasture lot, she seems as aimless as fog drift. But she is not. She is picking and choosing aplenty: from the goldenrod she turns gently away, to seek the succulent young grass shoots. She deceives you with the leisure of her movements. Genuine browsing is more commonly done by the goat, omnivorous, incessant, and truly playful. No goat turns from goldenrod to seek grass shoots— at least, not within my own range of observation, which has been limited to a very few goats. I get the impression that the goat nibbles lots of things just for fun. He wants to see what happens when they slip down his all-encompassing gullet. This has earned for him the libellous reputation of an eater of old shoes and glass bottles. I dare say that every up-and-coming goat has, at some hilarious moment of his youth, nibbled a beer bottle and licked the tip of an antiquated shoe. But never, never has he become a bottle

addict, never the ultimate consumer of the world's foot-
wear. He is simply a liberal learner. He is willing to try
anything once—and God gave him a body fit to stand the
shocks.

Now, here is the primitive spirit of turning life's trial
and error into a sport. Primitive, I repeat; for we must not
exalt it in our effort to give it fair play. Mental browsing
has a place in life, especially during the formative years.
It has, I grieve to say, been crowded out of the program by
the thick, buzzing swarm of duties and entertainments in
modern life. The schoolboy of today has all his hours and
minutes mapped out for him. Twenty subjects, sports, and
social affairs pin twenty shackles on his sprouting wings and
prevent free flight into the blue. And then there are the
movies and the summer camp and the comic supplements!
Poor child! He lacks the enormous advantages which I
enjoyed as a youngster . . . Fade back, old screen! And
flash a shot of forty years ago! . . .

Learned Goats, We!

My uncle, who lived with my parents all of his long life,
was a printer with a mania for good books. On such he
spent most of his money as well as his time, down to the
very last years of clear eyesight. I still see him at his old
desk, of an evening, poring over Homer, Molière, Balzac,
Thackeray, and all the other old fellows. He had a weakness
for three things, Carlyle, Ruskin, and the Encyclopaedia
Britannica. But this did not deaden his appetite for everything else in print.

He read for sheer amusement, never for prestige, never
in order to improve his cash status with the grocer, never
for edification. He read without system, principle, or aim,
forever browsing like the literary goat that he was, and
capering a little as he moved on from weed to flower, from
flower to fruit, from fruit to dead fish, from dead fish to

ambrosia. Of the many hundred volumes which he owned, hardly a one that he did not reread a dozen times in the course of his life. Yet, so far as I know, he never put to use a single item in any one of them.

Now, that was carrying the hircine habit too far into the realms of learning. And, even as a small boy, I disapproved of it. But I caught just enough of its charm— yes, its sometimes poisonous charm!—to play around with books and to nibble at all the green branches of learning with less seriousness than the leap of a grasshopper from leaf to leaf. Never have I regretted this. Many a time have I indirectly benefited from some of the most preposterous errancies. Probably the greatest advantage of all on which I can lay a finger is an appreciation of the infinite variety of human interests. It has never occurred to me that the subjects to which I devote most attention are intrinsically more alluring than ten million others which I neglect. I agree heartily with the lines which Stevenson should have written:

> The world is so full of a number of things,
> I'm sure we need ne'er be as wretched as kings.

Browsing Reveals Yourself to You.

Almost equally valuable is the self-revealing power of prolonged aimless reading and revery. Just as the "free association" tests in psychology disclose hidden states of personality, so does free absorption bring to light appetites and aptitudes which can be discovered in no other manner.

Here are ten million or more lines of human interest and activity. Can you find how each appeals to you by a few vocational tests, or by observing your reactions to subjects taught in school? No! You do no more than graze the invisible possibilities of your nature. The soft routine of sheltered days can never lead deep down in the chasms and whirlpools of any vigorous personality. You get there

only by exploring. Beat crooked little paths hither and
yon. Clamber here, descend there. Slip down a gully, scale
a steep. And let your itinerary be that of the goats of
which James Stephens has written:

> The crooked paths go every way
> Upon the hill—they wind about
> Through the heather in and out
> Of the quiet sunniness.
> And there the goats, day after day,
> Stray in sunny quietness,
> Cropping here and cropping there,
> As they pause, and turn, and pass.
>
> If I were as wise as they,
> I would stray apart and brood,
> I would beat a hidden way
> Through the quiet heather spray
> To a sunny solitude.
>
> I would think until I found
> Something I can never find,
> Something lying on the ground,
> In the bottom of my mind.

The Child's Way.

Is this not the way of the healthy child? Does he not
learn by tasting and touching and trying everything within
reach? Does he not run away from mother's apronstring
as fast as he can, to drift up and down his little cosmos like
the goat on a hillside? Does he not go lost in revery over
each new thing? And find a grand sport in it all?

Unless you can be like a little child, you cannot enter
into the heaven of knowledge. He and the goat, two brows-
ers, are both the children of Pan. Nature runs in their
veins. And Nature, being everywhere and all things, leads
to all places and everything.

The Trail of the Goat.

Today I saw:

Today I heard:

Today I learned:

The Wrong Attitude Is Worse than Instability.

It has been assumed, merely because it "seems reasonable," that a learner suffering from some emotional instability is heavily handicapped. But such investigations as have been made do not confirm this view. Rather do they qualify it heavily. At Colgate, Donald Laird and his associate, J. Bateman Young, find that the poorest students fall chiefly into two groups, one of which is emotionally stable and the other unstable. The former are pronounced extraverts, the latter equally pronounced introverts. It has also been found, however, in college studying at least, that highly intelligent introverts have a harder time of it than most other types. So the failure of many unstable introverts may in reality be traceable to their high intelligence. Thus nothing may be inferred.

At Colgate Young finds that twice as many emotionally stable as emotionally unstable students fail. Thus, the psychoneurotic is not handicapped in learning; or, if so, not nearly so much so as many other kinds of people. And this goes to prove that the poor learner is probably the man with stable emotions of a sort which predispose him to resist learning or to dislike it. The general trend of my own experiences with college students and younger people leads me to that conclusion.

The poorest learners among several thousand students who have passed within my ken seem to have been those who have taken one or more of the attitudes indicated by the following terms:

1. The listless learner.
2. The sentimental learner.
3. The reluctant learner.
4. The hostile learner.
5. The aggressive learner.
6. The too docile learner.
7. The fearful learner.
8. The egotistical learner.

Around these eight a sizable volume might be spun; but we must skim their fatal traits, alas, and fastest of all do we overleap the listless learner.

The Listless Learner.

He cannot get up steam. He may stick faithfully to his task but with leaden feet. Something keeps him weak. Is it ill health? Often. Or a native deficit of energy? Often. Or some bad emotional upbringing? Less often. He cannot command out attention here for long, simply because he will never throw himself into the art of learning. Why talk to those who stay beyond earshot? Let us forget him.

The Reluctant Learner.

The reluctant learner usually is a person who doesn't quite know why he dislikes to learn something. Seldom does he dislike it intensely. Under pressure he can be persuaded to take up certain subjects and, after a while, develop a mild interest in them. He never knows his own mind, hence is easily led. He follows a leader, if one happens to be around. Otherwise he runs with the herd. A severer analysis of a few hundred of this variety probably would dismember it into many small classes; for reluctance is a vague word that covers many negative attitudes and many inner resistances. I employ the term here as a catch-all, to spare myself the labor of making such an analysis. Every teacher will recognize the validity of the characterization. For every school gathers in a sprinkling of these learners who have to be pushed into learning and, when pushed, make the grade just well enough to continue in the institution.

To all such I offer specific advice. Many of you can overcome this reluctance as soon as you are able to see the injury of it. You are not necessarily so stupid as you seem, nor so flabby, nor so antagonistic to the finer activities of life.

You may be no worse off than an automobile motor which delivers little power. A few petty adjustments—a turn of the carburetor needle, a slightly better seating of one poppet valve, a lubricating oil one degree heavier, and whizz!—you take all grades on high. Cases like yours often baffle teachers and parents, simply because there is nothing seriously wrong with you. So do your own overhauling, please! What is too trivial for others to discern in your mental machinery may be easily seen by yourself.

Your trouble may go back to a long forgotten dislike of one teacher or one subject, as did my profound reluctance to read history. For many years I disliked histories and historians. And this, too, in spite of the fact that several other interests were repeatedly leading me to read ancient chronicles at great length. What caused the aversion? Chiefly a high school teacher who knew nothing of the art of learning.

He was a German of the old school. He pursued the intensive method of teaching in the oldest and worst manner. For weeks on end, during my first course in general history, this learned man assigned us from ten to twenty dates for memorizing daily. He would then go around the class, hurling at each individual a date, "January 11, 1347," and so on. The victim had to yelp back the event which, according to myth, had occurred on that day. Then the pedant would reverse on us, calling out the event and extracting from us the date. There was little else in his course beyond this monstrous perversion, and the marvel is that anybody who ever sat under the man opened a history book even once in after years.

This preposterous method committed two basic blunders. One, of course, is obvious; it focussed upon the least interesting and least important aspect of human events. The other error lies deeper; the teacher failed totally to convey to us, before he swamped us with dates, the larger significance of the entire study. Had we grasped the consequences of the Magna Charta before worrying over the day and hour of its arrival, what a different point of view we surely would have taken! Indeed, I have sometimes thought that one of the most effective ways of introducing a student to history might be to tell the tales of great events with no allusions to any names, dates, or places save those absolutely needed to convey a glimmer of the meaning. Bring out the human and dramatic values first, then advance to details.

Because authors and teachers fail to do this, many learners become reluctant, without being at heart either timid or hostile. Their reluctance is superimposed upon a healthy interest in things worth while and a corresponding antagonism toward wasting time and performing feats of memory comparable to the acrobatics of a well trained seal.

There are other subtler errors of teaching which induce this same reluctance. For instance, take the sentimentalist's mooning over culture in its awfullest four-o'clock-tea sense. The tough-minded person who hearkens to his teachings fails to see any connection between early Gothic dress reform and the things of our own day and age. The sentimentalist urges him to learn Gothic in order to appreciate early Gothic dress reform; he talks expansively about the wonderful thing, as if it were holy (or worse). And he develops a peculiar attitude toward all learning, which must now be described.

Cupid Is a Dunce.

The most annoying form of reluctant learning appears in life's second decade.

All the elemental appetites and passions raise the devil with young learners. The hungry pupil cannot learn well, still less the thirsty. But the erotic adolescent is hopeless as long as the sexual unrest persists.

And now we must say some cruel things about that ancient and honorable institution, love. Love is the foe of the art of learning. If you are well versed in theology, you know that the holy trinity is heat, light, and power; and that love is heat, while learning is light, and action is power. As you also know, there was a terrible family quarrel in heaven, ages and ages ago, in which love sought to be elected head of the works but was caught stuffing the ballot boxes and was ridden on a rail out of town. Ever since then, love has been running an establishment where everything is so hot that it has been called hell. The law of the place is: "Never think! Obey that impulse!" And the mayor of the chief city is a chap named Cupid, who, being the world's greatest dunce, gives complete satisfaction in his high office.

This theology is a myth, we all know, but, like most myths, it has a long lost foundation in fact.

The Sexual Giggle.

Rapid sexual development thwarts the learner, especially between the sixteenth and twenty-first years. Many college students waste four years simply because they cannot keep their minds off sex lures. In coeducational schools this is at its worst, of course; and, relative to the attendance in such institutions, their productive scholarship is exceedingly low—even contemptible at times. The social advantages of throwing hot youths in with hot maids probably do not outweigh the intellectual stunting. But that is a question into which we need not go here.

Many a bright girl giggles her sexy way through college, learning less than a decimal of what she might, but for her flirting and erotic fidgets. Many a clever boy receives his sheep-skin after four years of futility and necking parties during which he has not even learned how to be a wholesome male. As the teacher sees it, the later years of high school and the entire college period are probably the poorest of all for learning, save only the closing decade of life. Youth finds it hard to knuckle down to any solid job requiring mental concentration, detachment, and coolness. This explains the tremendous time allowed for the learning of a typical college course.

Adults Learn Better.

Four years at any institution, be it Harvard or the Titusville Baptist Academy, cover no more intellectual content than a fairly zealous and able person of thirty or forty might complete, even more thoroughly, in five or six months of sustained study. Many a man has said that he never learned anything until after leaving school. And in this there is much truth. With the passing of adolescence the mind steadies; then come the fruitful years, the years of less heat but more light and power. Fully nine-tenths of all that a mature citizen has learned has been acquired either before adolescence or after its storm and stress.

Children Learn Best of All.

Did you know that boys and girls in the fifth and sixth grades of grammar school read much more than high school students? That they spell better? That they show more spontaneous interest in finding out new facts? That they take books more seriously? And that they often give promise of attainments much higher than they later realize?

Our teachers and high school systems have been roundly abused for this slump. But I think less than half the blame can be placed upon them. The heavier charge rests against the inevitable maturing of sex traits. This brings new and violent interests which draw the youth and maid away from studies. It also appears that changes in endocrine growth actually arrest mentality more or less in these years. The girl who is boy-crazy and the boy who is girl-crazy sometimes have been, in earlier years, bright; and sometimes they regain at least some part of that brightness in adult years.

We have two masses of evidence to support this view. First of all, consider the huge number of students who drop out of high school and college through incompetence of some sort. It has been assumed—I think rather naively—that all these failures are endowed with inferior minds simply because they score poorly in intelligence tests during the adolescent period. Our second body of evidence brings that theory under suspicion. It reveals a large percentage of these school failures as succeeding later in work requiring more than average mentality and emotional poise. Does this not suggest strongly that all such suffered an eclipse during love's fitful fever but emerged from the shadow after the temperature fell? True, they seldom equal the college graduates; but they surpass their own college records by a considerable margin, thanks to cooling off!

Advice to the Love-lorn.

If you, dear reader, chance to be just now a pilgrim across the Sahara of Sex; if you are in the throes of adolescence, permit me to cheer you on your way. Do not be discouraged if you find it hard to concentrate, remember and use what you are studying. Do not rebel too fiercely against the compulsions of school and college. Allow me to flatter you with a sugary truth. If you have read in this book as far as this page, you have proved yourself to be far superior to 95 out of every 100 persons of your age. The typical adolescent cannot be persuaded to plough through volumes on the art of learning. He isn't eager to learn. He looks upon learning as an odious imposition invented by old fogies with false teeth and false hearts. He knows that life is meant for love—and that means dances, petting seances, joy rides, and cuddles. His judgment is unbalanced; but, like other lunatics, he thinks himself the sanest of the sane. Lucky you! Not to be befuddled by the process of growing up! Have patience! You will learn fast; if not today then soon.

A Scarlet Tanager; and I See Red.

Now for a dash of bile, to cut the sweet syrup of this discourse! It's a shame to do it, but it must be.

E. Ruth Pyrtle, an excellent educator in high standing, spoke before the National Education Association at its Columbus meeting on "Vital Values in Education." In the course of her remarks, some of which were penetrating and admirably sound, came this one:

> Once I asked a twelve-year-old boy about the scarlet tanager which was nesting within a stone's throw of his school. This modern rural schoolhouse was located in a beautiful river woods, a locality well known to ornithologists as one of the best in the United States *for making a big bird list.* The boy knew nothing of the tanager. He said his class did not have much time to study birds; they had so much arithmetic and geography 'to get.'

The speaker blames the teacher, and the school board behind teacher, for this lamentable ignoring of the art of making bird lists. But is this censure well founded? I fear not. To me it runs quite contrary to a sound art of learning. A school supported by the meagre earning of many small taxpayers chances to be in a spot frequented by many kinds of birds. Is that a good reason for taking time away from arithmetic and geography in order to make up big bird lists? Rather not!

How does a scarlet tanager figure in the normal life of an American, young or old? There is the key question. Its answer must set the educational policy of a public school in a country like ours, which strives to adjust school values to real life values, thereby avoiding sentimentalism on the one hand and empty intellectualism on the other.

Now it happens that I am at no loss for my answer to the question. Aside from having spent the best quarter-century of my life as a teacher and countryman, I have lived for almost that same length of time on a farm whose woods and brooks contain, in season, hundreds of varieties of birds. The pheasants eat in my back yard every winter. For a brief fortnight, the whippoorwill calls in the dark deeps on my spring woods. And the scarlet tanager flits about the marble bird bath under my appletree. Even the herons and the great silvery fish hawk drop in on me at long intervals; and, for years, I used to hang about the underbrush on a cliff's edge, half a mile from my house, and spy on the eagles as they wheeled overhead. All of which leads me to believe, quite firmly, that birds can be used by school folk and other learners in only one way that is to be encouraged by schools and in school; and that is as things of beauty, to be enjoyed.

But to enjoy a scarlet tanager, please do not put him on a bird list! There is no surer way of killing all the fun in life! What a horrible perversion! Yet how typical of the intellectualist! His notion of getting something out of the Metropolitan Museum of Art is to study the History of Art first, then buy a catalogue of the Museum, then go through and make a list of the Early German painters, the Flemish School, the Post-impressionists, and the Vorticists represented by canvasses on the museum walls. The list finished, the art has been taken in.

In reality, only the poor fool himself has been taken in. Having the priceless chance to enjoy himself, he has chosen to turn the day into the journey of a census enumerator.

A Sentimental Intellectualist Is Worst of All.

In all this we behold a dual sentimentalism. One-half of it is an emotional exaltation of the purely intellectual operations of collecting, listing, classifying, and analyzing; these are regarded as acts so precious that they must be performed toward all things and on all occasions. The other half appears in the silly exaltation of the scarlet tanager over history, arithmetic, and composition. Strange as it seems to me, thousands of cultivated people, the world over, firmly believe that, just because the scarlet tanager is a creature of lovely hue, there is something peculiarly noble in thinking about the bird; something edifying in studying its habits and habitat. Here we have a doctrine of Plato's which has been oddly perverted. It underlies a vast deal of contemporary miseducation. Among Americans it is still a vigorous superstition, as has been lately proved by the vogue of Abbé Dimnet's "Art of Thinking."

Confusing the Good, the True, and the Beautiful.

The good Abbé Dimnet and I will never agree as to the ways of appraising a man's thinking. We cannot simply because we disagree profoundly as to what thinking itself is. Here is Dimnet's notion, in his own words:

. . . The criteria of estimation of a man's thought are, first, the images on which it exercises itself; second, the likes and dislikes corresponding to these images; and lastly, the mental energy which enables us to combine intellectual data with more or less success.

It is evident that a person whose mind is filled with the images of petty pleasure, comfort, good food, good clothes, dancing, traveling, amusing company, in short, material well-being, is farther away from what we call thought than the person whose imagination will be engrossed by beautiful scenes—Italian scenery, for instance—with noble fabrics, with the quaintness or the appeal of antiquity, churches and museums full of the realization of beauty, and the recollections of great artistic lives everywhere. The superiority of an artist to a society man or woman who is nothing else is undisputed, and *it comes from no other cause than the superiority of one class of images to another* . . .

It is not difficult to go up the scale of moral values attached to magnetic images by visualizing in succession those characteristics of the patriot, the social reformer, the moral reformer, the saint or the great religious interpreter . . . What visions pass through our mind when it is at leisure, what scenes do we spontaneously imagine? . . . [1]

To me, all this is complete and unmitigated nonsense. But I know that millions of serious people have sincerely believed it. Analyze Dimnet's statements strictly, and here is what they mean: *The quality of one's thinking is determined first and foremost by the things one thinks about.* Your thinking is noble when it concerns itself with noble things. It is good when it addresses itself to good things. It is lovely when it deals with lovely things. It is swinish when it deals with swine, patriotic when it handles national topics, holy when it wrestles with theology, and—may we suppose?—infinitesimal when it studies infinitesimal calculus.

By these tokens, when Franz Schubert lingered pleasantly over images of his great predecessor, Johann Sebastian Bach, and his music, Schubert's own thinking was far superior to my own, when—as recently happened—I found myself alone at home unexpectedly and, having to get my own supper, had to ponder over the possibilities of evolving a square meal from flour, sugar, condensed milk, dried currants, a ham bone, and three eggs.

I have long striven to comprehend this lunacy, but in vain. The intellectual quality of my own mental processes surely does not derive from the subject matter—which Dimnet quaintly calls "images." It has absolutely nothing to do with that. *One and only one thing determines the quality of thinking, and that is the intellectual results of thinking.* If you start with a problem and solve it correctly, you have thought well. If you start with a problem and reach either a false solution or no solution at all, you think badly.

Dimnet says that we can rate people's thinking according to the *moral values* of the subjects on which they reflect.

[1] "The Art of Thinking," pp. 16 and 17. The italics are mine.

Here is what this means. William Jennings Bryan devoted all the years of his political career to the most sincere pondering over the great issues of American destiny and politics. He reached not a single conclusion worth an instant's serious consideration, and he reached many which were idiotic. But his thinking was far superior to that of an obscure college professor who works five years over the influence of diet on the development of rats' teeth, and reaches correct conclusions. Does this sound sensible? Not to me. And if it does to you, I think you had better not read further here.

Now, what are the intellectual results? How measured? By and large, we may say that they depend, for their quality, upon *what we start with as a problem* and, secondly, upon the *intellectual complexity* of the stages through which we advance to our solution. In short, work done! For genuine thinking is problem solving. It is not mooning over images. And it can be measured in pretty much the same way as an automobile engine can be—though of course with different units of measurement.

The Four Varieties of "Thinking."

Dimnet has not thought enough about the nature of thinking. Apparently he has not reflected upon Dewey's careful analysis of the four common meanings of the term. In the opening chapter of "How We Think" our American philosopher describes these; and his account discredits Dimnet's view.

A thought, says Dewey, sometimes is taken to mean anything that "goes through our heads." "To think of a thing is just to be conscious of it in any way whatsoever." A second sense of the word takes thinking to be any mental operation in which things not actually present and perceived with the sense organs are brought to mind; we think of things we do not see, hear, feel or taste at the moment.

In the third sense, thinking is believing with no particular effort to support the belief. "I think that there must be something to phrenology." "I think the world must have been created by some supernatural power." This, you recognize at once, is one of the commoner usages of the word in daily conversation. Fourth and last is the deeper and more precise significance: "the ground or basis for a belief is deliberately sought and its adequacy to support the belief examined."

We need not review here all of Dewey's keen elaborations of these four varieties. Enough to say that he shows the first sort is the only thinking of which "silly folk and dullards" are capable.

"The story is told of a man in slight repute for intelligence who, desiring to be chosen selectman in his New England town, addressed a knot of neighbors in this wise: 'I hear you don't believe I know enough to hold office. I wish you to understand that I am thinking about something or other most of the time."

That citizen had plenty of images. Dimnet would rate him as a thinker. And he would be praised as a good thinker, if the images were beautiful or noble. But, alas, that style of head work has precious little to do with the art of learning. Only the fourth variety is worth cultivating, and that is far removed from a flux of mind pictures. It is, to cite Dewey again, "the active, persistent and careful consideration of any belief or supposed form of knowledge in the light of the grounds that support it, and the further conclusions to which it tends." In brief, genuine thinking is an examination of evidence. It is best called reflective thinking, to distinguish it from the idle and usually futile sort which Dimnet extols. It is ever guided by "the demand for the solution of a perplexity." "The problem fixes the end of thought, and the end controls the process of thinking." Hence it is, as

Dewey concludes, that "to maintain the state of doubt and to carry on systematic and protracted inquiry are the essentials of thinking." Hence, too, any subject whatsoever may be intellectual in this higher sense. The facts and objects of themselves are neither lofty nor mean, neither important nor trivial, neither high-brow nor low-brow. You can think just as hard and just as magnificently about hen lice as about the Immaculate Conception; about cream cheese no less than about Einstein's space and time. It isn't the thing, still less your images of it, that counts; it is what you do with it.

The "Good" Subject: What It Is.

Just as thinking is not "good" according to the sort of images with which it deals, so learning is not "good" nor "worthwhile" according to the subject we select. Its final value resides solely in the purposes it serves. The playful learner who lacks all serious intent may find the hours spent over pinochle far more beneficial than those devoted to astronomy. The bereaved orphan who must occupy his mind with whatever lures him in order to readjust his entire life does well perhaps to become a golf maniac instead of a student of European diplomacy or the evolution of Bohemian glass. Nothing is noble save through service. And what the service shall be, there is no telling. Man needs a hundred thousand things between cradle and grave.

The Sentimental Learner.

Sentimentalism influences learning differently from all other defective attitudes. It may be only faintly harmful when it does nothing worse than direct one's learning efforts toward subjects over which one waxes sentimental. These subjects may be the best on earth. I know a few men who pour floods of feeling all over mathematics and dip their theorems in syrup before taking. All of which argues not a whit against mathematics nor, in these cases, against the men. But more often sentiment fixates upon the wrong thing, or else exaggerates the importance of a subject, or even sends the learner off in a direction which, if followed for long, loses him in nonsense.

The Hostile Learner.

As no hostile learner will ever open this book, it passes him by with a word. Our schools are crowded with his kind, and they are to blame, not he.

"I've got to take this silly course, to get a teacher's diploma. I'm not at all interested in it and I'm only going to work for a passing mark."

So a mature woman once addressed me. And I marveled at the true form she showed. She had not changed her own attitude toward required school courses since she wore pigtails down her back. She behaved exactly like her own grammar school pupils through the entire term, alternating between absence, sulking, spurts of forced work for the sake of the passing grade, and a thinly concealed contempt for the course and the wretch who gave it.

Of course, she ought never have been compelled to study the subject. On the other hand, having decided to seek a teacher's diploma, might she not have played the game with better spirit? After all, if you do sit in on a hand of poker, you're supposed to know the rules of the game and abide by them. Why not in learning, too? But I will not argue.

A hostile attitude toward a subject almost always blocks progress in it. A closed mind seldom comes out on the open road.

The Aggressive Learner.

Superficially resembling the hostile learner in some ways, the aggressive learner differs from him in every important respect. He comes at the subject like a warrior girded for battle. He is going to overwhelm the enemy, which now happens to be Fact. Just how he will do this is rarely clear. The attitude is sharp, the thought blurred.

It is hard to describe faithfully the weakness of aggressive learning, but it is easy to get the feel of it, once you watch it in action. I have had perhaps a dozen students of this extreme type in the past quarter-century, and all of them have displayed the same weakness. They pounce upon their subject, tear it to pieces, eat the pieces, and never capture the living whole. In a word, they concentrate on their attack rather than on the subject. They are like the private soldier in the World War: they never perceive the enemy as a whole, never grasp the stratagems of the entire front; and, after they take possession of all the details within reach, they scarcely know whether they have won or lost the battle, for they don't know what they have captured.

Let me be more specific. A successful engineer once asked me to teach him narrative writing. He believed it would improve his technical reports, which had been criticized as heavy. So we started, but made no headway. The man worked too hard conquering whatever came next in his lessons and assignments. He concentrated on hard details with visible ferocity. He was mentally unable to pause, ponder, sink into revery, and allow the new facts to present themselves to him, as a spectator. He couldn't be a mere spectator. He had to jump in and snap the handcuffs on the unruly truths. Would he listen to a general discussion about narrative? Not he! He would fidget and at length burst out with some remark like this: "Well, Professor! Let's get ahead! What am I to do next?"

Forever striving to "do something next," he never did anything now. So, you see, he was the reverse of the sentimental learner, whose chief defect is that he divorces his emotions from real action. This man let action dominate all his learning. He never understood that the deepest learning is a form of compliance, in accepting of things as they are.

It is my experience that there are not many such aggressive learners, although the world is packed with aggressive people. This can mean only one thing: most aggressive people will slow down enough and become compliant enough to make a try at learning.

The All Too Docile Learner.

It may ring strangely in your ears, this remark of mine that the learner who is thoroughly docile makes hardly better progress than the aggressive one. Yet every teacher knows it to be a commonplace of the schoolroom—and it is no less true among adults.

The submissive child loves his teacher, loves his school, loves his subjects. He does this, not as a matter of positive taste and out of a keen urge to learn, but simply because he is constitutionally affectionate toward man and beast and theorems. A charming attitude! Useful, too, in many human relations. But it is far from ideal in the act of learning, for it results in utter passivity.

Now, the passive learner seldom strikes deep into his lessons; and, when he does, he normally fails to do anything about his achievement. That is, he does not apply the new knowledge. He just sits around waiting to be told something else, and he will go on sitting around until earth's last encyclopaedia has been written. So he will never, never transform the raw material of his primary learning into fully assimilated knowledge and wisdom. In a literal sense, he "never knows what to make of it all."

But, as we know, we never learn fully until we live what we learn. The over-docile person is, at best, a half-learner because he lingers on the easy, lower level of contemplation. Quick to perceive, he is desperately slow to act on his perceptions. He is encouraged in this by the usual school practice. To pass a subject, he merely has to recite the contents of the day's lesson. His success at this often deceives him as to his abilities.

The Frightened Learner.

Fear will undo the best teacher in the world. Sometimes it prevents a person from beginning to learn a subject he truly yearns to understand. But more often it disintegrates his plans and programs after he has made a start.

Here is the testimony of a woman who, though graceful in all her movements and physically strong and dexterous, as shown in her skill in dancing and sports, has been completely thwarted in learning to catch a baseball. An extreme instance, no doubt; yet in every essential a revelation of the commoner effects of childhood fear.

I can't catch a ball or anything else, especially if I want to. It's because I was laughed at too young.

When I was five years old, all the children in our block would get out into large back yards and play rough-neck games of ball. Larry Deming was bigger than I. He'd throw a fine large baseball right at my nose. It came at me so fast and hard that I blinked my eyes and waved my hands in the general direction of the projectile. The ball would zoom past at a racing speed that utterly terrified me. And the assembled kids would whoop for joy. "Yah!" they'd cry. "Couldn't catch a ball if yuh tried—couldn't if-ya-tried, couldn't-if-you-tried . . . " For long dragging minutes they would chant at me, and I would run home bellowing loudly—only to be sent right back out to play with the children and not to be a baby.

Of course, the same thing would happen all over again. I was easy prey for ten active young devils. Games of ball got to be unbearable. I refused to join. I grew shy and self-conscious; and if everybody was going to laugh at me when I played, I'd stop. That was all. So I did.

Result: twenty-five years later I dodge when I see anything coming at me through the air—not so much because I'm afraid of getting hit as because I hate to be laughed at. But anyway, it keeps my waistline down to bend over so much picking things up.

A trivial misfortune? Not at all! It has colored this woman's whole life, even in matters far removed from catching baseballs. She is still shy, still timid when confronted with a new task of learning. She attacks such with a curious caution and hesitation, the hang-over of a genuine fear. She never goes at anything with a whoop and hurrah, though physically and mentally her health is such that one ought to expect some high enthusiasm.

So much has been written of late on the devastation caused by fears that I shall not rehash that old story now. Enough to insist that there is not the slightest sanity in being afraid to tackle any subject, even one which happens to be far beyond you. If you soon reach an impasse in it, what of it? Nobody will shoot you at sunrise. And whoever taunts you for your failure is a thick fool.

The Egotist.

It was not far from Belleau Wood. The raw American troops were coming up to take over a sector from the French. There was a bridgehead which vexed the high command, for the Germans had concentrated artillery upon it so that Allied attacks were out of the question; and everybody knew it. The American captain there was under orders to hold back his men until the enemy had been dislodged through attacks farther along the line.

One night things began to happen. The American captain was suddenly transferred. A stranger came from behind the lines to supplant him, an old-fashioned sergeant of the regular army who, largely because of his brilliant record in training camp, had been promoted. At first glance the junior officers saw trouble in the offing.

The new captain spent a day or two looking around. Lieutenants explained the situation to him. He sneered noisily at them. The French liaison officer described minutely the tremendous power of the German position.

"I'm going to ford the river right there," said the new captain. "We'll drive the Huns out before they know what's happening."

"But, Captain, there's a gun trained on every spot of the shallows. The French have tried again and again."

"Shut up! I'm doing the thinking here."

The orders were issued. Every man who had been in that sector as long as a week knew that an advance spelled death. The junior officers got together and decided to make a polite joint protest with full explanations. The French liaison officer hurriedly reported the alarming news to his superiors. But too late.

The ex-drillmaster glared at his subordinates when they respectfully objected to his mad project.

"I'll court-martial the man who says another word!" he yelled and pounded a table. "You lily-livered saps! I know more about this man's war than you would learn in ten years. Nobody can tell me where to get off. Out of here! Make it snappy."

The advance began. Men were shot down like rabbits. Scores fell—and hundreds would have fallen, had not the French managed to interfere and call a retreat. Thus good soldiers died simply because their superior officer was so thoroughly poisoned with egotism that he could not learn new facts from subordinates. Who knows how many other thousands have died, since the dawn of history, from that same cause?

The egotist of this type scarcely surpasses the moron as a learner. And this too, in spite of the fact that many an egotist is endowed with magnificent intelligence. The antagonism between this set of traits and the ego is perennial and irreconcilable. For to observe, to analyze facts, and to draw clear conclusions, a man must be humble and, in a peculiar sense, passively neutral toward everything. He must come to his data with an open mind. He must check every impulse to do something about these until after he has considered them in cool detachment.

Look at him from this point of view, and you see that the learner must put himself temporarily in an "inferior" position with regard to what he is studying. It is this which irks certain egotists, especially when there are other people around watching him submit to facts.

"You can't tell that man anything." This remark is often made about the egotist who cannot learn. Should such a person chance to open this book, he will make neither head nor tail of it, and it will profit him nothing.

Brilliant Failures Often Egotists.

Years ago there appeared on the horizon a seemingly brilliant youth whose high promise set many a publisher's heart a-throbbing. He leaped to fame with a few vivid stories and then grazed the best seller field with a short novel which won high praise from casual critics and inspired the deeper observers to advise the author to study human nature more thoughtfully. They said he was blessed with every literary ability but lacked insight into people.

His second book proved it even to his admirers. It failed miserably. So did several more stories. He worried over it all, as well he might. Several of his closest friends suggested that he devote himself to an orderly study of psychology and the history of social institutions, by way of overcoming the limitation. He agreed. At one of the best universities he enrolled under its ablest professors, some of whom felt flattered by the presence of the budding genius.

But they soon recovered. The young man proved a sorry pupil. He glowered at his instructors. He spoke up in class challenging some statements and sneering at others. Now and then the other students, who had become accustomed to the budding genius, took to smiling whenever he piped

up. Some said that there seemed to be a worm in the bud—
which was quite true.

"I'm willing to learn anything." remarked the young
man one day. "But nobody is going to teach me. I can
do my own thinking."

Soon thereafter he quit all classes in a huff. An instructor
told him frankly that some of his pet ideas were nonsense
and that he had better knuckle down and study in a humble
spirit. That was the last straw.

Like the ape Kipling described, "there was too much ego
in his cosmos." No wonder he made a monkey of himself
in the halls of learning! He construed every effort of his
teachers to instruct him as a reflection upon his personality.
He was cock-sure and puffed up with poisonous pride, the
sort of pride which goeth before a fall.

Some two years later he was recognized on every hand
as a total fizzle in literature. He disappeared from all save
the shoddy magazines, for which, so I am told, he still
scribbles just enough stuff to keep him alive.

A man whose ego blocks his learning is foredoomed.
Not all the wise men of his generation can save him from
himself. While he may succeed magnificently in some line of
work which calls less for knowledge than for some other
aptitude, he is shut off from every intellectual achievement.
He may become a clever and prosperous salesman, an
acrobat, an artist's model, a sculptor, or a comic columnist;
but with such vocations he must stop.

What's Your Philosophy of Life?

When all is said and done, your success as a learner depends enormously upon your philosophy of life. Your
perspective determines what you are going to do about it;
and the energies which emerge in your attitudes and emotions give vigor and scope to your ways of learning.

Do you see life as a mere struggle for money? Then you will shun all study which pays no quick cash dividends.

Do you look upon yourself as a creature of blind chance, helpless in an all-engulfing chaos of futility? Then you will probably find no pleasure in well directed intellectual effort.

Do you consider this world of yours and all its creatures simply as a curious, lovely, alarming, grandiose, noisy, gaudy, thrilling spectacle, which you contemplate as an innocent bystander? Then you remain forever an esthete and contemplative, uninterested in the deeper forms of learning.

Do you itch to understand every machine you see, every odd act of a friend, every absurdity of politicians and actors and debutantes, every obscure news item, and every strange light in the night sky? Then you have it in you to master the whole art of learning.

There are scores of other outlooks upon life, hundreds of distinct attitudes; hence as many varieties of learners.

Learn a Better Philosophy, if You Have a Feeble One!

Don't cherish the moth-eaten idea that a man's philosophy of life is born with him and in him, fixed from birth to death, and beyond his power to improve. There's nothing to that notion! You can learn a philosophy of life quite as surely as you can learn algebra. But it involves many peculiar disciplines not invoked by algebra. Above all, you must reeducate yourself emotionally—a large order and still somewhat baffling, even to psychologists.

Where begin with this task? Plainly, in the cultivation of the first, the deepest, and the most important attitude of all, the attitude of openmindedness. I have been calling this a form of compliance; if the term rings strangely in your ears, forget it for the moment, but keep the fact in mind. It is a way of acting. What does the openminded person do? He allows the facts to lead him to his conclusions, both in theory and in practice. He never bars a new fact simply because it upsets an opinion already formed and cherished. And, having accepted all the relevant facts, he acts on the basis of their implications.

How to Drill Yourself in Openmindedness.

It isn't easy to draw up a program for the learner who would like to achieve openmindedness. The trouble is that each man carries in himself his own unique handicaps and obstacles. One person cannot accept certain facts simply because some childhood fear blocks him. Another one is thwarted by certain presuppositions of which he is wholly unaware; few of us, indeed, ever know just what we are tacitly assuming when we observe and reason. So I must move warily here. A scheme that works well for one may ruin another.

Here's the simplest procedure.

RESOLVE TO CHECK UP ON YOUR STRONGEST CONVICTIONS DURING THE NEXT YEAR. START AT ONCE A SEPARATE NOTE-BOOK DEALING WITH ONE BELIEF. AND PROCEED ROUGHLY AS FOLLOWS:

1. Select, for the first attempt, some belief that can be verified or disproved through a careful study of facts now published in scientific works. To be sure, you may make several false starts here because you do not know in advance where the evidence may be found. But you will soon hit upon a clear trail if you scrupulously avoid beliefs about religion, metaphysics, and morals. Stick to simpler matters of fact such as the belief that the weather of the world is slowly changing, or that cancer is a germ disease.

2. Write in the note book, first of all, your precise opinion.

3. Next write down all the evidence you can muster in support of this opinion, without looking up any references. (I think you will be amazed at the results right here!)

4. Now begin gathering further evidence for and against the belief. Draw on every accessible source. Arrange the facts under two headings, one for those which support your belief and the other for those which throw doubt upon it.

5. At the same time, copy all other beliefs about the same matter which you come across in your reading and inquiries. Make a note of the persons who have advanced these.

6. Study the arguments such persons have used to support their beliefs. Can you find bad logic in them? If so, make a note of each instance.

7. With all these other views clearly in mind, return to the facts you have collected. Try to arrange them so that they will reveal their implications. As you think about them, take nothing else into your reckoning. THIS IS MOST IMPORTANT. YOU ARE TO FOLLOW THE FACTS ALONE.

8. Finally compare the conclusions you here draw with your original belief.

The more thoroughly you carry out such self-criticism, the better. Perhaps you can analyze three or four beliefs in the course of a year. I have done this with at least a hundred ideas, ranging from certain youthful convictions as to the nature of visual perception down to amateurish notions about the commercial value of wind mills as a source of electric power. The method proves both pleasant and useful. It has enlightened me greatly.

BOOK V

METHOD IS EVERYTHING

METHOD IS EVERYTHING

The way you tackle a task of learning is, in many respects, much more important than what you study. It is so especially if you think deeply about your subject; for that leads you afar. Before you know it, you are learning many things beyond the supposed boundaries of the original enterprise.

That brilliant scientist, Karl Pearson, says in his book, "The Grammar of Science":

> I have no recollection of at least 90 per cent of the facts that were taught me at school; but the notions of method which I derived from my instructor in Greek Grammar (the contents of which I have long since forgotten) remain in my mind as the really valuable part of my school equipment for life.

Many another man can say the same. Method is a system of habit formation. The habits live on, long after their original incentives and materials fade; and, to a certain degree, they are transferred to other subjects. The better the method, the more widely can it be readapted later.

The Three Parts of Good Method.

Most methods have three phases, all simultaneous in practice except perhaps at the very outset of a new study. They are:

1. Working into the subject; or the technique of approach.
2. Choosing and pursuing a project within the subject.
3. Getting and using the necessary equipment, such as tools, instruments, charts, and books.

Sometimes a man cannot work into a new subject until after he has found some project which excites him. He may lack knowledge and training necessary for success in the venture but, as a result of lively enthusiasm, finds study easy and pursues it hard. More often, however, the learner cannot grasp the value of a project until after he has advanced a considerable distance in the study. This is why we give first consideration here to the technique of approach.

EXERCISES

What facts that we have mentioned earlier in this book have a direct bearing on the problem of the psychology of the consumer?

Have you ever been reluctant about studying some subject? If so, try to analyze your attitude toward it. Can you discern the deeper causes of the reluctance?

Can you recall some subject which you found distasteful or at least painfully hard but still most useful in later years? What was it? And what were its subsequent advantages?

What great forces in modern American society are now aiding the art of learning?

During the past thirty days how many hours have you spent in bridge, backgammon, and similar innocent pastimes? Had you devoted that time to serious books, reading about 15,000 words an hour, how many volumes of 100,000 words each would you have finished?

Is It Worth the Time and Trouble?

Before you start a serious course of training, ask yourself bluntly whether it is worth the trouble. Many, many things are not. They resemble one of my old yearnings, which was to be able to bring down flies on the wing with a fly swatter. It has always appealed to me as a rare form of sport and marksmanship; and I have, now and then, made a feeble try at its art. But I always weaken and forsake it; for I find that flies are most devious and darting while in transit from point *A* to point *B*, taxing the eye, arm, and hand to a degree quite beyond my patience, and probably also beyond my skill.

Learning such things as Assyrian, the history of postage stamps, the evolution of theories of logic since Socrates, Druid architecture, Ancient Chinese politics, and several thousand other matters beloved by the worshipers of culture are even worse than swatting flies on the wing. After you have swatted even one fly, the world is somewhat better off for your triumph. But suppose that you have conquered the intricacies of the cuneiform; what then?

Dear lady, you who have a tutor call, on your lazy afternoons, to drill you in French conversation! Tell me! Just how does this endeavor of yours differ from swatting the circumfugacious fly? What if you learn to ripple off, in that dulcet voice of yours, perfectly smooth French chatter about Napoleon and Molière? What if you converse freely with a railway porter as to the handling of your luggage as you arrive in Paris? If you intend to live in France, all well and good. Your time and money are being well invested. I congratulate you. But what is this I hear about your intention to remain in Keokuk, where your husband runs a successful mushroom cannery? How will you use your mellifluous French in Keokuk?

"At the French club," say you.

"Hooey!" say I. (And I'll not say it in French either!)

Twenty women babbling tutorial French at one another on the banks of the Mississippi! What could be more foolish? It is nothing but a thin smoke screen for a mutual admiration society, and you know it!

Fit your learning to your life. Then it is healthful and lovely. Then too is it worth much time and trouble.

Pure Fun Is Worth Some Time and Trouble.

Am I not contradicting my own earlier remarks? Did I not say that it is quite all right to study some things for pure fun and other things for sheer esthetic delight? Why then not take up French conversation in such a spirit? Or Druid architecture? Or ancient Chinese politics?

With that I have no quarrel. And if you think I am condemning the fun motive or the esthetic, you misread me. All I ask now is whether you can spare the time and effort for such difficult subjects which have absolutely no relation to your life and your place in the world. Some people can: rich people, old people, clearwitted invalids, and perhaps a few more. In general, however, we seldom come upon a man or woman who can, in the larger sense, afford to delve deeply into abstruse, remote, unserviceable subjects.

The Social Slum.

Julian Huxley, the distinguished biologist, recently traveled up and down Africa studying animal life. Some of the strangest observations he made were of the bipeds of whitish color which huddle together in colonies, somewhat after the manner of termites, and pass their lives in a singularly monotonous ritual pretty much as the lesser ants do. Speaking about these creatures, Huxley comments thus:

It is a matter of great surprise that more people in Africa do not take up some branch of natural history as a hobby. If you have the collector's instinct, there are still thousands of new species waiting to be discovered and described. There is always the chance of enduring fame

. . . in having a new animal baptized *Smithi* or whatever your name may be . . .

And yet ninety-nine out of every hundred white men and women in Africa neglect all this, prefer to spend their superfluous energies on golf, tennis, and bridge, and when not pining for their next leave home make their lives as faithful a copy as possible of whatever they would have been in a London suburb, . . . instead of taking advantage of the unique opportunities which Africa spreads before them.[1]

The art of learning will never appeal to such inhabitants of our social slums. The brand of the stupid is graven deep upon their besoaped brows and their talcumed noses. The stupid never learn and never forget. The British dominions and colonies swarm with their breed, which has contributed its bit to the crumbling of the once great empire. You know the old story about the British in India who inflexibily dressed for dinner and promenaded about in silk hats and black frock coats, even as in dear old London. Well, the social attitude of such as these makes them impervious to new sights as well as to new ideas. They do not wish to learn anything, thank you. As the ant in its hill, as the hog in its wallow, so they.

But Americans dare not brag. For, with each advancing year, millions of them adopt this social attitude and come to desire nothing beyond conformity, nothing beyond thinking what everybody else around is thinking, playing at games which everybody else plays, reading thinly the thin reading that all other thin readers read. Do you doubt this? Then read that newest little classic, "Middletown." There shines forth the full length portrait of the socially poisoned American.

For those (in Middletown) who look wistfully beyond the horizon a hobby tends to be like a heretical opinion, something to be kept concealed from the eyes of the world. One family, unusually rich in personal resources, has recently built a home a little way out of town, set back

[1] *Harper's*, October, 1930, p. 623.

from the road almost hidden in trees. So incomprehensible is such a departure that rumors are afloat as to what secret motive can have prompted such unprecedented action . . .

An inquiry as to the interests of young people, outside of school or working hours, reveals the same blight of the social slum. A few, a tiny minority, have favorite subjects which they pursue alone; but "standardized pursuits are the rule; with little in their environment to stimulate originality and competitive social life to discourage it, being 'different' is rare, even among the young."[1]

The Eager Doer Is the Eager Learner.

As Thorndike has said, the best time to learn something is just before one wishes to use it. The rule works out in devious ways, some rather startling. For instance, it helps to clear up the habits of the precocious learner. It is the child who craves to accomplish some unusual deed who studies unurged to that end. Autobiographies are packed with evidence. G. Stanley Hall, in his precious "Life and Confessions of a Psychologist," tells how, as a young boy, he toiled for hours learning new words and their precise meanings, just because he wanted to arise in school and astound his classmates with learned essays and oratory. Hendrik Van Loon confesses that, when only eleven, he conceived a "Universal Encyclopaedia of Historical Knowledge" to which he proceeded to devote all of his time, cash, and horse-power. His first step was to save money to buy twenty blue copybooks in which to indite the colossal opus. Sad to relate, school work cramped the young historian's style; so the task was neglected, but the thought lived on, and at length emerged in the form of that best seller, "The Story of Mankind." Who will venture to estimate the years of learning which went into that enterprise? And all as the sprouting of a child's fancy?

[1] "Middletown," New York, 1929, pp. 309–310.

How Do You Use Your Time?

The ambitious learner, no matter what his field of study, must first learn one great lesson, namely, the skillful use of his time. Must we dwell here upon this ancient exhortation? Alas, yes! For each minute brings into the world fresh learners to whom it is strange.

You have already been told that much can be learned in little time, with well organized efforts. A few minutes a day suffice to make you master of a language or a branch of science within a year or two. Where will you find the few minutes? And how much time can be devoted to intellectual progress? It is all a matter of cunning. Are you keen enough to outwit the clock? Are you nimble enough to get in a vicious jab at wisdom, even for a minute or less, while doing nothing in particular?

The Housemaid's Ne Plus Ultra.

Are you one of the ten million American women afflicted with housework, and quick to protest that you cannot find a moment to study anything serious, what with brooms and mops and dirty dishes and the children's school work, not to mention Monday's wash and Friday's fish? Madame, you kid yourself. Madame, you haven't even learned housework properly. Why, Madame! You have confessed that your heaviest obligation to your family is to begin learning at once the modern science of Home Economics. Enroll under Martha Van Renssalaer's banner! Learn how to cut in half your daily mileage from sink to bedroom, from cupboard to dinner table, from garbage pail to parlor rug! Learn how to get breakfast in one-half the time you now manage it! Install labor-saving devices from cellar to attic, even though you drain your purse! Within a few months you'll find leisure enough to learn half a dozen sciences, with fancy dancing thrown in for good measure. This is guaranteed. Hundreds of women have done it.

At the same time, practice the art of grabbing the fugitive second as it leaps airily past you. Grab enough of them, and you'll soon have a fine litter of minutes in which to study whatever you like. Nobody comes upon more stray bits of time than the American housewife. And it is all nonsense to suppose, as so many do, that such wisps cannot yield a harvest. It's all a matter of system.

Relax, O, Tired Business Man!

The tired business man has an office. Let this be furnished with books and whatever implements of learning suit his needs. Let him learn the subtle art of browsing at odd moments, suffering no interruption in his day's work but rather heightening his efficiency by these many pleasant digressions.

Most business executives work intermittently. It is common to find gaps of ten, twenty, or even thirty minutes in the day's routine. Why fill them in with a mere cigar or a dirty story? Why not study a few minutes? Or, if orderly learning seems too hard, why not have good magazines and books at hand for brief perusal? Figure for yourself how much ground you might cover in a year if you were to utilize those vagrant lapses.

The Railways: Our Undeveloped Unnatural Resource.

When I hear men and women bewail their lack of time for earnest study, I recall certain figures from the Inter-State Commerce Commission. It seems that we Americans travel on railways every year to the extent of nearly 37,000,000,000 miles. The average distance of each journey is close to forty miles. This probably works out to about an hour and a quarter, perhaps a little longer, on board the train, for most trains are locals and branch line, hence slow. In the roundest of round numbers, then, this means that we Americans, every twelvemonth, make nearly 900,000,000 train trips averaging some seventy-five minutes each. I like to wonder what would happen if, on all those little journeys, we travelers booted the train butcher and his trashy magazines and books off the rear platform and devoted our idle time to learning something.

What a pleasant fantasy! Let's see! In seventy-five minutes a moderately zealous learner easily covers 10,000 words of very stiff reading, such as a textbook in economics contains. A dull learner covers 4,000 words. In good literature and the arts, it would not be hard to cover as many as 15,000 or even 20,000 words. So, being pitiably conservative, we calculate that our train learner might complete one serious book every seven trips of forty miles each. And he takes seven trips a year! In fact, half a trip more than that. Thus, you see, we Americans might use time utterly wasted in moving from town to town so that we would absorb thoroughly 120,000,000 books every year! I refuse to make all the necessary statistical corrections here. For I have only one point to score: we fail to turn to account about 1,125,000,000 hours every year. If we don't waste this much time on trains, we waste it on street cars, in taxicabs, and in motor busses. Enough to create a new civilization!

Prepare to Seize the Moment.

Many of us waste our share of that time simply because we fail to anticipate the event. We go aboard the train with no materials of study in hand. A pencil? Yes. Scratch paper? No. A notebook? Rather not! A volume to be studied, or some other task to be performed? We never thought of that! How careless such a way of life! Correct it at once by slipping a pocket notebook into each suit of clothes or each dress, along with pencils or fountain pens. (It is advisable to have ink in the latter.) Keep a few solid books or lesson courses in your valise for long journeys, and in handbag or portfolio if you are a commuter.

A Study Schedule

Beginning today, do all of your studying on a regular schedule, but beware of making this schedule too severe. Better an easy one at which you can succeed than an over-ambitious one at which you are bound to fail.

Your schedule will depend entirely, of course, on the subjects which you are learning. If you are making a serious study of the origin and chronology of the oracles at Delphi, you will need a schedule very different from that which you would use in learning some new variations of famous routines used by tap dancers throughout the ages.

Make your study schedule, therefore, entirely relative to:

1. Your subject matter.
2. Your regular daily routine.
3. The time of day at which you work best.
4. The hours when you are least likely to be interrupted.

If you divide your study period into four intervals of, say, thirty minutes each, you may get the best results. But that is for you to decide in the light of your own interests and habits. *Learn* all that you study. Think about it. If possible, write your thoughts about it soon after each study period. Experiment freely until you hit upon the best schedule.

My Study Schedule

Morning

7 to 8 o'clock
8 to 9
9 to 10
10 to 11
11 to 12

Afternoon

12 to 1
1 to 2
2 to 3
3 to 4
4 to 5
5 to 6

Evening

6 to 7
7 to 8
8 to 9
9 to 10
10 to 11
11 to 12

The Trail of the Goat

Today I saw:

Today I heard:

Today I learned:

Intensive and Extensive Learning.

The Old World has long championed the intensive method of learning, while the New World has favored the extensive. Each method has its uses, as well as its serious limitations. Neither, taken alone, constitutes a sound basis for the art of learning.

Suppose you pursue the intensive method. You master everything as you go. This means more than simply committing details to memory. It embraces also the most thorough reflection and analysis of the material. I was taught Greek by this method; and, though it was a cruel and unusual punishment, its benefits were great and enduring. Henry Sherrard, the teacher in the old Detroit High School, compelled us to commit to memory five lines of the Iliad every day, over and above the regular stiff assignments in grammar and prose composition. The student who failed was personally insulted, or even put out of the room; and on one occasion within my memory a debonair youth of wealthy parents who came to class calmly admitting that he had not studied his lesson at all was taken by the collar and thrown bodily into the corridor and part way downstairs.

There was no happy medium between total disaster and letter perfect in that Greek class. Either you knew your verbs or you didn't. If you knew them, that was fine. If you didn't, that was rough on you. When I think of the namby-pamby habit, in American schools, which allows students to slip through with credit when they score 70 per cent in a subject, I wish we had a few thousand more teachers like Henry Sherrard (and police to protect them against the dull herd and its politicians). Learning as intensive as the sort he demanded has a value far, far beyond the subject learned.

The other aspect of this Old World method is even more significant. It appears in the prolonged, serious musing over material which has been committed to memory. It must be thought through. All its significant aspects must be pondered. It is to be related to all that one has previously learned—and not until such elaborate intellectual operations have been consummated should the learner advance to new fields.

The American tendency is in the opposite direction. Our learner "hits the high spots." He cultivates the black art of skimming. Now and then, he goes as far as a certain eminent professor in an Eastern college, who has a habit of giving students a passing mark in his classes if they can tell where to find the facts asked for in the examinations. "Knowing where to get a thing when you want it is just as good as knowing it," he stoutly maintains. Need I add that the gentleman's eminence as a scholar is not great, in the opinion of his colleagues? But how the senior classes vote him the most popular Prof!

A rare case, this, and fortunately for North America. But the milder forms of this superficial learning are to be found in every walk of American life. It is a mistake to suppose that they indicate nothing more than slovenly minds and a love of bluffing. True, all the slovens and fakers indulge in surface thinking and surface learning. But thousands of able people pursue a special variety of extensive acquisition that is valuable and solid. It is not easy to describe it without seeming to condemn it. The phrase that comes to one's lips most readily is "learning by the bird's-eye view."

Getting the Gist.

It is much more than that. It is also a way of learning by getting the gist and letting the details go. And it is a way of learning by mastering a little, then trying to use it, and then learning by practice, alternating with learning by rote and by reflection. Finally, it is a way of learning by trying to master the whole business at one shot and then straightway applying what has thus been learned. Let me illustrate it out of my own experience.

Three things I learned, after this fashion; playing the piano, handling an automobile, and plowing with a team of horses. All the advantages, as well as all the weaknesses of the method, have developed in the course of these disciplines—if you will tolerate that noble word in this context.

When I was young, I had no interest in learning to play the piano, and that too in spite of a strong love of music and of much urging on my mother's part, she having been an excellent player. I never took a lesson in those early years, but would spend perhaps an hour a day picking out tunes with one finger, later with two and three, and at last with all ten. Not a thing would I bother to learn about keys or the technique of using my hands. I would try to reproduce, entire, tunes which I had heard and enjoyed; but, lacking a superior musical memory, I could never reproduce more than the bald outlines. And I was not sufficiently interested in mastering the details and the finesse.

Not until some fifteen years later did I sigh to learn the piano. Then I lacked time for thorough drill. The best I could do was to take three lessons a week in sight reading and in fingering. With the former I made excellent progress, with the latter scarcely any. The early bad habits were fixed, beyond correction except under tremendous pressure; and I still lacked the interest to put myself under such pressure. The result is odd and not a little enlightening.

Today I derive immense pleasure from idly thrumming errant tunes. And, above all, I enjoy improvisation. Yet, if I were offered a thousand dollars in bright new dimes for playing even some absurdly simple melody before an audience, I should falter and stumble in some passages; and these would not always be the hard measures. In all the years I have dallied with the instrument, I have probably not rendered any piece exactly as written by the composer more than once out of every hundred tries. Then it has been mainly luck that every note came out right.

In every stern technical sense of the term, I am strictly no pianist. Yet, as a result of this superficial dalliance with the keys, I have a curious ease and playfulness with them that sometimes works out into pretty good original compositions. But it is absolutely unreliable; and there you have the profound weakness of the method—or lack of method. I have not the faintest doubt that, by devoting one-half of the time I did spend over the piano, from boyhood onward, to a more scientific method of mastery, I would have progressed ten times further than I have.

In learning to run and operate an automobile, this hit-and-miss procedure was much more successful—and for reasons imbedded in the subject matter itself. My first car was Pleistocene, I think. It was the second ever seen around our end of the county, and fearful was its mechanism. No book of directions came with it, the previous owner having lost the same in some rainy ditch. In all the environment there was not a garage nor a mechanic who had ever laid curative hands upon the contraption. We had good veterinary surgeons who came around to heal the pigs and cows, but none of those worthies would prescribe a pellet for the car. So I had to learn by the hit-and-miss method, or else by none. I tried everything—once. And somehow I still live to tell the tale. At least three times the differential was ripped out bodily, as a result of my experimenting with some maneuver. Once, for some reason still unknown, the entire drive-shaft fell clattering to the pavement midway up a steep hill; and I saved myself and son by a wild leap from the running board, while the bus went through a rail fence. So we lived and learned; but we lived more than we learned. One finger was mashed to the point of losing the end—but I didn't quite lose it. If there was anything we didn't try out, it was because we lacked a wrench or jack or some other instrument with which to try it. And, little by little, the cold gray light of Truth dawned out in the old shed which served as a garage in those dim days of old.

What were the defects of this schooling? The bodily hazards, above all. Next to that, the sheer physical discomfort. Lastly, the difficulty of working back, from skill in handling the car to genuine understanding of engineering principles. And the advantages? The greatest one is complete familiarity with the object of attention: not a nut, bolt, washer or piston ring in the ancient bus escaped us, and the picture of the entire device became so clear that we could work on it with closed eyes almost as well as with clear vision. This is literally true. Next to this, though perhaps an integral part of it, was the capacity to interpret noises and unusual behavior generally.

Americans favor variations of this method of trial and error largely because it is our tradition. Every pioneer must resort to it, through the necessities of his ill furnished environment. No schools, no experts at beck and call, no fine shop equipment are his. Alone in his wilderness, he fights Nature with bare hands and bare brain.

In no small measure, the American youth of today who skims, bluffs, and dabbles is, quite unconsciously, carrying on that grand old tradition—but, alas, in such a degenerate form that Daniel Boone would never recognize it. The still lusty habit of sneering at experts is a hang-over of those primitive days. For, in a pioneer age, most men who posed as experts were patent-medicine fakers, shyster lawyers, and knavish exhorters. Politics and the law are still dominated to a large extent by fraudulent experts.

The young American who leaves school to take a job commonly tends to bluff his way along, in the guise of a competent worker, while he strives to learn. The European,

on the contrary, calls himself an apprentice up to the very
hour when he proves to his employer that he has mastered
every detail of his trade or craft. Which course shall we
follow, we who seek the art of learning?

Neither! The ideal is a blend of both; the particular
combination varies with the subject no less than with the
individual learner. The extremely intensive method carries
the beginner into a labyrinth of details which clog his
memory and bewilder him as he reflects over the larger
aspects of the matter in hand. The advanced student
suffers less from this; for he has a well organized background
of information which lends meaning to the details and
therefore facilitates their assimilation. In this fact we find
a clue to the proper use of the method. It suits the later
stages of learning far better than the earlier. Conversely, the
extensive system is best at the outset. To acquire the feel of
a subject, to nose all around it, to sniff its salient features,
and to shun minutiae—that is the novice's shrewdest move.

American Schools Mix the Two Methods Badly.

Teachers have generally failed to appreciate this. So our
schools, especially in the higher levels, have ruined courses
and students alike by imposing a double demand upon the
latter, from the very first class session. They have required
mastery of immense masses of fact in the shortest possible
time that could be allowed for rapid reading of the matter.
Thus both the wider view and the thorough grasp have not
materialized. If you would like to see this erroneous
technique as it is now pursued in a Western university, read
the enlightening tragi-comic confessions of a German
girl, Eva Schwidetzky, who, after a childhood spent in the
intensive method, came to our land and was plunged into
the most superficial and chaotic of extensive perversities.[1]
Here are a few high spots in her testimony.

[1] Her article appeared in the *Survey Graphic*, September, 1930, pp. 458*ff.*

She had grown up with the Old World habit of thinking straight through to the heart of everything as she learned it. At our Western institution, this embroiled her in a trice. Lights in the dormitory were turned out at ten o'clock. Two hours were allowed for study in each course assignment. Enormous blocks of reading were given out. Only fast readers could race through these, yet the quizzes in class covered details, often trifles. So she had to give up every attempt to assimilate.

It was a desperate cramming of facts in a compulsory, piecemeal fashion which paralyzed all the interest and satisfaction that could have come out of the same work under individual initiative and under more continuous, deliberate and intensive study . . .

I manufactured my papers, triumphantly watching the increasing output in pages . . . I dropped the more subtle problems that had fascinated me and wrote down what came first into my mind, without much scrutiny, following the authorities I had read, instead of passing judgment myself on every point . . .

I learned . . . to divide my days into those tyrannical little units in order to get everything done in its proper time . . . I learned to read assignments at top speed, whether the thought was perfectly clear to me or not. I learned to shut the book promptly after two hours' work and dismiss the subject from my mind, no matter whether I came across some interesting points over which . . . I should have liked to ponder long . . .

Often the teachers in this crazy institution complained that the students were not able to think for themselves. How could they, under such a lunatic régime? This method was neither the extensive nor the intensive; it was one which combined the worst features of both and none of the good. Is it to be wondered at that the graduates of so many of our more popular colleges testify, in later years, that they learned absolutely nothing at those institutions except the art of cheating and skimping?

EXERCISE

How about Insurance?

Owing to the hazards of the following occupations, many life insurance companies refuse to give policies to people so employed: steeplechase riders (horse racing), caisson workers, divers, explorers, circus trainers, white-lead workers, compressed-air workers. There is great hazard in the following occupations, although it is possible for the most part to get insurance even though you may follow them: prize fighting, wrestling, aerial-circus performing, being a jockey, being a powder and dynamite worker in a cartridge factory. But it is easier to get insurance if you follow one of the following businesses or professions, for here the mortality rate is fairly low: astronomy, auditing, writing, clergy, farming, instructing in golf, landscape gardening, law, journalism, teaching, etc.

Form Many Habits!

Whenever you learn anything, you form a habit. The more you learn, the more habits you possess. Conversely, but in an imperfect measure, all your habits tend to serve as some sort of learning. Even the habit of smoking a pipe involves you in a little lore, such as information about briars, tobacco blends, and prices of the weed. Still more emphatically does every habit, save perhaps the most trivial motor varieties, color your emotional attitudes and your philosophy of life. Tell me all the important habits of a man, and I can read off most of his beliefs. Nor is this necromancy. Any good credit man could do the same. Thus intimately does action fuse with thought!

All this has a powerful influence upon the art of learning. "Unto him that hath shall be given." The man of many habits learns most easily. I am not saying what he learns. That all depends upon the habits. A large set of bad habits makes him a fast learner of more bad things. A large set of good habits facilitates his mastery of more good practices.

W. F. Book's Achievement.

A few years ago, at Indiana University, W. F. Book gave a special course for freshmen in which they were taught how to study.[1] Before the year's work had ended, the efficiency had increased amazingly: in one group it rose from 76 to 96.3 per cent, while in the other it went up from 84 to 98.1 per cent. The speed and accuracy of reading difficult assignments improved 102 per cent, which surpasses the belief of laymen who have not followed recent research in rapid reading techniques.

One of Book's students who was working his way through college applied this art of learning to his off-campus activities with extraordinary results. He pushed up his weekly earning power from $10 to $17.25, while adding ninety min-

[1] A full report of this appeared in *School and Society*, Oct. 22, 1927.

utes nightly to his sleeping time and taking on three extra hours of class work. In spite of the added burden of studies, the young man made grades of B plus and A in all his courses.

Inasmuch as new habits are most easily formed during the first fifteen to twenty years of life, the person who makes the most of his youth reaps the richest rewards in his maturity. A lead, even though slight, if established before he casts his first vote, gives him an advantage that grows with each elapsing year. Here we lay bare the secret of the poor boy who has to go to work at the age of fourteen. How does it happen that he turns out to be a better business man than his more favored friends who go through high school and college? (He doesn't always prove out thus, for many stupid and unambitious boys have to go to work, of course.) His success is due largely to the early formation of many habits of office work, thrift, orderliness, responsibility, attention to details, familiarity with market trends, and the like. He picks up new ways and deals with novel circumstances in business more deftly than the man who first enters the field at twenty or later.

Unlearning Bad Habits.

Knight Dunlap, the Johns Hopkins psychologist, has recently set the pedagogue's world on end by coming out with a rule of habit breaking which reverses all previous methods. The old schools commanded us to resist bad habits every time they raised their reptilian heads and hissed at us. Beat the horrid things down often enough, said the wise men, and in time the heads would cease to lift. Now comes Dunlap with the strange advice to encourage them as they lift their heads; when they fail to lift, force them to it. This, you may recall, is the way the mongoose slays the cobra. He wears the great snake out by teasing him into lifting its head and striking at Ricky-Ticky-

Tavy until totally exhausted. Whereupon the mongoose
pounces upon his ancient enemy and ends his career.

Some psychologists have laughed at Dunlap's doctrine.
I do not. It has a substantial truth in it for certain types
of people; and, it is my present opinion, prior to investigation, those types are all emotional, not intellectual. That is
to say, all depends upon the attitude the learner takes toward himself and his problem. If, for example, he can laugh
at himself or despise himself or generally acquire a feeling
fringe which tends to make the habit more and more
obnoxious, and the task of beating it more and more
laudable, Dunlap's method will probably succeed. But if, on
the other hand, the sufferer fears the habit, or if he tends to
fall into a senseless rage toward it or toward himself for
giving in to it, or if, finally, he inclines to flee perils and
hardships and hence is unable to force the recurrence of the
habit, then I doubt the benefits of the treatment.

Try it out for yourself. And if you learn something valuable, please let me hear about it.

Many Uses, Much Insight.

The more ways you use what you have learned, the more
securely do you retain it. Your knowledge becomes a living
part of you only after you have read it, talked it over
with friends, criticized it, written about it in a journal, and
turned it to some practical account in your personal
affairs. Men often deride "book learning" and correctly, if
they mean by that whatever a person has merely read. For
reading is little more than an eye impression unless its
content is taken into one's system and converted into
workable energy. Indeed, a man who has not in some wise
worked over read facts cannot penetrate to their essences
nor comprehend their many vital relations; all his knowledge is of the surface.

Genuine learning cannot be divorced from genuine use. This is one of the few immense truths which American thinkers, above all John Dewey, have brought to light. It is one which most Europeans and all Americans who trail the older European culture cannot grasp, still less accept. The Old World has always supposed that knowledge consists of a nebula of memory images. The more images, the richer the fund of intellect. The nobler the images, the loftier the thinker. But it can be proved (though not here!) that this is a profound error; and it is, furthermore, an error responsible for a vast deal of miseducation and fake culture.

It is the variety and number of definite connections that determine the thoroughness of learning. But what kind of connections? Two sorts. First, the connections of fact with fact in the subject learned. Secondly, the connections of mental act with muscular behavior in dealing with the subject learned. Neither kind of connection suffices alone. The two must occur together in close harmony. Link the facts to you, first of all! That is the primary stage in learning. You pick up information as a hen picks up grains of corn. Then link yourself to the facts! That is the next stage. Now you digest and turn into some form of work all that you first picked up.

How to Use the Unusable.

"This is all very well," says somebody, "but it applies only to subjects which are alive, practical, and of manifest value to you and others. It cannot work with such things as Latin, a dead language. Nobody can use Latin nowadays. Nobody will talk to you about it. It's idle book learning. You can't do anything with it."

Half true, my friend! Half true! Latin cannot be used as chemistry can. People are less interested in it now than in miniature golf. I am not urging anybody to learn it. But those who wish to master the language may still use, in a mild form, all of its treasures. The best way to show how is to let a Smith College woman tell us how she did it.

Here is her own report. I may add that she learned Latin well enough so that, after twelve years of disuse, she is still able to read many of the simpler works in that language.

I began my study of Latin with a simple elementary grammar and a book containing easy selections of Latin prose to be translated into English. I memorized the regular verb forms. I learned fastest when I would recite to myself aloud, so I would sit for half an hour at a stretch saying aloud, "Amo, amas, amat; amamus, amatis, amant," going on through the other forms of the same verbs and of others. I did the same thing in learning vocabulary. When I wished to learn a new word, I would say it aloud first in Latin and then in English. During the whole time, however, I tried to get the feel of the word in Latin. I made mental images for concrete nouns. "Cave canem" (beware the dog) brought to my mind a large fierce hound about to leap at the skirt of a Roman toga. As much as possible, then, I tried to experience things *in Latin*.

By this time I was ready to read simple prose, I used to sit down and read aloud in Latin, not translating as I went but endeavoring to get the meaning of the words and sentences without going through the mechanics of translating into English. The method was so successful that within three or four months I had a fair working vocabulary and I could translate at sight with a good deal of ease.

I thought about the words as I read them, and often used to write down all the English derivatives of Latin words that I could recall. It got to be a kind of game, and I spent hours with the dictionary just to find out how many English words came from Latin sources, to discover what variations in meaning had arisen with the change from one language to the other, and to work out as much as I could the pattern of these changes.

I recall one prose selection which gave a vivid description of the Roman streets and houses and the way the people dressed. So I bought a clay modelling set, built a Roman house and peopled it with little clay Roman ladies and men, dressed in togas and sandals.

As I looked through current magazines, I would seize upon references to classic myths and Roman gods, and I made a huge scrapbook of all the allusions I could find, in articles and newspapers and advertisements.

In this way Latin became to me a vital language. It had far more meaning to me because I had used it and carried the knowledge I gained over into fields of motor activity. For ten or twelve years I never looked at a book written in Latin. The other day, just for fun, I picked up one of Cicero's essays. At first the meaning was pretty confused. But I read along, out loud, and the words began to come back to me. And in a week or two of reading a half hour a day, I had almost as much facility in the language as I had when I gave up its study years ago.

Here is an act of learning in which the intellectual processes were converted into many kinds of motor behavior. This student did with the language of Caesar just what many another does with French. Had she gone a step further and kept a journal in Latin—as I did for years in both French and German—she could easily have become fluent. (By the way, did you know that a few brilliant American scientists write Latin as a hobby?)

Be Your Own Examiner.

In most subjects, but not in all, any man may be his own examining board, even though he cannot grant himself a diploma. If you have studied enough to give you some idea of the subject, you surely can frame questions about it; if you can frame these, you can endeavor to answer them.

Go at this in a systematic manner. Write out your own questions, set down the answers, then file the records, with date attached. In time you can use these as a progress chart. In subjects in which the answers can be verified only by a teacher, do not follow the method, of course. I doubt its usefulness in mathematics except in connection with the learning of theorems. The solving of problems must be checked up by somebody else, as a rule.

In history, literature, and similar studies the method is at its best. It serves pretty well in language study so far as rules of grammar and vocabulary are concerned; but not at all well in pronunciation and prose writing.

Language: the Basic Equipment.

Before you set out to learn a new language, it will profit you to learn something about language. There are few important matters about which the well educated American knows less than this one.

First grasp the well attested fact that man cannot think effectively except through the medium of symbols; and all symbols are language, even those of arithmetic and of the ritual of the Ku Klux Klan. Some psychologists and philologians go further than this: they insist that man cannot think at all save with language. But this is a controversial point which need not harass us here. For we are learners now, and as such we think of language as an aid to learning. It is indispensable to all forms of higher learning, though possibly not to those simpler varieties which consist mainly of the mastery of some dexterous movements. Some feeble-minded persons whose grasp of language is slight manage to play the piano or violin with rare skill. But none of them has ever shone as a mathematician or as a political theorist.

Corrective Learning of English.

It is astonishing how little most people who use English poorly need learn in order to make the grade in ordinary conversation and letter writing. Sherwin Cody, who has long specialized in the peculiar problem of such persons, states that the average American fills one-half of all his speech and writing with only sixty-nine words and their repetitions. Cody also shows that there are not more than a dozen basic rules of punctuation and about twenty-five typical errors in grammar which constitute fully nine-tenths of the ordinary blunders men make.

Any able-bodied, able-minded youth can vanquish these bad habits of speech and spelling in a few weeks, by spending only a few minutes a day on them. But from that point onward he will progress at a steadily diminishing velocity,

no matter how clever he may be or how able his instructor.
The "law of diminishing returns" gets in its dirty work.
When and where will it bring the learner to a full stop?
That depends entirely upon the degree of mastery he craves
and is willing to aspire and perspire toward.

To master English well enough to serve well as a telephone operator, a young lady of imperfect language might
have to study no more than ten hours, in ten-minute periods
for sixty days. Would she succeed as a floorwalker in a
fashion shop? Then she might have to spend forty hours on
her speech. Is her dream one of teaching in a grammar
school? Surely she would be compelled to labor over her
sinful habits for a hundred hours, until she handled, with
smooth accuracy, a vocabulary of at least 20,000 words.
And what if she hoped to write popular stories for cheap
magazines? Perhaps another hundred hours would be
filled with her blood and tears. As for handling English as
Joseph Hergesheimer handles it, do not forget that it took
eight to ten years of his life to rise to that smooth color-
fulness which marks his style today. And remember also
that, during those long years, Hergesheimer wrote every
day from breakfast up to noon, as methodically as did
Jack London and many another master of prose. Here we
are carried far, far beyond corrective learning, in its usual
sense—But the argument remains clear, for all that.

Meanings Derive from Contexts, Not from Items.

How do you gather the meaning of each letter in the
words of this sentence? How do you arrive at the significance of the content of this chapter? Only by "putting one
and one together." Only by pulling all the letters, words,
and sentences together while you keep clearly in mind what
the whole book is about. This vast mass is the context,
or what Dewey would call the situation. It determines how
each item is to be construed.

Let me give you a comic illustration. What does "Jew" mean to you? And are you familiar with "Jeet?" No? Well, let Susie and Mame give you a meaning of "Jew" which, I'm sure, you haven't met before; and let them infuse "Jeet" with genuine significance.

Susie and Mame clerk in a department store. Friends, they lunch together whenever possible. Today Susie edged around to Mame's counter and said: "Hey, Mame! It's a quarter past twelve. Jeet?"

"No," replied Mame. "Jew?"

Don't take this as a frivolous episode. It illustrates a principle that runs through all language and discourse.

The Larger the Context, the Richer the Meaning.

The more you know about a situation, the larger the significance of everything you observe in it and about it. A friend of yours is ill. You visit him while the physician is calling to diagnose the ailment. You see your friend's flushed cheeks, hear him wheeze, and note his emaciated appearance. What does this all mean to you? Measles or mumps? Elephantiasis or fleas? Luckily, you don't have to commit yourself. The physician receives a pittance for that service. He sees the relations among the things visible in your friend. You see only a few of the things and not their relations. The medical man has spent his years studying the larger contexts of flushed cheeks and wheezes. You haven't. Of course, he grasps symptoms as you never can.

This is the only essential difference between the expert and the layman, between the professional and the ordinary amateur, between the veteran and the raw recruit, between the aged and the juvenile, between the well balanced mind and the crank.

Alekhine's Thinking in Chess.

Alekhin, the champion chess player, told the correspondent of the London *Observer* that he never sees the chessmen in his mind as mere images of the ivory figures which his hands move about on the board. "I see them as force symbols—as nearly as I can put it into words." This is a penetrating account of the highest type of abstract thinking. Alekhine rose to mastery by virtue of his intellectual ability; he learned chess as a system of meanings, not as a bald set of rules. Is this remark obscure? Let me try to throw light on it.

Take the knight on the chess board. Your eyes perceive it as a horse's head set on a pedestal. Your fingers feel it as a certain shape of hard stuff. Your muscles push it along two squares, then one to right or left. You learn the rule that, alone among the chessmen, the knight hops any other piece unhindered, provided only that the square on which it alights is clear, or can be cleared by taking its occupant. Is this enough to make you a competent player with the knight? Not at all!

YOU MUST LEARN TO BEHOLD THE HORSE'S HEAD AS THE SYMBOL OF A BEHAVIOR PATTERN. IT MEANS LEAPING IN ARCS OVER OTHER PIECES. THE ARC OF LEAP IS ALWAYS FIXED AS TO CURVATURE AND LENGTH BUT NOT AS TO DIRECTION.

Close your eyes and imagine the real behavior of the knight. Watch it hop about the board. Make it hop five times in succession. Can you see where it lands? What is its potential in terms of two moves? That is to say, how many different squares can it attain by all possible combinations of two moves? If you can visualize that clearly, you are on the way toward grasping Alekhine's vivid phrase, "force symbols." The real knight, in the real play, is a force. It does things. It moves. The horse's head on a pedestal is a mere sign of that force.

Your Three Vocabularies.

Everybody has three vocabularies, at least. (Some of us have four, five, or even six.) First and solidest is the outfit of words which a man *uses* in daily affairs. Next comes the considerably larger group of words which are not often employed but can be quickly *recalled* when the need arises. And lastly we have the immense treasury of words which are never used in common dealings and seldom, if ever, recalled but are all *recognized* whenever seen or heard.

Each vocabulary represents a distinct level of learning. Words used are best learned, words recalled come next, and words merely recognized are least well mastered.

Americans, because they live intensely, tend to reduce their practiced vocabularies to a telegraphic code. This is inevitable, if men speed up their transactions and communications. Much American slang is merely a result of exaggerated cravings for brevity. It is neither funny nor, in some cases, lucid; but it does cover ground at an appalling rate.

You narrate to me your marvelous experiences in escaping from gangsters who held you up and robbed you. When you have finished, you look at me, awaiting my response. I say just one word: "Baloney!" It speaks volumes. And our friendship ends on the spot.

The American Telephone and Telegraph Company recently eavesdropped on 3,800 people as they carried on telephone conversations. The purpose was to count the different words which they used over the wire. The statisticians found that nearly all speakers got along with only 1,421 words. I confess that this staggers me. Had the number been five times larger, it would still have been astonishingly small. In judging it, we must make due allowances for the subject of most telephone talks, which serve to make or break engagements, to give an order to the grocer, and to gabble with Mrs. Jones up the street, while waiting for the coffee to cook. But, even so, what a feeble command of the English language it reveals! And what a meagre content of the human mind! Conversation which functions within such limits cannot rise far above the chatter of monkeys in the trees.

Test Your Vocabularies on This Book.

Go back to the beginning of this book. Run your eye alone the lines until you come to a technical word or phrase. Can you define it precisely?

Day by day, check through the pages. Write a list of the words you cannot define. Look up each word in the dictionary.

If you are in deadly earnest, carry a memorandum book and enter in it every new word you encounter. I know several brilliant lawyers and business men who have done this for years. It calls for little effort and yields excellent returns.

EXERCISE

SELECTIVE READING

Here is a short selection from *"The American Credo"*[1] by George Jean Nathan and H. L. Mencken. But mixed in with it are the names of departments and various important divisions of the United States Government. Pay no attention to anything but the department and division names listed.

The American Credo

That the philoprogenitive instinct in Executive Department rabbits is so intense that the alliance of two normally assiduous rabbits is productive of 265 Department of State offspring in one Treasury Department year.

That there are hundreds of War Department letters in the Dead Letter Office whose failure to arrive at their Navy Department intended destinations was instrumental in separating as many lovers.

That the Italian who sells bananas on a push-cart always takes the Postoffice Department bananas home at night and sleeps with them under his bed.

That a man's stability in the Interior Department community and reliability in Department of Commerce business may be measured by the number of Government Printing Office children he has.

That the Department of Agriculture lions in the Department of Justice cage which a lion-tamer enters are always sixty years old and have had all their Department of Labor teeth pulled.

That when one takes one's best girl to see the Interstate Commerce Commission monkeys in the Muscle Shoals Commission zoo, the General Accounting Office monkeys invariably do something that is very embarrassing.

How many of the above-named governmental divisions do you recall? If you can remember all sixteen, you have a very superior type of concentration.

[1] Reprinted from "The American Credo," by H. L. Mencken and George Jean Nathan, by and with permission of and special arrangement with Alfred A. Knopf, Inc., authorized publishers.

Trail Words Back to Their Realities.

Words, so far as they aid in learning, stand for things and relations. You have not mastered a word until you have followed it back to the realities it symbolizes. And to do this, you cannot rest content with a glance at the dictionary. The printed definition there is itself a bundle of words. More symbols! Hence, a medium that hangs betwixt you and the truth! You must slash through its seven veils and touch the naked facts beneath.

What does this imply? Simply that if a word stands for something that can be seen, you ought to see it and identify it as the thing meant. If a word stands for something that can be heard, then hear it. If it stands for something that can be smelled, smell it.

If you like, you may turn this precept into a ludicrous mummery. What! If a word stands for murder, shall I go out and slay a man, in order to master the word? If a word stands for leprosy, shall I sneak around seeking a leper to touch? My reply to such twitting is straightforward: *observe the universal law of economy, and do no more than is needed in order to transform the word into an experience of reality.* But surely do that much!

Nobody can trail back to fact every new word he encounters. At best he may look up some in his dictionary and guess from the context of his reading the precise shade of meaning which the word carries. Hence our literary vocabulary is not only much larger than our practiced vocabulary, but it is sure to be hazier. Bookish people are ever in danger of misusing many words with which they are, on a purely literary level, quite familiar. Practical men have always criticized the bookish for being out of touch with realities; and the censure is sound.

I am willing to hold myself up here as a horrible example. For reasons which I have never been able to analyze, I was never able to work up the slightest interest in botany,

in the days of youth and early adulthood. Plants concerned
me only in so far as they lent beauty to landscape and
flavor to soup. I was content to leave their structures,
functions, names, and interrelations to other people. In
reading books, however, I frequently ran across allusions
to trees, flowers, herbs, and shrubbery. Then had I to look
up the things in the dictionary. Little by little I amassed
a botanical vocabulary. I was never proud of it, and I
never used it appreciably; for I never used things botanical
except cabbage (which is best when slightly fried with
brown sugar and a dash of spice) and lettuce (which cannot
be improved upon by flavorsome additions) and potatoes
(which few chefs understand even yet).

Now this vocabulary is still full of thin fogs. Can I
conjure up instantly a gardenia, when the word is mentioned? I cannot. Indeed, as I write these lines, I am, as
usual, wrestling with a host of dark images. A petunia?
A rose of Sharon? A Shasta daisy? I roll the mere words off
glibly. Yet, for the life of me, I cannot distinguish between
one and the next in terms of realities. Take me into a
garden, and I'd be put to shame. Which names merge with
fact? Geranium, zinnia, dahlia, tulip, chrysanthemum,
dandelion, goldenrod, peony, and one or two more. What
makes them stick? Simply their presence in my mother's
flowerbeds, long years ago; and their reappearance in our
ragged farm garden nowadays. They have taken root in
my experience; and there they thrive like wild carrot and
the unconquerable morning glory.

Translate Everything into Your Own Words.

Each man has, then, a vocabulary whose words are
realities to him. Let him make the most of this. Let him
translate every new, strangely phrased fact into his own
personal speech, as far as this can be done. (Often, of course,
it is impossible.) Beware of being victimized by other

people's language! You may fondly suppose that you understand it when, in truth, you have only parroted it.

People who teach and write and lecture on serious topics have to put things into their own words, in order to convey the substance to other people; and this makes them learn thoroughly. If everybody else could be persuaded to play the role of a teacher while learning, it would smooth many a rough spot in the upward path.

Master Each New Vocabulary.

Would you take up a new subject? Then first of all master its vocabulary. It has been found that many otherwise bright learners waste much time and bring themselves to a state of discouragement simply as a result of poring over books full of words which they do not clearly understand. This slows down their reading, makes skimming impossible, and only too frequently leads to the forming of profound misconceptions.

So we insist upon vocabulary drill: first in the less common words of ordinary speech, and then in the special words of whatever subject you wish to pursue. Save time and trouble by beginning thus!

Accept this rule with common sense. It does not mean that, if you are about to take up radio, you ought to commit to memory every term in its technology. The practical procedure would be to learn the basic terms first and then to keep several laps ahead of your learning of the subject as a whole. You will be surprised, I am sure, at the amount you will learn as an incident to the mere looking up of terms. Even after I had spent several years at psychology and had advanced far enough in the science to teach it, I was bewildered by the mass of fact I was able to pick up simply by poring over the pages of Baldwin's "Dictionary of Philosophy and Psychology" now and then. Had I spent much time thus before having grasped the funda-

mentals, I would have profited less, to be sure; but even
then it would have been worth while. Words have a singular
capacity for stimulating revery and criss-cross associations
which seldom pop up in orderly study. They help to fill
in gaps.

The Monuments and Memorials of Learning.
    Says John Dewey, in his epochal little book. "How We
Think":

> The very essence of civilized culture is that we deliberately erect
> monuments and memorials, lest we forget; and deliberately institute, in
> advance of the happening of various contingencies and emergencies of
> life, devices for detecting their approach and registering their nature . . .

We go even further. We hire professional memorizers
to carry around, for the use of those of us who cannot
or do not happen to know, a multitude of facts, precepts,
and advice. Some of these hirelings are teachers, others are
historians, archivists, and librarians, and still others run
information bureaus. The services of all are invoked in the
process of learning, too. And what Dewey says about
civilization is true of that part of it which now concerns us,
the art of learning.
    The civilized learner is he who leans most heavily on the
most serviceable "monuments and memorials," thereby re-
lieving his own nervous system of as much strain as possible.
A well organized filing system is such a monument. So is a
notebook. As the mass of important facts grows, the need
of easing up on one's absolute memory becomes more
urgent. True, we sometimes find geniuses who never have to
go lightly here, for they are endowed with photographic
eyes and ears, as was Theodore Roosevelt, who could glance
at a page and not only repeat it, word for word, but retain
its essence for an indefinitely long time. Most great statesmen are of this rare type: witness Raymond Poincaré, whose

memory makes even Roosevelt's seem ordinary. So are some unusual business men; witness Charles Schwab, who remembers the name of almost everybody he meets and who, according to his own statement of several years ago, regularly commits to memory the weekly balance sheet of the Bethlehem Steel Company in a few minutes. But the rest of us frailer mortals must fall back on physical aids or perish.

I cannot over-emphasize the usefulness of appropriate material helps to the learner. Our schools never stress this fact enough. Indeed, many teachers err in the direction of encouraging the learner to carry as much as possible in this memory. In so far as this is done for the sake of memory drill, all well and good. But there its virtue ends.

The material aid has a double value. First of all, it carries much of the burden of fact. Secondly, the learner fixates its content better and better by the simple act of using it. Odd as it may sound, the mere act of writing out a file card under "H" and inserting it as a further note on hippopotamus serves to impress that noble animal still more deeply upon you. Fill out a hundred cards about him, file each properly, pull the batch out occasionally, and— presto! abracadabra!—first thing you know, all of the cards are in your head, as well as in your file, thereby proving how easy it is for Truth to be in two places at the same time.

The Art of the Outline.

How can one practice the bird's-eye view? How apply the broad vision to literature, history, science, and other subjects which are not visible in quite the same sense that the city of Paris is when it spreads before your sight from the towers of Notre Dame?

You do it best in three steps.

First, skim the entire field as fast as you can, noticing only the large design, order, or arrangement of facts.

Next, attend to those facts which stand out in any conspicuous manner, ignoring all others; and observe how these are related to one another.

Finally, consider the relative importance of these facts, together with such lesser items as you have time to study. With regard to each one, ask yourself point blank: "Is this more significant or less than the last fact I noticed here?" Finally bring together your judgments in the form of an orderly outline.

Let us see how this works out in the reading of a book.

Hitting the High Spots.

For several years I followed a simple method of "hitting the high spots." Statements would be graded as to their general importance; sometimes inks of various colors were used to underline passages, sometimes letters were used. After having finished a chapter or two, I would go over it again, noting only the statements which I had first appraised as being of the highest significance. If the subject warranted such a procedure, I would then do likewise with statements of each lesser rank.

Now, the valuable part of this method lies chiefly in the mere doing of it, not in the accuracy of results. The effort to appraise is, at the middle stage in the art of learning, more fruitful than any appraisal one might make. For the effort, repeated often, becomes a habit; and the habit eventually sharpens the appraisals.

Select a chapter in some solid book or periodical and try this system out on it. Possibly it may not suit your temperament. But if it does, you will soon discover its benefits. Make a game of it. That helps. For instance, hunt down the author's original assertions and give them a mark all their own. Hunt down his errors and brand them with the brand of Cain. Use a series of question marks, some as little as this one,   ?   , and some as big as this,

♭ . Set the wee one opposite the slightly doubtful statements and reserve the big fellow for the seriously doubtful.

Books Are Made to Be Marked Up.

This method became, long ago, such a habit with me that, on more than one occasion, I innocently bedaubed borrowed tomes and brought down wrath. Of course, it is useless to apologize. I find the best retort is to overwhelm the wrathy one with rude remarks about people who are so unlearned that they think good books are corpses and should be interred in air-tight coffins or urns. Add that an unmarked book indicates a witless owner, and the latter is usually crushed. If that doesn't shut him up, quiz him on the contents of the book.

It's an old story that many people buy books to expose to the gaze of visitors, in the hope that the latter will be impressed. There may be sillier forms of exhibitionism, but I am not acquainted with them. A book should be used like an automobile. When it becomes tattered and torn and well digested, turn it in to the junk man with a kindly word for the author.

Transcribing the Outline.

After having surveyed and marked out the contents of the book, proceed to detach the essential outline. This should be, at least in its first form, much shorter than the array of sentences and phrases you have underlined in the book. Furthermore, it must be cast into a logical structure something like this:

   I. First main proposition.
      1. First special argument.
         a. Illustration of this argument.
      2. Reply to critics of the argument.
  II. Second main proposition.
      1. How distinguished from a similar argument.
         a. Other argument quoted.

And so on. Whatever the subordination of parts in the logic of the whole exposition may be, follow that as well as you can. Usually you may find a method I use helpful here. In taking up a book on a new subject or a hard one on some old issue, I jot down the high spots, with page references, on the fly-leaves, and then mark in the subordinate points throughout the text. This saves quite a little time.

EXERCISES IN OUTLINING

Do you play any game like tennis or baseball? If so, outline its rules entirely from memory. Then try to outline the principal methods of skillful playing.

Do likewise with your city government—if you live in a city. Prepare a formal chart showing the relation between the head of the municipality and each important department under him.

Prepare the outline of an argument either for or against a bill in Congress to bring the regulating of all automobile traffic in the United States under the Federal Government, thereby depriving cities and states of the right of enacting local traffic laws.

Without looking at the table of contents, draw up an outline of everything that you have read thus far in this book.

Preparing Briefs.

After you have acquired skill in outlining the subjects you learn, advance to the next higher level. Write briefs. Here is a technique of immense value. Indeed, few teachers appreciate its possibilities. You simply cannot draw up a good brief without first grasping the thought and structure of the material you are briefing. So you have to learn a good deal as a briefster.

In a sense, a brief is merely an expanded outline. But that hardly describes the thing fairly. For, while the outline may be nothing more than a set of heads and subheads, each condensed to a single short proposition or phrase, the brief has to read well as a piece of prose. It is, in short, a summary which preserves something of the flavor of the original.

A few simple exercises will start you on your way in brief writing. Take any serious articles in current periodicals which interest you. Estimate their length. Then, after careful perusal, write a brief on each that is exactly one-tenth the length of the original for a 6,000-word article, a brief of 600 words; and so on.

After having done this a few times, double the relative length of the brief. Repeat this with the same articles, for thus you will discover the graded importance of facts and arguments in it. I mean that, as you add new matter to your brief, you must pick and choose among all the items which you could not pack into the first and shorter brief.

Next Comes the Paraphrase.

You are now ready to work at a considerably harder form of learning—the paraphrase. This too is grievously neglected in our schools. Newspaper men have to master it sooner or later; and to it they owe no small fraction of their facility as learners and writers.

In the paraphrase, you preserve the gist of the original article or lesson but none of its literary form or phrasing.

To acquire skill here, you ought to lay down, as a first rule of the game, that you translate the original entirely into your own words and phrases. Thus you penetrate to the realities; for, as I say in the discussion about vocabularies, you never truly grasp what somebody else means until you have cast it all into words which mean something to you. Here is the supreme merit of the paraphrase.

Let me illustrate this in short order. I pick up a copy of that invaluable magazine, *Science*, and open it at random. Here is the first paragraph that greets my eye:

Tissue resistance against bacterial invasion generally finds an explanation in the production of specific bactericidal and antitoxic substances on the part of the organism or in the increased activity of certain wandering cells of the infected host. The resistance which may develop in the higher animals against certain drugs and chemical poisons cannot be explained by any of the above-mentioned mechanisms.

This may mean nothing to you. Surely the average citizen would flee such passages in dismay. The 62 words, ponderously concatenated, serve only to bewilder him. Yet they may be paraphrased, about as follows:

Animals slay harmful bacteria in two ways: either by secreting substances which kill the invaders or else by attacking the latter with cells that wander up and down the blood stream. But these methods do not protect the higher species against certain drugs and chemical poisons.

Try this procedure on whatever you happen to be learning. Repeat it early and often. Its results are guaranteed.

You might begin by paraphrasing this very book, chapter by chapter. Confine each exercise to one-tenth of the length of the original; and use no words nor phrases which are not your own.

To make sure that you are conveying the thought of the original chapter, ask some friend to read your paraphrase first, then the original. See whether he catches the essence of the latter in your report.

If he misses something which strikes you as important, discuss it with him.

Be Your Own Book Reviewer.

As soon as you have read an important book, write a review of it just as you would if some editor had offered you fifty dollars for such a contribution. File your copy of the review. Long afterward, run through the book again and then write a second review, without looking at the first one. Now compare the two reviews.

Express yourself freely here. Do not reduce the review to a mere summary. Whatever you doubt or dislike, attack. Whatever pleases you should be praised, and with reasons well set forth. In this manner you react fully to the subject and develop a clear attitude toward it—which is one of the major goals of all learning.

For about six years I thus reviewed almost every serious volume which I studied. Sometimes I'd write 3,000 words or more at a shot. Not a line was ever offered to a publisher; it was all done merely as a means of learning. And I feel amply rewarded. So will you if you follow suit.

File Everything!

Unless you are temperamentally unfit for such a life-long adventure, organize and file everything you learn. I know this is the counsel of perfection. Not one man in a hundred thousand has the time and persistence for such work, especially if he learns much. Nevertheless it is a goal toward which the thorough learner must toil, even though he never reaches it. For knowledge that is not organized is only half-knowledge. And knowledge that is not available when needed is scarcely more useful than blank ignorance.

How organize? How file? There can be no universal answer. The subject determines the method, and so to does the individual learner. If you happen to be studying concrete objects such as minerals, birds' eggs, postage stamps, flowers, or typography, the organizing and filing ought to center around a collection of specimens. A poor collection is far better than none at all. For it lends solid reality to your body of information. Each specimen becomes a firm hook on which to hang endless imponderables.

I have sometimes tried to imagine how I would arrange things, if I were to study minerals and had money enough to install whatever I wished, regardless of expense. First of all, I should equip one large room with shelves on all four walls. These shelves would be subdivided into sections corresponding to the best known classification of minerals. Each subdivision would be clearly labeled in large letters easily readable from any position in the room. Each specimen of mineral would stand, also well labeled, on its own shelf; and next to it would be the books and pamphlets describing it, as well as all of my own notes about it and related minerals. Naturally, in a large collection, there would be many specimens accompanied by no such literature. My own notes would embrace references to books, present and elsewhere, as well as my comments and observations.

Were I studying a new language, regardless of expense, I'm sure I'd rent a sound-recording apparatus such as is used for rehearsal in the talking picture studios; I'd engage a native teacher, listen to him, record his more important conversation on disks, and then try to imitate him, recording my own efforts in like manner. I would later listen to both set of records, comparing his with mine, point by point; and repeating this until I felt sure that I had grasped my own errors in pronunciation and diction. All such records would be kept in chronological sequence, so that I could listen to my own progress (or lack of it). At the same time I would commit stories, poems, arguments, and what not to memory in the language and recite these at the helpless disks. I should classify my errors, with reference to records which embodied them. And from that point onward, all would depend upon developments.

I should, of course, pursue a parallel policy with the written language. After penning as many thousand lines as possible, I should arrange the work in part chronologically and in part topically. The former method would serve as a progress chart, while the latter would aid in rounding out a vocabulary in terms of subjects. Here again I confess to handing out the counsel of perfection. Few learners have either the time or the patience to write endlessly in a strange language: and of those who so have, only a handful would face with courage the further task of toiling through their own exercises as described. Then too, it must be granted that the method I find best would not suit those who are predominantly ear-minded and throat-minded in matters of language.

EXERCISE IN COMPREHENSION[1]

This exercise will test your ability to understand what you read. You are to read the following paragraphs with care. Then answer each question listed below by writing after it the number of the italicized passage in the text which contains the correct answer. The correct answer to Question 1 is indicated below. Answer the other questions in the same manner.

All higher mental acts are *chains of reflexes* (1). When you *multiply two numbers "in your head"* (2), you are linking up perhaps a hundred reflex acts. Suppose that each reflex runs its course in 0.01 second less than the same reflex in your friend, Jones. Then it is theoretically possible that you will finish the task of multiplying one second *faster* (3) than he can.

Do you see why people naturally incline to argue that *an alert person is intelligent* (4), while a sluggish one is not? We judge people in everyday life by their results. Results occur in time. The more results per unit of time, *the higher the ability* (5). The natural man feels that time is life, and in that he is not far from the whole truth. Much activity in little time means an intense, fruitful, positive living—and that is what he regards as a *superior* (6) human type. Conversely, *little done in much time* (7) means an inert, fruitless existence—and that strikes him as an inferior variety.

An oak grows for two hundred years, and, so far as we can see, accomplishes nothing but the bringing forth of acorns. A man, twenty years after birth, may devise a *new principle of international law* (8), as did Grotius; or discover mathematical laws which revolutionize a score of engineering techniques. The oak's activities in space-time are very meagre, relative to the man's. In two respects man enormously surpasses the tree. First, *he organizes his energies to a very high level* (9) which we call intellectual. Then too, *he consumes those energies so as to get end-results* (10) which project far beyond his own personal affairs, far beyond the span of his own years, and even far beyond all his wildest anticipations. Two centuries of an oak result in nothing but propagating the species. Two decades of a man have transformed the environment of the human race.

Now, this *capacity to do work* (11) is *energy* (12). And it is the surest single measure of achievement, as well as its main determiner. As man differs from oak in energy level, so man differs from man. As man differs

[1] PITKIN, W. B., "The Psychology of Achievement," pp. 130–131.

from oak in end results of energy expenditure, so man *differs* (13) from man.

Answer these questions by number. Number 1 is answered correctly.

Number of
passage

1. What illustration is given of the linkage of reflex acts?   2

2. What is the relation generally assumed between speed of mental action and its quality?

3. Define all higher mental acts.

4. In what two ways does man surpass a tree in his activities?   — and —

5. Define energy.

6. What did the twenty-year-old Grotius achieve?

9. What is the capacity to do work?

10. Fill in the appropriate passage here: The more end-results per unit of time, the ————

11. If each reflex act in multiplying of a given person runs its course faster than the same reflex of another, how will he compare in his rate of multiplying with his competitor?

12. What kind of person acts much in little time?

13. What is a striking characteristic of an inferior person?

On Journals, Scrapbooks and the Like.

To assimilate any subject, you must—as the psychologist would say in language elephantine—react to it as a whole with your whole personality. What does that mean? Well, you must work up a certain feeling toward the matter. You must smell out its difficulties and poke about in its dark corners with the torch of your understanding (unless you happen to own a flashlight of genial penetration). You must let the thing lead you outward into the world and establish there all sorts of connections with affairs that formerly seemed to have little to do with it all. You must crave to collect further facts and to preserve these in formal fashion.

The simplest form of doing this is the scrapbook; and after that comes the journal, which may be anything from a glorified diary to a majestically informal autobiography. Our schools have never utilized either of these devices— probably because few pupils have the energy to work at them systematically. One must warm up to a subject clean through to the marrow if one is to sustain the task. Then too, considerable fluency is needed. Perhaps it would be unwise to urge every learner to adopt the journal as a form of self-drill. We may find it beyond certain abilities. But for those who can, it is a godsend.

Ever since my eleventh or twelfth year I have used either a regular journal or some modification of it in connection with studies. The advantages have been quick and obvious. Many another can testify likewise. The Smith College graduate whose method of learning Latin we report elsewhere worked up a most remarkable scrapbook in conjunction with that language. As you will find, she cut out of current periodicals every allusion to Roman culture and history, along with every Latin word and proverb. Did she find such in a soap advertisement? That was no bar. Into the scrap book it went. In time she had a unique mirror image of ancient Rome in the blurred and twisted glass of our own day. As she looked through the queer pages, she derived both pleasure and insight from their entries.

It isn't what goes into such a book that counts, nearly so much as how much and how often you clip something and paste it in. The action fixates the lore.

Advice about Your Journal.

Go at your journal as seriously as Heywood Broun prepares his daily newspaper column or H. L. Mencken his *American Mercury.* These men write journals, in large measure; they set down the day's events and their own reactions to such. They are not studying anything in particular, and they are under commercial obligations to be public entertainers. Yet the learner may well profit by their example.

A journal, even though it be on your progress in the study of economics or physical geography, can be made a work of art and a basis for accelerating insights. Make it your own "Pilgrim's Progress." To that end, observe a few simple rules.

First, write in ink; better yet, typewrite the job.

Secondly, leave extra wide margins, like those on legal cap sheets. This enables you to add later annotations.

Thirdly, if convenient, use a loose-leaf note book, so that you can add long inserts at will and rearrange the material in topical form.

Fourthly, read over your recent notes at least two or three times a month. Check up on your progress in learning, as well as in writing.

Fifthly, study your literary style at long intervals. Watch for improvements and deteriorations.

Sixthly, rewrite important topics at long intervals and then compare the versions. The results will astonish you now and then.

Seventhly, use new words every day.

EXERCISE IN COMPREHENSION[1]

Do this exercise just as you completed the previous exercise. Write the answers to all questions by number, as before.

To succeed in great affairs, *think early and often* (1). For your brain *improves with use* (2).

This isn't poetry. It has been proved in the laboratory. Neurologists have watched *the nerve fibers change* (3) as a result of being stimulated to action. The harder and the oftener you think, the better your headworks become.

A babe is born with scarcely any *insulating material* (4) around its nerve fibers. That is why infants neither reflect nor remember much. For the *nerve currents do not flow properly through the brain* (5) unless they are kept in their courses. But what keeps them there? *The insulation* (6). And how does it get there? Only *as a result of stimulating the nerve* (7).

It is exactly as if you had your home wired with electric wires that were laid all through the walls bare; and, as you turned on the current, rubber were formed around the wires. Little by little the leakage would be flowing where you wanted to use it, in lamp bulbs and in toasters.

Our greatest brain physiologist, *Frederick Tilney* (8), finds that the insulation on brain fibers *grows in spurts* (9) at the first, seventh, tenth, and twentieth years of life. Thereafter it grows slowly until one is *about forty* (10). Not one brain in a million ever becomes completely insulated, so that all parts of it function up to capacity. It is, so to speak, full of bad leaks.

Some neurologists estimate that not more than *one-fifth of the average man's brain* (11) is ever used as it might be. Others think that perhaps *one-half* (12) of it lies fallow from birth to death. All agree, however, that all of us are equipped with mental machinery which we never, never use.

[1] *Loc. cit.*, p. 133.

ANSWER THESE QUESTIONS

1. What effect on the brain has much thinking?
2. What keeps the nerve currents of the brain in their courses?
3. What do the nerve fibers of a baby lack?
4. What is the point of the paragraphs you have just read?
5. Who is the greatest living brain physiologist?
6. How does the insulation on the brain fibers grow before the twentieth year?
7. How much of the average man's brain is used from birth to death, according to the estimates of various neurologists?
8. How long does insulation in the brain fibers grow?
9. What happens to nerve currents if insulation is not there?
10. How does insulation get on nerve fibers?

EXERCISE IN COMPREHENSION[1]

Read this paragraph:

Much of the world's greatest music has come from men in middle age. Handel wrote his "Messiah" when fifty-six. Bach completed the "Saint Matthew Passion" at forty-four. All of Haydn's best chamber music was composed after he passed fifty, and "Creation" was composed when he was sixty-seven. Beethoven was growing more and more prolific up to the year of his death in his fifty-seventh year; and among his papers were found outlines of tremendous symphonies which, in their rough forms, stand out as unfinished masterpieces. Brahms wrote his four greatest symphonies between forty-four and fifty-three. Wagner finished "Tristan and Isolde" at forty-six and "Parsifal" at sixty-nine. Finally, there is the oft-cited case of Verdi who composed "Aida" when fifty-eight and was still producing "Stabat Mater" and the settings of "Ave Maria" at eighty-five.

[1] "Psychology of Achievement."

NOW TURN THE PAGE

WRITE THE ANSWERS TO THESE QUESTIONS

1. What is the point of the paragraph which you just read?

2. Who composed the following music: the "Messiah"; the "Saint Matthew Passion"; "Creation"?

3. What music did the following composers write after middle-age? Wagner; Verdi; Brahms; Beethoven; Haydn.

Now turn back and verify your answers.

Memory Follows Interest.

One of the keenest attorneys I know whose memory amazes every courtroom in which he appears to plead a cause has a poor general power of recall and recognition. He cannot retain names, faces, dates, or episodes as well as the average man unless these enter into the web of facts which he must investigate as a part of a lawsuit. Several times he has striven to improve himself with the aid of one of those mnemonic systems so widely advertised some years ago. All in vain! Things irrelevant to his practice remained written in water.

Back of this odd incompetence lurked a profound indifference to everything outside of his law office. This showed in the man's attitude toward people he met in society no less than in the way he read his daily newspaper. His was a single-track mind; so he had a single-track memory. Those of us who run along several tracks usually remember fairly well along all of them, but not in other directions. A chemist who is also fond of bridge retains a hundred formulas of phenol derivatives and all the cards in a deal; but he cannot name the presidents of the United States nor the provinces of Canada.

What underlies this limitation? It is the organizing tendency in the pursuit of an interest.

Memory Depends upon Organization of Items.

Try to commit to memory a string of meaningless syllables or numbers, such as

	uk	il	ut	oz	tef	olk	yom	gid
or								
	15	7	98	5	33	0	1	6	2

How do you go at it? Watch yourself narrowly and you will discover that you try to connect the items with one another, in small groups; with some word each resembles, with remoter objects which they call up in your mind;

or with their own sounds as you pronounce them. If you take the first course, you may run the syllables together so as to form a few larger groups, as if they were words, thus:

ukilut   oztefolk   yomgid

Or you may intone them in some rhythm which sinks in easily. But always the same basic process recurs. You organize the meaningless stuff.

The higher the degree of organization, the more easily does any one item in the pattern suffice to recall all others. Integrate well at first, and the least part revives the whole. If there is no system apparent, the items must, so to speak, stand on their own legs, which are spindling indeed. Then you are thrown back upon "absolute memory," or "the photostatic image" which was imprinted upon your brain cells in the original act of perceiving. That doesn't help much, for there are trillions of such. Finding the right one makes the old task of looking for a needle in a haystack seem mere child's play.

We Organize Items around Our Interests.

When a subject interests us, we nose all around it. We get our general bearings in it promptly. We linger over details. We muse. Thus do we bring together all that we perceive and think into some sort of a panorama through which a design runs. The threads of design hold the minutiae together. Nor does our organizing cease there. We organize our attitudes and our general behavior around the interesting things. The lawyer joins lawyers' clubs. He buys law books. He reads legal periodicals. He takes the professional point of view toward the murders and scandals about which he reads in his morning paper. Each such act links up his entire personality more and more tightly with the law, and the law with his personality. It is in no poetic sense that we may say that the most brilliant and experienced jurists are the law, and the law these very jurists. Man and institution become more nearly one as the man "identifies himself" with the institution. Such a one scarcely has to remember anything about the law. He merely must "be himself."

Intrinsic and Extrinsic Organization Patterns.

To learn nonsense syllables and numbers, we are forced to invent some way of organizing them which, strictly speaking, is foreign to the data. We devise artificial tricks of associating, such as connecting each integer with a letter of the alphabet and thus spelling out the numbers to be learned; or adding some idea to a set of facts which ties them all together in some sentence. It is plain that all devices like these are infinitely less effective than the simple act of finding some sense in the matter and holding the meaning firmly. Things which hang together of themselves, in a state of nature, have meaning. Things which do not are meaningless. To retain those which have a meaning all their own, you merely have to be interested in them. To hold the others so as to be able to draw on them at will is an appalling job. By good luck, we do not often have to do it nowadays. But when we do, how proceed? One way is illustrated by Berol.

The Story of Berol.

Berol, an immigrant, tried his hand at many jobs after his arrival in America. He was discharged from each in short order, and always for the same reason: he forgot. He could remember neither orders nor ways of doing things. Steadily he sank: from good job to poor; from poor job to worse, until at length he became a dishwasher in a greasy restaurant down on the Bowery.

Then he paused to ponder. If he did not improve his memory, he would pass out of the picture. But how? He decided to go up to the Public Library and read for light.

As he said, he read everything on the shelves which dealt with the mysteries of memory. Little by little, he worked out a private plan of self-improvement, founded upon three fundamental procedures. First, never take notes of any sort. Do not even write down a telephone number you wish to keep in mind. If you do, that helps you to forget it; for man has become the slave of the written word, which should have been his slave. Secondly, find your own amusing association for each thing to be recalled; the funnier, the better. Never let the link be dull, if you can make it snappy. A mnemonic system based upon fun sticks best. Thirdly, never force the memory functions. If something doesn't bob up at the instant it is wanted, wait patiently; sooner or later, it will show its head.

Berol then adopted, in his own modified form, the old familiar tricks of mnemonics. He built up associations between letters and numbers, to learn such things as telephone numbers and statistics. He used the device of repeating slowly the content to be memorized, at the moment it was first presented, and, of course, he drilled himself in concentration. After some time, this man of evanescent memory became one of the best known teachers of memory training in New York City. I have talked about his courses with prominent business men who took them; and there can be no doubt that Berol's method worked, *provided all of the conditions he set forth as vital were strictly observed.*

Of these, by no means the least important was the prohibition of all written notes. Here you must not compromise, said Berol; if you do, you are lost. This was a keen insight; for it established a total situation in which you had to use your memory or fail altogether. Throwing away all crutches, the cripple walks. Berol saw that most men have seemingly poor memories simply because they have ceased to use them in an orderly manner. (He might have gone further and observed that most men have poor minds because they evade using them as much as possible; and they have weak wills for the same reason.)

Unfortunately, we waste too much time and introduce endless confusions into this strange world of ours when we try to get along without notes. Berol's system is suited to dire emergencies—as are many other systems. But there is no mental feat of retention which warrants our leaning heavily on it for the ordinary affairs of life. It is much better, in the long run, to reduce effort and save precious hours by inventing memorials of events and duties. The way of Berol is the way of the stone age.

Reciting Helps to Memorize.

No matter which way we memorize or what we attack, it pays to recite to ourselves at short intervals. Suppose that you try to memorize the gist of this chapter. If you merely read it over and over, you will probably remember about 16 per cent of it after four hours. But if you spend four-fifths of your drill period in reciting it to yourself aloud, you are pretty sure to retain, at the end of that same period, about 26 per cent of it all. (If you are specially interested, of course, you will retain considerably more in each case; and if bored to death, less.) To serve you best, let your recitals be spaced at least ten or fifteen minutes apart but never more than twenty-four hours apart, if possible. (True, some memorizing can be done through recitals two full days apart; but the safer general rule adheres to the one-day interval.)

The Emotional Factor.

We have already studied the emotions at some length and have learned how vital or fatal they are to learning in all its phases. Now it is enough to mention that the pleasant tone of one's attitude toward the task of memorizing makes all the difference in the world as to its speed and accuracy. Best of all is intense self-confidence. Worst of all is fear of failure that is bound up with some deep worry over the failure. Many beginners spoil everything by taking—often with a shred of justification—the unpleasant attitude toward lessons. Remember the four lions in the path as we entered upon it? Well, in each there is this wrong feeling, now of discouragement, now of helplessness, now of suspicion—and until the spirit changes, learning must lag.

The Four Types of Memorizing.

To learn well, find out your own type of memorizing and retaining facts. In a rough-and-ready way, we may group people under four heads:

1. Fast learners and fast forgetters.
2. Fast learners and slow forgetters.
3. Slow learners and fast forgetters.
4. Slow learners and slow forgetters.

This runs counter to the old notion, still held by many people unfamiliar with psychology, that those who learn quickly forget quickly. Truth is, though, that memorizing and retaining what has been memorized involve quite distinct functions and attitudes; and these latter vary more or less independently of one another. Consider, for instance, how you may seize upon some new article about your favorite subject, astronomy, in which a novel hypothesis about the formation of the spiral nebulae is advanced. You absorb it quickly; for to your interest in astronomy is added the immense reinforcement of knowledge about spiral nebulae and the opinions of eminent scientists concerning those strange formations of star dust, whose every mote is a sun. In half an hour perhaps you have assimilated the entire article and can recite it smoothly.

But, after you have pondered it and read other articles about it and talked it over with astronomers, you find that it is flimsy. The author is not a thorough scientist but an ingenious guesser. His hypothesis differs little from an old one put forward eighty-four years ago and totally demolished by Sir William Goofleberry, of the Royal Academy of Star Gazers. Thus, like spring's last snow beneath the April sun, your confidence in the article melts and runs off into the great sea of oblivion which doth embrace all worthless things. A week later you barely recall the name of its author. A month gone, and you can scarcely bring back the idea of the thing.

We Slough What Does Not Fuse with Our Total Natures.

What has happened? The sharp arrow struck your skin and stuck there. But it did not penetrate to your heart. It was an alien substance, so your blood built lymph around its tip and forced it out of the skin, then covered the little wound with scar tissue. Is this a fanciful analogy? I'm not at all sure. The mind receives many things on its surface; holds them to itself and even allows them to sink in a little; but, as soon as it finds that the new object is false, hurtful, or silly, or in any other wise out of harmony with the spirit of the entire personality, it begins casting the intruder off. No matter how perfectly we originally learned such matters, we throw them off and can no longer recall them.

Apply all this to your own problems of learning. It will guide you to your own best procedure. Never be disturbed if you find that recently learned material doesn't stick. This means either that you have not yet related it vitally to your own life and affairs or else that it is positively hostile in some unsuspected manner. Test the second possibility first. Ask yourself the following questions:

1. Does it antagonize some deep belief of mine?
2. Does it interfere with some old pleasant habit?
3. Does it arouse painful memories?
4. Does it conflict with some present desire?

If you will study the learned material minutely from each of these points of views, an astonishing event will soon occur. Either you will open your eyes to some aspect of it or of yourself which puts everything in a new light and fixates the whole business photographically in your mind; or you will find excellent reasons for giving up the study of it on the spot.

Try it!

Nobody who is a slow learner and fast forgetter will ever read these lines. For that is the pattern of an inferior mind. Thus the moron, who spends an hour learning to spell "house" and forgets it utterly two days later. (I once taught a high-grade moron about fifty one-syllable words like "cat" and watched him lose them all over and over, in spite of repeated drill.)

You may learn and forget fast. Do not let this discourage you until you have persistently asked yourself the four questions about each thing you forget. Should you, after this self-inquiry, still forget as fast as ever, that would be a bad sign indeed.

Should you learn and forget slowly, take heart! While you may never be able to hold the pace of geniuses who absorb and retain all things in a flash, you can move ever onward and become a highly educated, skillful person simply by applying the many little tricks of technique in the art of learning.

If you learn fast and never forget, perhaps you are wasting your time over this book. But it may have something to tell you; for not a few exceptionally bright learners abuse their ability and take unfair advantage of it. They find that they can keep abreast of the rank and file of humanity with little effort, so they never exert themselves. Little by little they sink to the dull average; and soon the demon habit has bound them in his shackles. Friends begin to say: "Oh yes! Smith! A man whose future is behind him."

Later we shall recur to this problem of memorizing. It runs through the entire repertory of learning methods. And now please apply what you have just learned by interpreting that charming and accurate little poem of Thomas Bailey Aldrich on "Memory":

> My mind lets go a thousand things,
> Like dates of wars and deaths of kings,
> And yet recalls the very hour—
> 'Twas noon by yonder village tower,
> And on the last blue noon of May—
> The wind came briskly up this way,
> Crisping the brook beside the road;
> Then, pausing here, set down its load
> Of pine-scents, and shook listlessly
> Two petals from that wild-rose tree.

EXERCISE

Here are President Wilson's famous Fourteen Points, with which every well-informed adult should be familiar:

1. Abolition of secret treaties and diplomacy.

2. Freedom of the seas in war as in peace.

3. The largest practicable extension of free trade.

4. Reduction of national armaments to the lowest point consistent with domestic safety.

5. An unselfish adjustment of all colonial claims especially in regard to the interests of native populations.

6. Good will toward Russia and the evacuation of its territories.

7. The absolute freedom of Belgium.

8. The restoration of Alsace-Lorraine to France.

9. The completion of Italian union by addition of the Italian-speaking provinces under Hapsburg rule.

10. Self-government for all the peoples of Austria-Hungary whose place among the nations was to be safeguarded and assured.

11. Liberty for the Balkan States, and especially free access to the sea for Serbia.

12. The Ottoman Empire to be confined to its Turkish parts, and the Dardanelles to be permanently opened.

13. The independence of Poland, made up of indisputably Polish-speaking populations, and with free access to the sea.

14. A "general association of the nations."

EXERCISE

On a sheet of paper draw, as well as you can, the outline of an oak leaf. Study the result carefully. Then draw a second one which is more accurate than the first.

If this second one still seems seriously wrong, write a criticism of it stating just how and where it errs.

Then get an oak leaf or a picture of one and inspect it in the light of your own recollection. Contrast it, feature by feature, to your sketch.

Without looking at any automobile, write down, as rapidly as you can, the differences between any cheap car and any high-priced car which you have often seen.

Who was the best school teacher you ever had? Describe his method of teaching.

Who was the worst one? Describe his method also.

EXERCISE

Here are some of Byron's loveliest lines. Read this poem through *once* aloud, keeping its content clearly in mind as you read. Then close the book and write down as much of it as you recall. Do the same thing each day until you can recall and write it down accurately. You should be able to do this within thirty days. If you do it in five or fewer, your memory is freakish.

She walks in beauty, like the night
Of cloudless climes and starry skies;
And all that's best of dark and bright
Meet in her aspect and her eyes,
Thus mellowed to that tender light
Which heaven to gaudy day denies.

One shade the more, one ray the less,
Had half impaired the nameless grace
Which waves in every raven tress
Or softly lightens o'er her face;
Where thoughts serenely sweet express
How pure, how dear their dwelling-place.

And on that cheek, and o'er that brow
So soft, so calm, yet eloquent,
The smiles that win, the tints that glow,
But tell of days in goodness spent,
A mind at peace with all below,
A heart whose love is innocent!

Forget It!

The learner changes something in himself when he learns. He also destroys that same thing in part, if not altogether. This is true of every kind of learning. In developing a new habit of conduct, in memorizing facts or words, in cultivating a new attitude, or in changing your mind, you invariably slough off something. Breaking down any form of behavior involves the breaking down of molecules and those constellations of molecules which we call cells.

So there is a sense in which we may say that the art of learning must embrace a certain art of forgetting. We might also say that it embraces a certain art of dying; if by that we mean what old Heraclitus did when he remarked that life is a perpetual flux in which everything is constantly coming into being and constantly passing away. The baby dies when the child grows up. The child dies as the youth comes singing. And youth dies the very moment man opens his eyes and sees the pretty mists of illusion lift from the battlefield of life.

The lowest form of animal life is the creature which can never learn and never forget. When men described the Bourbons in this phrase, they uttered the last word of scathing condemnation. They said, in effect, that the Bourbons were not even rats; for rats can learn and forget. You probably have known somebody whom the phrase fits. Did you ever return to a town where once you lived in your youth and meet on the street corner a man whom you knew well as a boy? He talks just as he did in the old days. He expresses the same ideas. He has not even changed his petty mannerisms, his gestures, the cut of his clothes, and his line of jokes. In a word, he is a little brother of the Bourbons. How related to the rat, perhaps you can say better than I. He is "the same old Bill Blubb. Just a little fatter and slower."

Some day, when microscopes are stronger, a scientist can peer into the nerve cells of men like Bill Blubb and see, with their eyes directly, just how it is that the molecules there cling together in their pristine patterns so tenaciously that no ordinary stimulation can change them. In that far-off day men will pity Bill just as we now pity a man born blind. Bill can't help it. His nerves are built too tough, too dull, too hard.

The Art of Forgetting.

Bill forgets nothing because nothing ever sinks in; and, if it did, there is no personality beneath Bill's skin that responds vigorously to the thrust of new experiences. Other men, however, forget even more than Bill ever heard and saw, and they do so in a way that enables them to retain more effectively whatever they wish to keep. Theirs is a selective forgetting. The shrewd politician remembers the face and name of every voter in his district, but most conveniently forgets his campaign promises. The statesman forgets the voters but keeps his policy and platform steadily in view.

You doubtless know the old tricks of exposing your wretched memory by asking you to describe the face of your watch, or to tell how many steps there are in the stairs of your home. Such questions betray the interrogator's ignorance of the laws of wholesome learning. When you look at your watch, you wish to know only the time; so you deliberately attend to the relative position of the hands on the face and ignore all else. A moron would notice all the odd details of the face for an instant or two, and certain freak memorizers would be unable to exclude them. So too with your stairs; when you approach them, it is to ascend or to descend; so you react by moving your muscles appropriately. You have no reason to count the steps. In fact, you have good reasons for refusing to count them.

Should they adhere to your brain cells, they merely clutter up the works.

You Can't Force Yourself to Forget.

Within narrow limits, you can force yourself to remember things; and other people can force you too, but it seems quite beyond mortal power to force oneself to forget. Concentrating on the thing to be forgotten only serves to keep it in mind. To forget usefully, you mustn't try! Rather must you attend severely to what you wish to retain. The rest will fade of itself.

An old joke among psychologists illustrates this point. Would you like to be able to cure yourself or any friend of any disease or physical injury by sheer mind power? I will tell you how to do it. Stand in front of the sufferer, look him in the eye for two minutes, and during that entire time never think even for a thousandth of a second of the word "hippopotamus." If you can do that, you can do anything!

EXERCISES

MAKE THINGS EASY FOR YOURSELF

Here are some exercises which will not only drill your memory but will establish mental habits which save much time and energy.

1. Memorize the following telephone numbers:

Your bank.

Your family doctor.

The nearest drugstore.

Three stores or offices which you telephone regularly.

Three of your friends whom you call often.

2. Memorize ten street addresses which you regularly use in correspondence and which you now look up each time you write.

3. From now on, each time you are introduced to people, make an active effort to remember their names. To do this, you must be sure to hear the names correctly at the time you are introduced. If you do not understand them, ask to have them repeated to you. By steady drill you will be astonished at your increased facility in recalling names.

4. Toward the close of each day, for several weeks at a stretch, tell somebody what you have seen, heard, read, or done during the day. Give exact details! Observe how much easier your memory is after such practice.

The Trail of the Goat.

Today I saw:

Today I heard:

Today I learned:

To Keep It, Pass It On!

One of the surest ways of keeping what you have learned is to pass it along to somebody else.

Sounds idiotic, doesn't it? But this is the ancient experience of teachers, among whom the saying runs: "You never truly know a subject until after you have taught it a year or two."

To this I subscribe, with a minor qualification. You do not have to go into a class room and formally teach a subject in order to learn it through and through. But you must do something that is fully the equivalent of transmitting the entire body of lore; and there are few methods which equal teaching.

As only one American out of every 150 or thereabouts ever has the chance to teach in classroom, some other way must be found to pass along what has been learned. What may be suggested? For one thing, writing for the newspapers. To be sure, you cannot expect the editor to publish articles from your pen on quadratic equations or the use of the ablative in Horace. Readers are strangely prejudiced against such subjects, and we shall have to put up with them. It is possible, now and then, however, to pick up an odd fact within your realm of learning and turn it into an entertaining contribution.

Conversation.

Far more promising for the average learner is well managed conversation. Not that antiphony of noises which too often passes for conversation! Not the disguised sermon delivered by the spouter while all other diners suck soup or puff their weeds! No! Rather that playful target practice of the mind—never done with blank cartridges and never with shrapnel or poison gas!—in which all present pop at everybody else. The soul of conversation is the friendly exchange of personal opinions, attitudes, and beliefs, not for the purpose of informing the world or to convert anybody but primarily to disclose the personality of the speaker and to excite others to disclose themselves.

To converse well, then, you must have crystallized what you have learned. You must also have developed thoughts and attitudes toward that information. But that is not all. A good conversationalist must be a good listener. He must take the compliant attitude toward what others have to say; and to that extent he must learn as he listens. He must then relate what he hears to what he has previously learned and effect a quick synthesis. Alas, how few can react at such velocity! Many, however, can do much better than they now do.

Finally the good conversationalist must be dexterous in expressing his opinions and in challenging others. He must have learned how to say one and the same thing in a score of elocutions, one to enlighten the stupid, one to charm the hard-to-please, one to crush Bombastes, one to sear the pedant's hide, one to arouse the unsympathetic—indeed, there is no end to the wraithlike shadings of utterance. And each shading forces the speaker to pass on what he has learned about the subject at hand. As the evening advances, he must shift his stance toward it—and sometimes come at one man with a brassie while the next one calls for a feathery putt. What can consolidate all that he has learned more effectively?

The Need of Conversational Groups.

So valuable is frequently repeated sessioning at conversation that I believe thousands of study clubs would do well to change over into conversational groups. This is not said in criticism of their present activities. These, however, might be furthered more easily if members studied by themselves more than now and then came together in a jolly, informal party to talk about whatever interested them, even small gossip. I am only too keenly aware of the hardships confronting the audacious soul who launches such an enterprise in the typical American community. If the group is made up of women, the conversation is ever in danger of degenerating into a squaw chorus of remarks about the price of sirloin and the new neighbor up street. If the group is male, it drops into smoking room stories or else the sad state of business in these dull days. I offer no preventive for these diseases, but if a fine of ten cents could be imposed for every lapse from true conversation and the collections pooled, we would soon have an endowment fund for a university of creative learning.

Our Schools Need More Conversation.

Just because no educator has yet discovered the art of learning, all of our schools continue to groan under the boredom and stiffness of set lectures, periodic quizzes, written examinations, and routine recitations. These leaden habits serve only as sinkers; they carry the bait down to the depths but entice no fish. Indeed, sinker is usually larger than bait and so frightens the fish away. True, here and there, some rare teacher makes a course more natural by talking with the students rather than at them; but as yet the practice has left no impress upon our school system as a whole. Nor can it make itself felt as long as the young learner must walk into Room 47 at ten sharp, prepared to deliver facts set forth between pages 177 and 194 in the textbook. To converse, he should have no inkling of what may come up during the hour; nor should he feel under the faintest obligation to say anything. All of which runs counter to our crude notion of education, does it not?

Teachers miss a tremendous opportunity when they fail to train the young in the ways of artful conversation. True, our mass education methods thwart the instructor at every turn; and from these only the robustious can break loose. Nevertheless, those who decree the methods must be taught that the brilliant teacher must and will find a more informal and more human way of inspiring young minds. Once in a hundred times, one teacher may actually talk, not to or at, but with the learners; and not on set topics but about anything which crops up. Free associations are thus stimulated, and so is a swift shift of attitude, a tolerance toward all sorts of new and queer opinions, and an eye-opening in all vistas.

Conversation in the Home.

Make it your business—and a solemn one, too—to converse at home whenever possible and as long as possible. This precept runs counter to the trend of American life, I know. So do many other excellent rules of living. So much the more loudly then ought we shout them from the house-tops! The talk that goes on within the walls of most homes resembles the grunt of hogs around a trough full of food more than human converse. Home has become more and more a mere trough and sleeping wallow. What with the auto, the miniature golf course, the roadhouse, and the dance hall, the old family unit has shrunk and shrunk and shrunk until it approaches zero, except in the matter of monthly bills, of course.

If there are learners there, how different it may become! I have known perhaps half a dozen homes where conversation flourishes; and these stand out like mountains among the mole-hills of the typical American family. There somebody is always learning as a result of what somebody else says; and there is a tingle in the air at table. Needless to add, some members of those families are brilliant learners.

Farmer Burns, Frank Gotch, and the Art of Learning Movements.

Out in the exuberant Middle West, where rainbows end in back yards and all things are possible, even though not always profitable, there thrive sundry geniuses, among whom two stand out in my own memory as having taught thousands of young Americans how to box, wrestle, and ply the ju jitsu racket, all by mail. A lesson a week, delivered at your door by the postman! Each lesson brings a new blow, twist, or body hold. At the end of the course, the learner is supposed to be competent to meet all comers of his class in prize ring or up a dark alley.

I have often sighed for time to sign up with Farmer Burns and Frank Gotch. Not that I dream of winning heavy-weight championships. No, I do not even aspire to throw a giant bully on Broadway, simply by applying ju jitsu to his left ear. I am genuinely interested, however, in discovering how far these Pedagogues of the Artful Thump can go in teaching such muscular proficiencies by mail. I refuse to believe that they are fakers or jokes; for they have never landed in jail nor, so far as I know, been barred from the U. S. mails. Hence their army of learners must feel that they are getting something out of the courses. Their success, such as it is, raises an important issue in the art of learning. To what extent can intricate movements be learned by reading minute descriptions of them?

Of one thing we may be sure. However much can be learned in this wise, it is trifling beside what is easily acquired through personal practice with a trained teacher who is able, not merely to tell you what to do, but also to demonstrate the right action himself. And the way of Farmer Burns and Frank Gotch is manifestly far inferior to learning with the aid of a well prepared motion picture, especially one accompanied by the talk of a competent teacher.

It can no longer be doubted that virtually all teaching of difficult movements in the future will follow a simple design. First of all, the teacher in person will explain and demonstrate. That done, he will throw a talking picture on the screen and, at certain points that call for special analysis, he will stop the view or else slow it down very much, so that every eye, even the slowest, can perceive each least detail. While exhibiting this, he will talk about the significant points. If some learners wish further explanations, he will run the picture over again and clear up whatever is needful.

So much for the ideal. But how about learners who live far from good teachers, or cannot afford that luxury? What can they do? If possible, let them rent films. If not, let them use a home motion picture to reproduce their own movements as made on the basis of faithful imitation and book study. If such equipment is not available, then let them practice before a mirror, not as Narcissus but as a cold-blooded spectator of a show for which he has paid admission.

Unfortunately, both the motion picture companies and our school authorities still lag a generation behind events in the use of motion pictures for this type of education.

Every Little Learner Has a Movement of His Own.

Caruso, you may recall, had the bad luck to fall into the hands of a pedant at the outset of his musical career. The pedant insisted that the youth use his singing muscles in one particular way, which was, quoth the pedant, the orthodox and only correct mode of singing. Caruso struggled to obey, but brought forth only raucous tones. The pedant pronounced his new pupil a flat failure; and some of Caruso's friends sought to dissuade him from operatic adventures. Fortunately for the world, Caruso sought a better teacher, one who followed the oldest Italian tradition of encouraging the learner to sing in his natural manner as far as possible and to develop that same manner to its utmost.

American piano teachers, I grieve to report, all too frequently err in striving to impose on their pupils a rigid system of postures and movements, especially in fingering. They have much to learn from Josef Hofmann, who declares:

> A correct fingering is one which permits the longest natural sequel of fingers to be used without a break. By earnest thinking every player can contrive the fingering that will prove most convenient to him. But, admitting that the great diversity of hands prohibits a universal fingering, all the varieties of fingering ought to be based upon the principle of a natural sequel.[1]

This applies to all sorts of muscle learning, such as type-writing, dancing, running, high jumping, and swimming. There is no one correct method *except in terms of the results to be obtained*. Hands, feet, and limbs vary in length, thickness, strength, and native nimbleness; hence they can be used only with due regard to such peculiarities.

Learning a Foreign Language.

The movements of tongue and throat muscles required for the pronouncing of foreign speech raise a new difficulty. Many of the sounds are unnatural to you. They simply cannot be made unless you force yourself to make strange, even uncomfortable noises. Many instructors have aggravated the difficulties here by drilling the student unmercifully in phonetics. This not only discourages him but confuses him. It is wiser to help him along by coaxing him to imitate the teacher's pronunciation and thus gradually improve his own. As I have said, the learner is helped greatly by speaking into a recording phonograph, then listening to his own voice. More and more, this method must be adopted.

[1] From his book, "Piano Playing," Chap. XII, p. 35.

With the best of methods, however, the adult learner must not expect to master a foreign language to the point of deceiving natives as to his birthplace. Ease and precision of speech come in childhood. True, the older person can conquer vocabulary, grammar, and idiom quite as deftly as the youngster; but he cannot reeducate his muscles without immense effort. And usually the game isn't worth the candle.

Can You Catch a Ball?

In this experiment, you will need the help of some one else. How great improvement can you make in tossing balls?

Using two balls of the same size and weight, you and your assistant (who will learn much through practicing with you!) are to keep both balls going, using one hand only, catching and throwing one while the other is in the air. You are allowed ten trials a day. Each time one of you fails to catch a ball, you must begin a new trial. Count the number of catches you make for every trial, between which you are allowed to rest if you wish.

Always stand about the same distance apart, let the distance be at least six feet, and preferably ten or twelve.

As you improve in your skill, the number of catches you make for each trial will, of course, increase, until at the end of a month's practice you will probably have learned so well how to toss and catch a ball that you will not have time to use the ten trials which you are allowed.

And be sure to keep a record of your progress!

Learning an Art.

Learning an art is utterly different from learning to enjoy the products of an art. Many people fondly fancy themselves "artistic" on the ground that they love good music and paintings. They might just as well declare themselves to be great baseball players because they like to watch Babe Ruth knock out home runs; or brilliant thinkers because they are fond of reading articles on science and philosophy. For some reason unknown to me, Americans have failed to distinguish between art and esthetics. Grotesque confusions flow from this bad thinking.

A man is an artist in so far as he himself sings, paints, carves, writes tales or plays, or does anything else of his own devising for the sheer urge and satisfaction of it, quite apart from ulterior aims, such as fame or fortune. He is not an artist but simply a performer in so far as he sings the songs which others have composed, copies the canvasses of the masters, acts a part in a play somebody else conceived. Beethoven was an artist; Paderewski is a very great performer, but not an artist. Shaw is an artist, John Barrymore no artist at all but an extraordinary performer-manager. Yet such is the blurred thought of most Americans on this subject that we tend to rank the eminent performers among the genuine artists.

All this has befuddled the art of learning. It strikes too deeply into the American psyche ever to be cleared up in a few pages in a book like ours. Many readers, no doubt, will hotly challenge what I have to say on the subject; for they have learned differently. Some will suppose me to be attacking our national sports and pleasures; but nothing lies further from my intentions. On the contrary, I think that an excellent argument can be framed to prove that Americans have advanced a long stride ahead of the Old World in matters of art and esthetics, no less than in political understanding, in industry, and in the spirit of play.

Americans are, beyond all doubt, the best all-around esthetes on earth. This is the pretty phrasing of it. If you want to be acid, you say the same thing by calling our countrymen the best listeners and the finest innocent by-standers in all history. You call attention to the steadily rising popularity of the sedentary sports—that is watching baseball instead of playing it, or listening to a report of a game over the radio instead of exerting oneself to go to the bleachers. You allude to our well established habit of traveling the wide world o'er and looking at pyramids, nautch girls, surfs, temples, and icebergs in total intellectual passivity, retaining no more than the simple pictures and their equally simple pleasure. You remark our canned music, our willingness to listen to talking pictures and their filmed orchestras, and the almost complete non-existence of musical composers. You point out that no land goes in more vigorously for musical decomposition, in the form of Jazz, Irving Berlin, and third-rate imitation of second-rate hymns. And you end up, perhaps, by defying anybody to name one American painter worthy to be mentioned as the peer of any one of the best one hundred now living in Europe.

I refuse to quarrel with these assertions. But I protest with full lungs against their tone. True, passive enjoyment is typical of our age and land. It will increase steadily, with the lengthening hours of leisure and our rising stand-ard of living. It is the resultant of many forces, not the least of which is the intensity with which Americans work. No Europeans approach our pace. They go through their office toil and their mill grind in a lackadaisical fashion. Careful analyses have shown that the output of the average American workingman surpasses by at least 50 per cent that of an Englishman in the same work and using the same equipment; and the Englishman surpasses in like measure the continental toilers, all of whom are mere dawdlers beside ourselves. The aftermath of labor is no less conspicuous. We let down laxly. The European does not. He is more active in his play, in his sports, and in his artistic tendencies. We become listeners and onlookers. This is part of the large price we pay for strenuosity.

Now, what has all this to do with the art of learning? Simply this. IT IS USUALLY A WASTE OF TIME TO TRY TO LEARN AN ARTISTIC ACTIVITY WHICH IS NOT AN INTEGRAL PART OF YOUR DAY'S WORK. After working hours the American is an esthete, not an artist. The pleasures of the spectator and listener are the pleasures of relaxation. They are, in the sense stressed by psychologists, detached from all practical affairs and indulged in purely for their own intrinsic pleasantness. Art, on the contrary, is hard work, a career, a high adventure which exacts the keenest concentration and the fieriest zeal to create. It is always based upon techniques which must be mastered to the finest detail.

Turn Your Work into an Art!

Hence people who work as fiercely as Americans have no energy left to pour into genuinely creative work after office hours. Loafers, dawdlers, and dilettantes may do that—not we! The American must be an artist in his business or not at all. There he often becomes a great artist, but in manners so untraditional that people who think of art in terms of its traditions cannot see the new creative forces at work in the American's achievements. But the Europeans can.

For example, in architecture, probably three out of every four distinguished Old World specialists agree that there is virtually no new spirit, no breath of life in this great art outside of the United States. And whoever studies at close range the churches, the private dwellings, the schools, and the office buildings of modern Europe finds it easy to side with the architects themselves.

A further proof of this is that nearly all of the foremost European architects adopt American effects and methods as far as their clients will permit them. This occurs daily in lands as far apart as Greece and China and England. Nor am I talking solely of the skyscraper, which is being imitated for economic reasons rather than artistic. I have in mind rather the amazingly vital American home architecture, which is the key to a democracy. What the cathedral was to the Middle Ages, the office and the home are to our own day. And it is likely that tomorrow will see a creative architecture of the highway store and hot dog stand. For Americans tend to live more and more on or along highways.

The motion pictures are almost entirely American in their art, especially since the advent of the talking screen. Only a few eccentric (and ill informed) critics believe that the Germans or the Russians surpass us. Those who—like myself—have spent scores of hours in projection rooms watching the much vaunted German and Russian films know, to their sorrow and eye pain, that, whereas American artists produce perhaps only one magnificent picture out of every thirty or forty emitted by Hollywood, the Germans produce only one out of a hundred, and the Russians one out of two hundred. We hear only of the fine products of the European studios. We never see the run of the mill. With only one exception, and that an unimportant one, every technical advance in the artistry of the film has been America. The French stand lowest in the scale here, with the Italians and English close seconds. We make a business of the movies over here! That's why we excel.

The art of still photography, which has almost displaced painting and sculpture, is one which owes much of its recent triumphs to the hard work of commercial photographers who have exalted their day's work to something finer. Visit a European exhibit of art photographs; you may find much to enjoy in it, but rarely as much as you can find almost any day in our best periodicals, including of course, the art journals themselves.

It is no answer, of course, to argue that Americans have drawn much inspiration from ancient cultures and Old World art. That misses the entire issue. Of course, our artists in landscape architecture, motion pictures, typography, and dress designing have learned from every source available. So have others, the world over. My point is that wherever Americans fuse their artistic efforts with their business, they create new beauty more richly than most other people, who, scorning the commercial forms of artistic expression, which they deem sordid or base, stick to pure art, which is only a name for musty tradition made holy by edict of those who teach the subject. The truly great art of Europe sprang from the Middle Ages and was almost wholly religious; for in those Middle Ages religion was genuinely the chief business of life, absorbing the state and most of its citizenry in one manner or another. Only the priests ordered stained glass windows. Only the bishops commissioned designers to fabricate cathedrals. Only the loot of holy wars and the fines of the confessionals paid all the bills. So inevitably those men of affairs who got the fat contracts for murals, windows, rugs, pews, stonework, and chalices put their heart into these and, dashed with a little religious frenzy, rose to high levels of art now and then. Hence Rheims, hence Notre Dame, hence Cologne. These are no more a piece of modern Europe than you are Pharaoh's cousin. They are far more alien to the spirit of contemporary Europe than are the designers of those fearsome things, the motion picture houses of Balaban & Katz.

The Impulse of Artistry Cannot Be Learned.

Why dilate at such length on this subject? Is it close to the art of learning? Yes. In America too many of us have been misled by false teachers. The tired business man, having amassed a competence, sighs to enjoy his income for the rest of his successful life. He sighs over his imperfect early education. He feels himself to be a nomad in the desert of commerce and yearns to enter the dominion of culture. Somebody assures him that the way to acquire this elusive culture is to walk for miles through art galleries, to loiter in famous churches, to read Homer, and to patter through Pater. Bowing to authority, he does this, but he comes through the ordeal keenly disappointed, sometimes fearing himself to be inferior, insensitive to finer beauties.

What's the trouble? He has divorced his art impulse from his own personality and his active life. Hence it dies stillborn. For it he has substituted a simple esthetic attitude, which is a wholly different thing: it is passive enjoyment, rather than creative fantasy. If our tired business man seeks nothing but a long rest from an active career, then let him stop, look, and listen! Let him eye paintings, stroll through churches, and listen to song! That's a worthy enterprise under the circumstances. (But don't call it art!) If all this leaves him dissatisfied, it is safe to guess that he has a genuine creative urge which has been thwarted. What can the art of learning do for him?

Nothing at all, so far as the developing of that deep impulse is concerned. Absolutely nothing! If that urge is not strong enough, of itself, to burst forth into some activity, we cannot teach it strength. Men are born with sensitivities and special energies fitted to artistic creation, or else they are born without them. No school ever gives a pupil an ear for music. No magic of pedantry ever endows a youth with an eye that links with hand in the handling of a portrait painter's brush. True, anybody with a feeble endowment of this sort may teach himself much, if he has intense will and boundless energy; but even so, the foundation is just that feeble endowment, reinforced by vitality.

*But a Certain Appreciation of Art Products Can Be Learned—
and Easily!*

But, as I said when we began this subject, developing
artistry is wholly different from learning to enjoy the
products of artistry. And there is a larger enjoyment of
these which comes through thoughtful study. This can be
learned by almost anybody whose mind and sensitivities
have proved able to get him through high school. For
every person gifted enough to create significant art there
must be ten thousand gifted enough to perceive sundry
delectable qualities in what that one rarity has created.
It is to these ten thousand that we now speak. To them we
say: "Play at artistic creation, if you get fun out of it.
Paint, sing, pen verses, act, dance! But don't expect to
shine! Learn all you can about whatever you do. And,
long after you have given up the little fling at art, the
appreciations will remain as the permanent treasure."

Perhaps one lucky dog out of every such ten thousand will
tap unsuspected powers. He may follow the career pattern of
Louis Untermeyer, who, while managing a jewelry factory,
dabbled at poetry until his power and feeling for self-expression overwhelmed the jewelry business and forced him, from
within, to abandon his commercial life. This, however, is the
rare exception. It will be more in the order of human events
to expect that the student, while working for a railroad company, studies painting and paints up to the point at which he
understands precisely his own heavy limitations as a creator
of canvasses worth looking at—so he drops studio work. But
for the next forty years he applies what he has learned to the
beautifying of dining-car decorations, to the painting of railway bridges, and to the criticism of designs for railway
stations, thereby improving the sightliness of our land.

The Peculiar Case of Music.

A whole volume might be filled with comments and
counter-comments about music as a subject for learning.

I accept a grave hazard by bringing the matter up here, for it cannot be settled in a page or two. But I dare not evade the issues entirely, for they drag their weary length clean across the panorama of American education.

Would that some new Harriet Beecher Stowe would arise and pen an "Uncle Tom's Cabin" around the American slave to music! The scene would open in some kindergarten, bright and early of a Monday morn. Simon Legree, teacher, lifts a hand, which is the signal for all the children to burst forth into song. They burst. School over, they go home; there mother awaits them and guides them to the piano, at which they must practice an hour. Sundays some of them go to church and Sunday school; there too the bloodhounds trail them. Again they must stand up and sing. High school and college continue the serfdom. Years later, they join the Rotary Club; and at every luncheon they must arise and yowl the Rotary songs. They subscribe to concerts and oratorios. They buy phonograph records by the score. For music is the soul of culture. Must not every citizen who isn't fit for treasons, stratagems and spoils go in hard for music?

Strange! Americans are more extensively and intensively drilled in music than any other people. They spend more money on music lessons and on performances than all of Europe combined. And yet they create no music worth listening to. True, we have an astounding number of competent parlor performers. But playing Chopin dazzlingly is no more creative musical art than is singing the national anthem. It is something else, quite commendable, quite enjoyable, quite uncreative.

Music Has Been Harmed by Over-exploitation.

What's wrong? Many things! The situation is frightfully complex. Above all, we Americans have ruined music by standardizing its study, by socializing it artificially, and by ballyhooing it. We seem never to have glimpsed that both the enjoyment of music—an esthetic event—and the creating of music are peculiarly a matter of private mood. A healthy person can no more appreciate Bach at 10:30 A.M. every Monday, Wednesday, and Friday than he can fall in love on the same schedule. And if somebody drives him to the schedule, by that same act he drives the would-be victim away from the music.

I echo the verdict of every mature and well informed music expert in our land when I say, as they all have said, that our schools and our private teachers, aided and abetted by parents, have rendered the larger cause of the musical arts far more harm than good. Of the millions spent on private music lessons, almost all has been pure waste, so far as developing positive abilities other than skill with an instrument is concerned. System has ruled. Social pressure has ruled. The mood has been ignored. And, to make matters worse, few American moods invoke musical expression.

Modern Work Rarely Induces Song.

The musical impulses seem to have sprung from the natural rhythms of the day's work, particularly from group effort. When not from such, then from some mysterious private yearning, some vague wish to have what one has not, some dark aspiration made articulate but not comprehensible through tone. Often this may belittle more than the desire to vanquish the external silences, which become oppressive. The lonely herder on the far plains still sings to himself to shatter those awful stillnesses of unpeopled places. But in America neither man's work nor his noisy environment encourage musical spontaneity.

True, some black stevedores along the lower Mississippi merge song with toil as they chant their extempores while rolling cotton bales aboard the night boat. College boys can sing songs at football games, even though they need a yellmaster to organize them. Dancing masters and night club hostesses are also able to fuse their jobs with melody, but the rest of us cannot.

An orchestra would be miscast in the New York Stock Exchange. Henry Ford doesn't whistle as he muses over a new model of his car. Mr. Hoover surely doesn't improvise merry little tunes while organizing relief committees on unemployment. Not even in the home can the housewife find the ancient stimuli to voice. The telephone is always ringing, the electric icebox purrs, the mechanical dishwasher clatters away, the world is full of pleasant little noises, all the household bills are paid, the neighbors drop in, and everything is too smoothly serene for the lyric cry.

The greatest music seems to grow out of repressions, distress, and their engendered emotions. It finds itself in silence. But American homes and workshops are brisk, noisy, bright, and crowded. Their dominant emotion is the enthusiasm of doing something fast and profitably. The brooder is not found there. And if he were accidentally present, he would create no music; for the din of passing autos, the rumble of mighty machines, the giggle of shop-girls, the clatter of typewriters, the jangle of a thousand telephones, and the bright lights would muffle the inner melody and kill it at its source.

To me, at least, this is one of the sorriest features of our common life. It can be obliterated only after many years of progress toward silence and toward a way of life freed from the pursuit of profits and filtered free of the thick poison of school tyrannies, jazz bands, and the Metropolitan Opera House. The reader who feels within himself the faint thrust of song must now be left with the mildly melancholy thought that, if he will achieve musical expression, he must first turn his back firmly on all the pleasantest phases of our own national life.

EXERCISES

If you work in any business or profession, study it with regard to its artistic possibilities.

What phases of it might be developed with fresh beauty?

Could you undertake any sort of creative artistic endeavor in it?

Analyze every aspect of it. Make a formal report to yourself about each.

Can you recall the forces described earlier in this book which are driving people more and more to study the art of learning?

What are President Wilson's Fourteen Points?

If you cannot recall some of them, turn back to the page where they are listed and notice your omissions. Can you detect a reason for them? Why are some of the points harder to retain than others?

EXERCISES IN MEMORY

On the next page are eight geometrical figures. Allow yourself only ten seconds by your watch to look at these figures. Then close the book and try to duplicate them on a sheet of paper.

Now compare your drawings with the originals and observe with care each error in the former.

Repeat the test at once. Compare results again.

Do some errors still persist? Then make another try!

EXERCISES
Learning to Estimate Areas

Here is a square inch with ten other figures. Once a day for thirty days practice at estimating the areas of each of these figures. Write down, with the date at the top, each day's guesses. At the end of thirty days, check up on yourself. How much have you improved by practice?

Do not measure the areas until the thirty days' practice has been completed.

Do not refer to your earlier estimates at any time. Let each day's practice be fresh and independent.

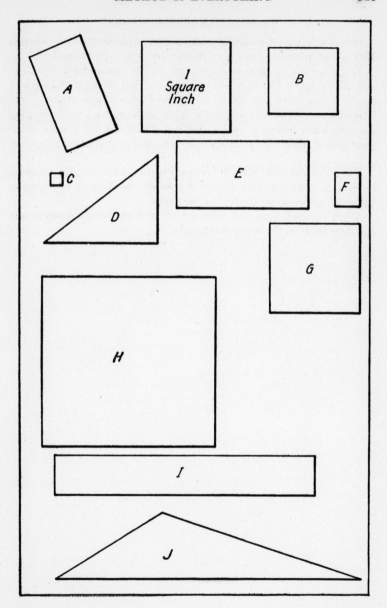

Weighing the Grocery Order!

People's judgment in sensory discrimination improves with practice. How about yourself? Here is an interesting experiment to make.

The next time the grocery order comes in, see how accurately you can estimate weights. Lift each loaf of bread and bag of sugar and see how nearly you come to judging its weight. Write down your estimates, and later compare them with the real weights as shown on a scale. You will discover many things about yourself—and perhaps a few more about your grocer! Keep this up for several weeks, and note your improvement.

If this interests you, carry it further. Practice estimating the weight of everybody you meet; and, whenever possible, check up on your guesses by inviting the victim to step on the scales.

A few hundred tries, and you may vie with the weight-guessers who ply their trade in the amusement parks.

Can You Estimate Lengths?

Here are twenty lines, each of a different length. How many inches in each?

Before measuring the lines, make ten sets of estimates, a set a day for ten days.

A Test in Substitution

You are to practice substituting numbers for letters in the following passage. Using the following key, practice ten minutes twice a day for two weeks substituting the numbers here indicated for the letters in this short paragraph. Keep a careful record of (1) the errors you make in substitution, and (2) the length of time it takes you to complete the passage. Do not try to commit the key to memory. Use it freely as you work on the cipher.

HERE IS THE KEY YOU ARE TO USE

Letter	m	c	f	i	r	x	n	z	a	q	w	e	h
Number	1	2	3	4	5	6	7	8	9	10	11	12	13

Letter	s	v	b	o	g	d	p	u	j	y	l	t	k
Number	14	15	16	17	18	19	20	21	22	23	24	25	26

AND THIS IS THE PARAGRAPH

Not even in Aesop's fables are there enough names of animals to use up all the letters of the alphabet. And that is why, little children, we are forced in today's lesson to fall back on the typewriter repair man's ancient text: the quick brown fox jumped over the lazy dog. And now that we have used up the alphabet, what have you done in ten minutes?

The Trail of the Goat.

Today I saw:

Today I heard:

Today I learned:

BOOK VI

PROJECTS

PROJECTS

Start Something!

Of all known ways of learning, the very best is to begin by doing something. Commit yourself to a program of action. That done, study the steps in the program as you go. It makes little difference what you start, so long as you like it.

Please don't imagine that you must start something immense, something noble, something difficult. Not at all! Get under way! That is the key to the learner's success. He may vow to beat his next-door neighbor, the fat codfish merchant, at golf within one year. He may, to this end, buy golf clubs and, in his own back yard, lay out a miniature course on which, rain or shine, he practices every morn and eve. Or, if his taste runs to ancient history, he may save his money for a trip to Mesopotamia and an archaeological investigation there which, according to plan, is to secure the first complete set of photographs of a certain ruined city. To this end, he begins by studying aerial photography and Assyrian; and he arranges, in his study, a collection of maps and pictures relative to his impending excavations.

Such painstaking planning is itself learning; and it induces still more learning, in the surest manner. This is why teachers of late have turned to the so-called Project Method, which is this very same thing in elementary form adapted to class-room use. The child must do something; build a model airplane, rearrange the seats in a study room, paint the walls, go to the city park and work out a plan for changing the flower beds there, design a dress, paint a picture. Thus, through exciting deeds and illuminating blunders, something solid is grasped.

Americans Are Always Starting Something.

The European needs urging to start something, but most of us Americans do not. We are self-starters. Indeed, our own critics and authors love to poke fun at us for going off half-cocked, for launching all sorts of societies, reform movements, clubs, and what not, on the slightest provocation. They accuse us of trying to bring Utopia to pass by enacting new laws, drawing up resolutions, and passing the hat to create a new political party. In this they are only half correct. They miss the deeper biological trend.

The urge to do something is largely the urge to learn. Not entirely, of course; but largely. For, as we have seen, learning in its widest sense is simply the double act of broadening and deepening one's personal experiences, or "life more abundantly." To discover things, you must go after them and, once contact is established, deal with them. The European dislikes such strenuosity. He has been brought up to believe that human experience can be converted into language and served in packages. He is an idea addict. He lives in a world of ideas and thinks this to be reality. In a word, he is an intellectualist at heart. As G. K. Chesterton, himself a perfect European, has so charmingly put it, men of the Old World have always been ready to fight and even to die for an idea, which sometimes boils down to a single word; "and why shouldn't they? Is there anything more worth while?"

The American thinks there are many things more worth while. He is suspicious of ideas and words. He regards a man's behavior as vastly more significant than his verbal beliefs. And he is sure that living is more comprehensive and more precious than any single part of living, even the finest part, which is thought itself. Dewey has given lucid expression to a deeply rooted American attitude when he declares that all intellectual operations are simply instruments of a living creature, all developed to serve his creature purposes. Now, what has this to do with the art of learning?

It has everything to do with it. When a Frenchman wishes to learn geography, he almost never travels, unless he is both wealthy and quite exceptional intellectually. He reads whole shelves of books on the seven seas and the isles thereof; he may, if audacious go so far as to study a few maps. If he is a rare bird, he may join a geographical society, attend its meetings, and read its solemn procedures. There he stops, firmly convinced that he knows the world.

Nobody has summed up this weakness of his compatriots more neatly than Abbé Dimnet, who remarks, among other things:

In absolute opposition (to the American) French schools turn out young people convinced that nothing, except the attainments of intellect, has much right to respect . . . The passion of the French for ideas makes them imagine that when an idea has been expressed, its own virtue will be sufficient to get it realized. Properly analyzed, this fallacy can be reduced to the notion that some practical person will do what we are too superior to undertake . . .

I have not forgotten the verdict which, when I first visited the United States in 1908, a famous American politician passed in my presence. "The French are bright," he said, "but they are not intelligent."

Ideas count more in France than facts, and as long as education is at one with the national bias to prefer the art of living to the struggle for life, this one-sided view will go on.[1]

The American politician was wise in his penetrating remark. A man may know, in the academic sense, all the ideas in the world and still lack intelligence of the higher type. He is an imperfect learner and, in a crisis, will surely run into trouble. His ideas will get in the way of his actions. The thoroughgoing intellectual develops a peculiar stupidity which well-rounded practical men always smell out and override. It is an insensitivity to bald facts, to imme-

[1] "Art of Thinking," New York, 1928, p. 70 ff.

diate necessities, and to the sublime inconsistency of most intelligent behavior.

In a rather subtle sense, the intellectual learner is always looking backward, while the American pragmatist looks forward. For, after all, what is an idea? Simply the precipitation of innumerable past experiences, good, bad, and indifferent. It is, indeed, just what a word is; and the word is the outward sign of the inner essence of meaning. No word adequately fits all the situations to which men apply it in speech. Neither does any idea conform wholly to any truth. But you can never convince a sincere intellectualist that this is so. And he shudders when somebody quotes James Harvey Robinson's brilliant statement that, by and large, the older an idea is, the greater the probability that it is unsound; the older a belief, the more likely that it is full of error.

Work on a Project!

As early as possible in the course of learning a new subject, set yourself a large task the accomplishment of which requires months, if not years, of further study and reflection. Let it be, not the command of a taskmaster, but the most interesting venture you can imagine. Regard it as an integral part of your career. Spend all the time and money you can on it. And don't weaken whenever you recall that, after all, this is just a stunt in the art of learning. If you do it well enough, it may turn out to be highly profitable in some other manner. A proof? Well, I'll draw that from my teaching experience.

For many years I have assigned long-term projects to journalism students at the beginning of their college work. The one which has proved most interesting as well as most profitable requires the aspiring journalist to advise the owners of the chief paper in his home town concerning the entire management of the publication, on the basis of a complete analysis of the community, including the whole circulation zone. This calls for a fairly minute investigation of local geography, industries, population make-up, shifts in local business affecting the economic and social character of the inhabitants, the policies of rival newspapers, transportation facilities, income classes, the influence of politics on editorial matters, and a hundred more intricate problems. Nobody can make the slightest headway in such an assignment unless he spends from four to six months on local surveys, supplementing these with a study of reader psychology and general newspaper policies.

Now, you may well ask, how could a beginner in journalism make headway with such a staggering task? And how could he profit by doing something wholly beyond him? The answer is, first, that the practical reality of the assignment enthuses him; and the fact that he is investigating his home town enables him to draw upon a huge background of information, so that he learns new items easily. Secondly, while the task is certainly beyond him, in one sense, it is not so in another. Were he aided only by textbooks and by the ascertainable facts about the town as furnished by the Chamber of Commerce and the U. S. census, he would indeed be in a sorry plight. While he studies the town, however, he is also studying the psychology of human interest, the history of newspapers, city room management, and sundry related subjects, all of which throw light on the larger project from some angle. So he progresses perhaps even faster than would a more seasoned newspaper man who, unaided by such parallel reading and lectures, might be called upon to make such a study.

It has often happened that students have found, midway in their research, an unsuspected opportunity back in the old home town; have returned thither, instead of seeking fame and fortune in New York City; and, within a few years have established themselves as managers or even owners of a paper—now and then, of the very paper they investigated.

Don't think that every project leads so straight to cash benefits. Disabuse your mind of the notion that you, as a beginner, cannot gain by tackling a large order from the outset. I admit that some people are terrified by the thought of undertaking anything sizable; for them this recommendation is ill adapted. But most learners get fun out of it. Fun adds to the zest. Zest adds to one's power of concentration and assimilation.

Now, let us see precisely what I am advising you to do. Suppose that you set out to learn carpentering. As soon as you have reached the point at which you can lay off a right angle by the ancient rule of 3, 4, 5 and know the difference between toenailing and hitting your thumb with the hammer, set out to build something that is far beyond your abilities. This does not mean, of course, that you are to start work on the final construction; it means rather that you are to address yourself to the problems of that construction, as a preliminary to success. You may resolve to erect a garage large enough for two automobiles. Very well! Start at plans and specifications. Look into the problems of cost and location. In this connection, check up on all the various kinds of lumber suited to a garage. What does each kind cost? Would Douglas fir be better than spruce? Would some composition board be better than either? On which wood would the carpentering be easiest? On which the hardest? As a partial answer to such questions, practice at cutting a mortise and tenon in four or four varieties of commercially available wood. Also experiment at driving nails and inserting screws and dowel pins in each variety. In a word, carry out the learning of the trade parallel with a thorough survey of garage building; and, not until you have reached the sense of competence, should you start erecting the structure. That is, you shouldn't unless you can well afford to use up many board feet and many kegs of nails in practice work.

Now take a less matter-of-fact subject. What if you wish to study economics? That brings you to all sorts of abstract principles not at all like the carpenter's craft. To go far, you must have "a head for figures," especially in statistical form. Where will you find a project?

In whatever field of industry or business your own bread and butter lie. You may be a young woman still living at home with your parents. What is your father's occupation? Manager of a small department store? Fine! Perhaps, then, you can set for yourself the problem of ascertaining how the chain stores which have lately opened up in your city are causing trouble for your father's establishment. Investigate each separate commodity which his store sells, barring only the trivial. In the end, strive to prepare a trade report in which you will advise the department store how it can best meet the new competition.

You'd be clever, if you could finish that in two years, starting from scratch! But how wise you would be at the finish! You might even break into the business!

Perhaps you are a railway conductor and wish to master the history of the United States. Can you not find a point of connection between your work and that history, say in a project to write a book on "The Role of the Railroads in the Development of America"? What if you never publish the work? What if you drop it when half done? Even so, you will have learned American history in the best of all possible manners; for you will see it as a living record, not as a dead hodge-podge of dates and names.

Or do you live on a farm and do you wish to study biology? Find a project within the biology of farm animals. Set out to experiment on crossing various types of chickens and recording all the variations in plumage, egg-laying capacity, weight of fowls, and general behavior of the hybrids. It is fairly within the reach of common probability that such a pursuit might, within two or three years, lead to a useful discovery.

EXERCISES

Answer the following questions at once. After a few weeks, come back to this page and answer them all over again.

1. I should like to study..

....

2. What projects appeal to me in this field?....................

....

....

....

....

....

....

....

....

....

3. Which of these projects lies closest to things I already know?....

....

4. Have I any acquaintances who would inform me about this project?...

....

5. Do I own any books or documents dealing with it?............

....

6. How would I organize the work, were I to undertake the project?

....

....

....

....

....

....

....

....

....

....

....

Here is an outline map of the United States. Do not refer to the map printed in an earlier section of this book.

You are to mark in on this map the following things:

1. The names and boundaries of each state.

2. The following rivers: Mississippi; Hudson; Delaware; Ohio; Rio Grande.

3. The following mountains—Adirondacks; Catskills; Rockies; Cumberland; White Mountains.

4. The following cities: Chicago; New York; Detroit; Atlanta; San Francisco; Los Angeles; St. Louis; New Orleans; Boston; Philadelphia.

5. The following lakes: Salt Lake; the Great Lakes (naming each).

What do you think of your geographical knowledge? See page 80!

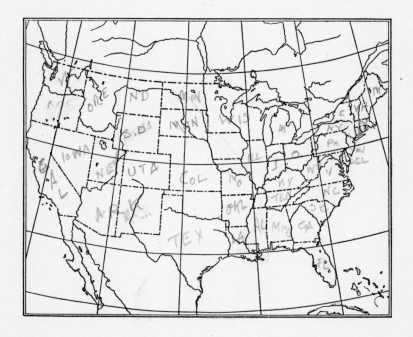

Many pages earlier we told you a little about the chances for insuring your life if you followed certain business or professions. How good are the chances if you are:

1. A writer?
2. An astronomer?
3. A prize fighter?
4. An aerial circus performer?
5. A diver?
6. An explorer?
7. A landscape gardener?
8. A teacher?
9. A circus trainer?
10. A jockey?

Wanted: 100,000 *Home Laboratories!*

Before I quit learning things, I'd like to see at least 100,-000 attic rooms, remodeled woodsheds, old garages, and unused basements cluttered up with test tubes, balances, microscopes, spectroscopes, home-brew seismographs, barometers, rheostats, incubators, mixing machines, anemometers, and what you will. I'd like to be able to step off my airplane at Amarillo, Texas, and watch a retired cow puncher measure the tensile strength of six new beryllium alloys which he has just cooked up. I'd like to come in out of the rain at Spokane and watch a former school teacher sort seeds she has just plucked from 644 new specimens of a hybrid pine tree in her back yard which promises to revolutionize the lumber industry. I'd like to—

But you get the idea. In a word, I'd like to see our people rise to the cultural level of the English, who for centuries have encouraged and respected amateurs in all the arts, sciences, and techniques. I'd like to rid our country of the silly notion that, to conduct important investigations, you must start out with:

1. A Ph. D. degree.
2. A University fellowship.
3. An endowed laboratory.
4. A grant from the Rockefeller Foundation.
5. A college professor as adviser.
6. Inability to write comprehensible English.

Not one of these is at all necessary. Each may even prove a terrible handicap. Not that such things do not have their uses. They do; for there are certain kinds of enormously specialized investigations which cannot even be started without a huge budget underwritten, a staff of super-experts, and the collaboration of a scientific society. But for every such costly enterprise there are a dozen which an ambitious housewife with a college degree and a moderately keen interest in snooping somewhere except up the backstairs could launch, all on less than half as much as her daughter spends for face-smear and in less time than she now spends on bridge and manicuring.

Those 300,000 *Carbon Compounds.*

Let me get down to real cases. Chemists tell us that there are nearly 300,000 compounds that can be built up around carbon. Once I asked several eminent men in industrial chemistry where I could find an account of the nature and behavior of the compounds. They told me that only a few thousand of that total had ever been made, and that nobody could tell what the others, still unmade, would do.

"Why hasn't some chemist set for himself the life task of making the whole batch?" I asked. "Or why hasn't some university done it as a five-generation job for the whole faculty of chemistry?"

One man declared that research was set on such a lofty pedestal that few chemists who wished to earn a reputation would spend time on such routine work, which almost anybody could perform, at least to a large extent. All of which suggested to my vulgar mind the notion that, if the big men in chemistry were passing up this work, then it ought to be done by a few hundred amateurs. And why not?

Many of the compounds couldn't be made and properly tested in an attic laboratory for a few dollars—still other thousands could be. And it is literally true that many of these will *probably* have some valuable practical application on which the discoverer can cash in richly, if he is at all business-like. I'd estimate that the odds are at least five to one in favor of an amateur chemist winning fame or fortune or both through the discovery of the properties of one compound out of, say, one hundred which he investigates.

And if he didn't, what of it?

Research in a Twenty-foot Greenhouse.

Eh? You don't know chemistry and just hate the awful smells of its stuffs? All right then. Let's smell something sweeter. How about posies? You think of flowers as ornaments on a dinner table or sick room sedatives. Why not consider them for a moment as an outlet for intellectual energy?

The world has not yet probed to the secrets of more than one plant out of a hundred; and we have not yet found much about the possibilities of making and using variants of existing plants, shrubs and trees. Women have developed magnificent new varieties of peonies and roses in their gardens, after patient years. But they might just as well attack the larger problem of developing super-beans, super-cabbages, and super-potatoes, after the manner of Luther Burbank, whose work was a mere beginning of a new epoch in industrial botany.

Nor does research halt there. Think of the many other factors of plant growth and variation which are investigated by great institutions such as the Boyce Thompson Institute, where the effects of all colors of light, all degrees of heat and humidity, and all sorts of food in the soil are being watched over the years. Any one of these problems, if patiently conducted from start to finish with some plant not already investigated would have substantial scientific value. A twenty-foot greenhouse in your back yard would more than suffice for the work.

Cats and Dogs and Genetics.

Are plants too tame, too slow, too messy, with the watering and manuring they demand? Possibly you prefer dogs and cats. You may even know somebody who has a fine small kennel and occasionally wins a medal at a show. Why not go him one better? Raise dogs yourself (or cats, if you prefer), but study them. Nobody has ever kept adequate records of the mental development of a normal dog from birth to death. I'd read a book on that with delight. Nobody has ever systematically trained dogs of the same litter along several widely different lines, with a view to showing how far the traits which seem to be native to the variety (breed) can be varied by education.

As for studying the variations in families of dogs, the new types which emerge from crossing various breeds, and all such matters of inheritance and mutation, the amateur can go just as far here as his purse will carry him. Such work is rather expensive and requires room. If you can afford it, you may add to the world's knowledge of life and evolution.

What One Woman Learned about Copper.

Women of means and leisure aren't doing 0.0001 per cent as much as they might in the higher domains of creative learning. Let them ponder such brilliant specimens of their sex as Carrie Everson, who revolutionized the copper mining industry of the whole world—and, after dying in poverty, won belated recognition.

Her husband lost his fortune in a copper mine which had plenty of ore but all of a sort which was so hard to refine that there was no profit in it. Mrs. Everson had studied chemistry before she married. When her husband's health broke down, mainly as a result of his misfortunes, she packed him off to Mexico to recuperate. While he was there, she took a course in mineralogy and then, all on her own, started experimenting with her husband's then worthless low-grade copper ores. For seven or eight years she learned all she could from these tests and finally came from her little laboratory with an ingenious method of using oil to pick copper particles out of the ore.

There are thousands of opportunities like the one Mrs. Everson found. And an amazing number of them can be seized fast by any housewife or business man who has half of a small room in which to carry on the study and a few hours a week of free time.

Why Not Learn about Yourself as Consumer?

Perhaps the largest group of problems now confronting business men and manufacturers is that which centers around the American consumer, his psychology, his habits, and his trends. Only a few students have yet learned anything about consumers, and what they have found is barely a drop in an ocean of startling facts. We must find out whether people can, without injury to themselves or others, increase the amount and quality of things they buy, so that our factories can be kept running to capacity. There seem to be no limits to production except such as are set by consumers. Here arise a hundred problems, any one of which can occupy all of your spare time for several years.

Solving the Surplus.

Do you know that one of the acutest problems of our twentieth century centers around our surplus crops? There's cotton! Thousands of bales of the fiber are, as I pen these lines, lying around on open fields, while other thousands are stacked up high in warehouses, where they may wait a year or two for a buyer—and then will sell so cheaply that the cotton grower will lose heavily. All over the world statesmen and scientists and plain dirt farmers are cudgelling their wits in search of new uses for cotton. Find such, and you open new markets, thereby saving tens of thousands of farm families from ruin.

Then, there's sugar. It's been a drug on the market for years. Immense tonnage can be produced at low prices all over the tropics. But, unless somebody finds new ways of using it, sugar growers must continue to make little or no money; and Cuba will go through crisis after crisis.

Or, if you prefer, look at wheat! Russia can grow enough of it to choke the gullets of the world. So can Canada and the United States. Shall we save our own wheat growers? Then we must hunt high and low for novel ways of turning the grain to account.

A score of other commodities call for attention. Who will lead here in the art of learning?

Next, the Parents and Their Education.

A colossal and most perplexing array of problems arise in the American home. They focus on the education of parents. How much mother must learn about little Willie! He is a large order and remains such for at least fifteen years. Mother ought to be a combination doctor-psychologist-trained nurse as well as a boon companion, guide, philosopher, and friend of little Willie—and all at the very same time while she is cooking, mending stockings, shopping, playing bridge, and carrying on some useful study. Can she be all that? Maybe not! But she can come much nearer to it if she learns all there is to know about child nature and applies her new learning to little Willie.

I know some mothers who have done this, with immense pleasure and profit; I know others who went at the job either in haphazard fashion or in the spirit of listening to a lecture on Shakespeare, and messed everything, little Willie included. Here is no enterprise to be managed frivolously. It makes stern demands upon the mother. Years must be devoted to it, and many hours weekly. And all that can be said about mothers applies equally to fathers, who have usually been left out of account in such matters of child training.

Over and above this technique, there is also a science of home life, still as raw as the general psychology of personality—and for the very same reason. To run any home intelligently, one must have a pretty deep insight into several personalities—and who has that? But who cannot study it and improve his insight?

I believe that the coming fifty years in America will see great changes here; and many of them will be brought about by scattered individuals studying in their own homes. A score of wholly original methods of child study and home study will be devised. Perhaps, among these, we shall see a neighborhood motion picture analysis of its children, as babes in arms, as tots toddling about back yards, and as schoolsters at play. Such pictures would be taken with a view to recording, for scientific analysis, the exact behavior of all sorts of children in all sorts of situations. It might overshadow the first attempts of John B. Watson and a few other psychologists to photograph infant behavior. Out of it might emerge the first solid monographs on the whole subject.

Can You Beat a Bug?

Man's most terrible enemy is the insect. We have not yet learned how to conquer the creature. For there are tens of thousands of varieties, each having its own food, life cycle, and peculiar way of being obnoxious to us. The world would never have to worry over food again, after learning how to hold in check the myriad of many-legged invaders of our fields, and probably some of the worst diseases would vanish with insects which carry them to man.

Any one species of insect probably will keep a learner busy for years; and the more one learns about it, the more fascinating the problem becomes. In time you see that you are playing a hand in a marvelously intricate game, which makes chess and contract bridge appear to be piddling pastimes.

For further details, see the U. S. Department of Agriculture or any State Experiment Station. Their experts compute that insects destroy about $2,000,000,000 worth of plants and trees every year.

The Rat Challenges You.

Another sinister foe of mankind is the rat. We have not yet defeated him, though progress has been made, especially since the cheapening of concrete, which holds the monster at bay. His cunning is terrible, his appetite vast, his progeny like the sands of the sea. He carries the plague and ravages house, field, and storage places to the tune of hundreds of millions of dollars yearly. A worthy foe! Can you outwit him?

Why Not Try a Weed or Two?

A weed is a plant for which no use has yet been found. Why not learn all about some weed, with the clear aim of finding a use of it? There is a magnificent labor of years, and one which might bring you fame and fortune. There is no difficulty in getting weeds. (I have millions for sale, all out on my New Jersey farm. Special rates on carload lots.) Nor should it be hard to discover the chemical ingredients of your weed—that is, provided you are willing to take plenty of time for finding them. Stupid people have laughed at Thomas Edison because he has spent years studying weeds in search of a domestic substitute for rubber. But the old man is wiser than his scoffers, as time will prove! Some eminent botanists declare that billions of dollars of unscratched wealth lie hidden in weeds; fertilizers, food, drugs, dyes, and fodder for cattle are all waiting to be taken by some ingenious learner.

And Then Nuts!

America may be revolutionized by some readers of these words who take them in earnest. One of our greatest potential sources of wealth is the nut-bearing tree, which makes possible what J. Russell Smith calls "three-story farming." By that he means that the farmer can make his life much easier by planting fine nut trees like the oak, walnut, hickory, and honey locust, turning in swine, sheep and cattle to forage on the grass and on the nuts as they fall, and later cutting the timber, which will always be salable at a good profit. Thus permanent agriculture will be established in place of the stupid kind now in vogue among our peasants.

Before this can happen on a large scale, men must find the varieties of hardwoods which grow fastest and bear the heaviest yields of nuts. Who will find these? Who will test out the trees? A thousand groups of people in our small towns and country districts ought to find this work fascinating. Slow? Yes, that's a great advantage. The study can be carried on without cutting in on your time. Important? Enormously so. In the long sweep of years probably a hundred times more important than municipal politics; and surely 543,094.78 times more important than French conversation and backgammon.

Whoever learns about nuts surely isn't one.

Chances to Learn How to Conserve and Utilize Our Forests.

During the next fifty years our country needs hundreds of keen students of a new kind of forestry. In spite of the Government's efforts to save America's once magnificent stand of trees, grafters, looters, stupid campers, and ignorant farmers have combined with bacteria and insects to destroy it at a rate of about six billion cubic feet of timber a year. The ravages of fungi increase, partly as a result of the immigration of new varieties, insect pests multiply; and small rodents, especially mice, kill millions of seedlings. (In one experimental tract under observation by Thornton T. Munger, director of the Pacific Northwest Forest Experiment Station, mice ate off the tops of 95 out of every 100 tiny trees within two or three days after they had been set out!)

Won't somebody please learn how to check such destruction? The study has a thousand angles. It leads into bacteriology, into botany, into soil analysis, into entomology, into ecology, and into a score of major industries. The work takes you out into the solitudes of the Appalachians and the high Rockies, up and down the Pacific Coast, through the vast man-made desolations of the stripped pine lands of the South. Or it can keep you, if you prefer, in a laboratory. In some of its phases, it is easily carried on at home.

Why Not Be the Historian of Your Own Place and Time?

It is unfortunate that in many parts of America the local historian has become an object of ridicule among intelligent people. But he has only himself to blame, as a rule, for he has done his job badly. He has seldom learned the historian's art. He has messed around with country courthouse archives, stirring together in one meaningless mass the trivial, the complimentary, the boastful, and the important—all of which is a great pity. Each region of our land deserves a competent historian. A good modern history of Texas is surely more important, on the whole, than an equally good history of Central America or Poland. But, to be good, it must rise above the stale twaddle about governors, political platforms, dates of inaugurations, centenaries, and all that empty show-off of politicians. It must be an independent observation of social and economic trends, of the influence of climates, the influx of races, the clash of religions, and so on.

Do you know that there has never yet been written such a genuine history of a single state? Who will undertake it? Much must be learned before a start can be made—but what a magnificent opportunity!

A few of our largest cities have had their historians, after a fashion, but a score remain to be done.

The Amateur Architect.

Relative to their income and their opportunities, Americans live worse than anybody else on earth. Only the well-to-do suburbanites and the high-grade farmers get their money's worth out of their homes in the dual form of use and beauty. Even the very rich are swindled to a fade-away, as some of them know. From personal inspection, I happen to know that some of the costliest apartments in New York City, among them some of the cooperatives, are jerry-built, shoddy as a slum tenement, and as uncomfortable as a conscience. Only the very poor seem free from the perils of the crooked contractor and the racketeering labor unions who serve him while they loot him and his customers.

Then too, the mad desire to have something just like the Jones' things leads to standardized houses, fireplaces, doors, lintels, sewer pipes, and toilet traps. The still madder craving to live in herds leads to the street of identical flats and duplex dwellings, such as one can see in the wretched Long Island sections of Greater New York. And poverty of a sort necessitates the standardized semi-slum, such as we see in various forms in every large American city, even Los Angeles.

Here is a tremendous problem which confronts every young man and young woman contemplating marriage and a home life. What can be done about it? In some cases, nothing, alas! The blight of the metropolis falls upon several million who cannot elude it save by giving up good jobs and seeking a more wholesome territory. For the rest of the country, however, is hope—provided there is also the will to live decently. Intensive study of architecture, building costs, and the incidental arts of exterior and interior decoration can be made by anybody of average intelligence; and, while one learns more than another, all may benefit much. Most of us find it extremely interesting too.

As Lewis Mumford recently pointed out, our country could return to a high level of prosperity if means could be found to supplant shoddy homes with good ones. Think that over!

Creative Town Planning.

Of the 3,000 American cities, how many lure the way-farer? How many make him sigh for the chance to dwell in them forever? Perhaps a score, surely not fifty. Always the traveler comes up against something ugly, nasty, or downright loathsome: billboards, oily garages, alien slums, dirty creeks, rotten pavements, factory chimneys belching thick smoke, open garbage dumps aswarm with flies, puddles and swamps full of mosquitoes, houses crowded on lots too small for them, public buildings full of cuspidors, streets at tag ends, a jumble of chance layouts, public squares as unattractive as the standardized chain store fronts which hem them in.

Well, what can be done about it?

Nothing, until the people affected by it have learned all there is to know about each aspect of the problem. But what a horde of things to learn here! You can't get results simply by launching a Town-Beautiful Club and electing the local banker president. You can't redesign your community merely by calling in a town planner, landscape architect, or popular lecturer. You must face the task of studying all the local factors so that you can make them clear to whatever experts you later bring in to help you, and that's a job calling for months or years of serious study.

The ideal would be reached if a small group in your town were to join with you, dividing the special tasks of study and field research among themselves; gathering statistics, taking photographs, analyzing costs, and investigating plans suggested for other cities by eminent authorities. Before any conclusions were reached, a complete exhibit

and report ought to be made. And the plan adopted ought
to give a distinctive air to your city. Above all, it should
not be a dead copy of some other city plan.

Then Think of Traffic!

Nobody has yet learned half of what must be known,
sooner or later, about the traffic on our highways and the
best methods of controlling it. The National Chamber of
Commerce committees who have been studying the problem
lately declare that we Americans "must charge off this
year a $3,000,000,000 loss and waste incident to automobile
accidents and traffic congestion." What an opportunity
for somebody to render a tremendous public service by
learning every detail of traffic! The facts, placed in the
hands of engineers and legislators, would soon lead to
important reforms.

The Neglected Science of Gastronomy.

For ever so many years I have yearned to appeal to my
fellow-countrymen on behalf of the neglected science of
gastronomy. Here I must reduce my petition to a few
shorthand notes, for the subject is immense. So too is the
invective.

Let us clear up, first of all, the difference between the
art of cooking and the science of gastronomy. Americans
have progressed far in the art, they know nothing of the
science—this with all due regard to the achievements of
Heinz and Campbell. The art of cooking is simply bound
by the exigencies of one's purse and the occasion. It is, like
all other arts, the application of facts and principles to the
wishes and needs of the cook and his hungry customers.
All cook books are compilations of somebody's art—or
artfulness. Somebody had to make a ragout. He found in
his cupboard a scrap of old steak, four cold boiled potatoes,
a wee onion, some milk, a tin of curry, and so on. In a frenzy

of inspiration he concocted out of these a blend which so pleased his palate that he wrote down the secret—thus from the humblest kitchen major of a sailors' boarding louse up to the renowned Savarin.

Savarin himself never had the faintest conception that there must be a true science of gastronomy. His own hunger and creative cookery were so strong that they drove him ever onward to the concocting of dishes. But that is not the way we of a wiser age advance to a genuine science of the laws of the stomach. There is a less exciting, more serious, and infinitely more protracted intellectual enterprise with sugars and spices, flours and pastes. Let me disclose it to you.

The science is a fusion of psychology and chemistry. It attempts to discover, by precise measurements under control conditions, the sensory and emotional effects of all the combinations and permutations of edibles. Let succotash be our example.

Says an old recipe: "Take lima beans, string beans, and green corn. Chop up together finely. Set to simmer in water with a piece of salt pork. Add a dash of Worcestershire sauce, to taste. Also put in a lump of butter, if desired." How would a scientist go at succotash? Not in this crude manner! He would collect samples of the outstanding varieties of lima beans, string beans, and green corn; he would select each vegetable at each age of its maturity; he would test the effect of cooking it in each known manner and for each period of time up to the moment when it fell away to a pulp from boiling over-long; he would try each proportion of the ingredients of the succotash on, let us say, a decile scale of subdividing; he would experiment with each of these combinations still more analytically by varying the cooking method and period of each ingredient separately; and what he would do next, I don't know. For this much would take a year or two, exhaust at least twelve common hired cooks, wear out three sets of kitchenware, and in some households be the best of grounds for divorce or homicide. (Thus doth society thwart science.)

A five-hundred-page volume could easily be filled on the Science of Succotash. I hereby subscribe to it, when, as and if published, regardless of price. And every other citizen of the world who wearies of the standardized food of immaculate excellence and wholesomeness which our canneries and fancy hotels purvey will some day rise up and bless me, if these few earnest words lead some genius to devote a career and a fortune or two to the Science of Gastronomy. I'd have undertaken the job myself, if I had been able to tap the fortune or two.

In the deepest of seriousness, I insist that ten thousand delights await the eater who lives in the heyday of this future science. Food then will surpass food now as food now surpasses the reeking raw mastadon cutlets on which the cave man gnawed. Arise, thinkers of America, and learn the secrets of food!

Begin with the Great French Amateurs.

Should these warm words of mine transmit to you something of their temperature, begin your gastronomic career by learning, first of all, from the best of the unscientific amateurs. I recommend the charming Paul Reboux and his "New French Cooking" and André Simon's enchanting "Art of Good Living." To any intellect which has the great good fortune to be attached to an able stomach, these books are the vestibule of heaven. The vestibule is presided over by rotund cherubs rich in sanctity and vitamins. But only cherubs! For neither of these admirable and sincere exploiters of the nutritive art has even grazed the science of gastronomy. Each has advanced far, far beyond the once great Savarin. And each deals with matters beyond the culinary of a woman's magazine. Yet neither has dreamed of doing even such a simple thing as I did myself a few years ago, when I took a fancy to experiment with the complex equations of "higher chutney." In the course of one week, I made small samples of about twenty variations of three Indian formulas—and, so my palate testifies and doth affirm, hit upon several which put old Major Gray to shame. Yet even I have not yet crossed the river into the Promised Land of scientific gastronomy.

And Then the Talkies!

The world-wide art of our age is the talking picture. In its intricacies of technique, as well as in its creative possibilities, it surpasses by the heavens' span all previous arts. Indeed these look feeble beside it, and only the blight of formal education prevents older people from appreciating this fact. The fakirs of culture still prattle at weak teas about the savage arts of sculpture, verse, and painting. For did they not learn in their own childhood that these were man's noblest modes of expression? And have they not waxed sentimental over them with the years? But the untrammeled taste of the younger generation shuns the dreary wastes of the Metropolitan Museum—which is a hybrid of multiple bastardy, a cross betwixt a mausoleum and a candy store. The young go to the talkies.

As soon as serious people of artistic power learn the new art, it will bloom like the desert after a rain. It is starting to do so even now, as slowly the older régime of silent-screen writers, directors, and artists pass into oblivion. Now and then you may see pictures which surpass the finest stage drama, but these are still much too rare. What an opportunity for vigorous imaginations! So much to learn! So much more to invent!

Community Movies.

I still wonder why so few people have been inspired to make their own motion pictures on a scale adapted to the needs of high-grade little theaters all over the world. I am not talking now about the amateur who photographs little sister and the family at the beach. I refer to the artist who, just for the fun of it all, gets up a story, finds a cast, hunts up his locations for the best shots, designs his indoor sets, arranges or even composes his music—and then shoots.

The possibilities of fine amateur pictures have not yet been even scratched. You may say that they cannot be because of the expense of a good job; but I reply that the cost can be held down surprisingly by a skillful producer— and there you have a nice problem for prolonged study!

To do a good job, there ought to be at least ten or fifteen people in your neighborhood having diversified talents and interests in the pictures. Is such a group hard to find? I doubt it.

Let such amateur pictures be produced, and the outlets for them will be found, without much delay. No doubt the Hollywood producers will subtly oppose any concerted movement toward amateur production and little neighborhood theaters; but that should only add zest to the game.

Creative Broadcasting.

Why not learn how to broadcast? The radio is still an untapped reservoir of possibilities for the person who seeks a new outlet for his ideas and energies, and there is a serious shortage of able performers and bright ideas here. What can be given over the air? Nobody knows, though the men in charge of broadcasting stations can tell you many things which cannot be successfully disseminated on ether waves. The medium has peculiar limitations which must be studied minutely by the aspirant.

Educators hope that much schooling will eventually be taken over by broadcasting stations. But how? Politicians and social workers sigh for great speakers on the air. Where are they? If ever opportunity yelled at its victim, it now yells at the top of its voice for help on the air; and, in time, thousands of people will answer.

A Neighborhood Laboratory; Well Why Not?

In many and many a large city and small town, there must be a handful of men and women eager to learn something wholly new. Hitherto they have satisfied this yearning by reading books, by taking home-study courses, and attending occasional lectures—but the results have not been solid enough. They acquire elementals thus, but they dream of pressing on to the frontiers and seeking things as yet unfound. What can they do?

Let me proffer a suggestion, which is, so far as I know, all my own. We have had literary clubs aplenty, and French conversation circles, and women's political leagues, and men's business associations. But has anybody hit upon the idea of a neighborhood laboratory? It is admitted, right here and now, that not more than one neighborhood in twenty contains people who would ever want such a strange institution. But there are at least 100,000 important, thickly settled neighborhoods in this titan land of ours; that would make, at a long shot, around 5,000 which might start some sort of community research.

Don't form a hoity-toity notion of research! It needn't be limited to inquiries such as those of the astrophysicist into the chemistry of Betelgeuse. Genuine, fruitful, and fascinating investigations of a rigorously scientific type may be concerned with the homeliest of problems. How abolish cess pools in the village? This might lead into a profound study of sanitary engineering and the devising of a new method of sewage disposal suited to local needs. What is the best way to exterminate poison ivy, which lines all the roads hereabouts and causes a pernicious amount of petty misery? Is there some simpler way than that of spraying every plant with old automobile oil? Has anybody ever found a bug that preys on the plant? Or is there perhaps a simple preventive of ivy poisoning?

A Cold in the Head.

Do you realize that, although the human race has sniffled and sneezed and coughed and groaned from simple colds in the head for 53,675,322 years, it was only last year (as I recall the date) that anybody had the bright idea of starting a laboratory to study the causes of these seemingly petty afflictions? Suppose that a physician's wife started a local group collecting case histories of colds, under the supervision of the physician himself. What if a hundred such groups gathered facts for five years? Is it conceivable that nothing of permanent value to the human race would emerge from those records? Hardly!

Make Music with Electrons!

During the next generation, thousands of music lovers will take up the strangest instrument ever devised, the invention of Leon Theremin which converts the electronic disturbances set up by a mere wave of the hand into musical tones. Already, though in its infancy, this device opens up possibilities of creative work far beyond any of the traditional violins, cellos, pianos, and organs. The tyro produces sounds never before created; shrill, harsh, smooth, loud, and continuously varying in each characteristic. As yet no masters have arisen. All are beginners. Yet even conservative musicians and musical critics declare that Theremin has given the world virtually a new art. Why not learn it? Nobody knows to what it may lead. To pursue it is an adventure.

Scientific Biography.

Do you realize that nobody has yet written a scientifically sound biography? Though thinkers have, for twenty-five

centuries, been echoing the thought that the proper study
of mankind is man; though all enlightened persons agree
that the "personal equation" (in its wider sense) is involved
in every acute problem of politics, social reform, and
business, nevertheless, *not one human being, living or dead,
has ever kept an accurate and complete record of another
human being in a form which could serve as the basis of a
reliable interpretation.* A modest approach to such was
made, of course, by Boswell when he devoted most of his
life to recording the behavior of Dr. Johnson. Of late a
more restricted but correspondingly more scientific move
has been made in France by Toulouse, whose "psycho-
graphs" of Poincaré and Zola are valuable indeed. Apart
from these, the writings of literary biographers are pitiful
attempts to penetrate personalities. Fascinating as they
are, they prove little or nothing.

A Chance for 10,000 *Sherlock Holmeses.*

Here you are, living in the world's center of crime, corrup-
tion, and depravity. No matter which town you exhibit,
you may be sure that it has ten to twenty times as many
murders, hold-ups, forgeries, and sneak-thieveries as any
European city of the same size. Reformers implore you to
do something about it. But when they get through implor-
ing and mop their fevered brows, you wonder what the
deuce you can do. After all, you haven't time to turn
Sherlock Holmes and go sneaking up dark alleys and climb-
ing back fences on the trail of wickedness—and you cannot
throw a gunman with ju-jitsu or anything else. So what
can you do to mop up the crime wave?

Well, there are lots of things which certain kinds of men
and women can do, and which nobody else can. The very
heart and center of American crime is the lawyer. Without
him, few crooks could carry on for long. A large fraction
of our lawyers are the arch-criminals. Some experts say

that one out of every four or five is a complete scoundrel. As for me, I don't know, but that estimate does not sound dangerously high. Anyhow, whether it is a million miles off or not, every well informed person will assure you that, if the American people could only exterminate the lawyer-criminal, we might trust judges and juries to make short shrift of most knaves.

Well, then, how about a little secret service sleuthing around your local lawyers? You don't have to wear pink whiskers and speak with a Bessarabian dialect, in order to indulge in that work. All you have to do is to attend court and listen to the members of the bar as they plead for their clients; then report your findings, with no prejudice, to a neighborhood group. See to it that all the respectable people learn about the lawyer who accepts criminals as clients and handles the cases in a suspicious manner. Pay no attention to the old hokum of the scoundrel lawyer who declares that it is his high moral right to defend a man even when he knows the latter to be guilty.

A community which watches its lawyers as a sanitary engineer watches the sewage will do much to check crime. Polluted water is said to purify itself after it runs several miles in the open sunshine. Maybe polluted lawyers will do likewise. (New York and Chicago papers please copy.)

Even Collecting May Become the Means of Learning.

Many a small boy has learned much through collecting postage stamps. I did that myself and can truly testify that no small part of my later interest in geography grew directly out of spontaneous studies of lands and governments whose stamps I sought so eagerly. Most of us slough off our collecting habits after we pass adolescence, probably because other tasks lure us more intensely. But the adult need not regard collecting as a childish thing to be put aside when we grow up. Every teacher knows that, in so far as the interest in collecting something is spontaneous and not forced, the collector is sure to learn much. Many a school encourages all sorts of collecting: stamps, eggs, bird feathers, rocks, flowers, souvenir post cards, and what not. Each item thus gathered becomes a center of attention and a possible focus of thought and further inquiry. (If made a part of required work, however, it probably defeats its own purpose. See my previous remarks on the scarlet tanager.)

So, to the grown-up who wishes to go on learning, I offer the collector's career as a possibility, always bearing in mind that, as compared to the varieties of creative learning which have been broached in the last few pages, such a career is likely to prove less rich intellectually, though perhaps more entertaining.

Poor People Can Become Great Collectors.

One of the most unfortunate notions that has ever gone abroad on the stream of gossip is the one which avers that much money is necessary for the assembling of any collection worth while. Book collectors assure me that the publicity given to the high adventures of Dr. Rosenbach in running down priceless tomes for millionaires' libraries has gravely injured the rare book trade. For it has strengthened the popular error about book collecting being a rich man's hobby. As a matter of cold statistics, a man who has only $100 a year to spend on books can, in the course of years, assemble a unique and valuable collection provided he learns as he goes, slowly becoming master of the entire background of the books and their authors. The trick is to find your own subject and field. Don't ape the rich by collecting the same rarities they seek; of course you'll lose out if you do that. But there are literally thousands of subjects many of historical or other significance—from which, after a cool survey, you may select one which nobody else has chosen.

What an Umbrella Clerk Did.

Many years ago a young man became salesman in the umbrella department of a large Boston store. As one may guess, his income was not enormous. In fact, the income tax collectors presumably have never known him. But, being thrifty and bent on turning his life to some pleasant account, he formed the habit of spending his noon hours in the second-hand book shops. Somehow the idea came to him that there might be more fun in collecting everything he could find there about George Washington. And, as luck would have it, in those days few buyers sought such material. So the old books and pamphlets were cheap, and our umbrella clerk assembled many of them out of his small savings.

He learned while he gathered, and learning made him ever more expert in the history and literature of Washington's day. So, after many years, one of the greatest collections of early Americana came into being.

What an Insurance Clerk Did.

In a little flat up in that horrible wilderness of brick known as the Bronx there dwelt for many years an insurance clerk, a poor bachelor and as unostentatious as a mouse with a guilty conscience. Only the landlord and the corner delicatessen dealer knew him until he died last winter, leaving his estate to the Metropolitan Museum of Art. Then the great collectors of the world sat up and rubbed their eyes. For this insurance clerk had, with mere driblets of cash, gleefully assembled a magnificent array of antique textiles, a round thousand Chinese fabrics so remarkable that the Museum authorities declare they must study them for a year before placing them on exhibit. Only the vast collection in the Imperial Palace Museum in Peking is said to surpass those thousand treasures which the insurance clerk kept in trunks and closets up in his Bronx flat. (Park Avenue papers please copy!)

The Endless Procession.

If you don't like any of these suggestions, you may enjoy learning something new about unemployment and trying to solve the puzzle of it in your own neighborhood. Or you may learn all about city noises and how to control them, thereby bringing peace, sleep and poise to your fellow townsmen. Or you may learn the ins and outs of military and naval propaganda, thus putting your friends on their guard against what they read in the newspapers and see in the motion picture news reels. Or you may learn the facts about jails and prisons in your community and help to clean up one of America's vilest abuses. Or you may turn joyously toward the conquest of dirt, which is now more than half beaten but still able to cause mankind trouble. Or you may see a great career in learning the problems of the millions of people who are partially deaf and handicapped just enough to suffer keenly.

I guess I'd better stop this line of thought. If I don't, there'll be no pages left for other matters I must broach.

Of learning there is no end, and you must find your own beginning. All that I have said here is purely suggestive. And not more than one good line of study out of a thousand has been mentioned.

After all, your best project is You! It springs from your unique nature. It becomes timely in your own good time and place. And it bears fruit according to your own energy, thoughtfulness, and enthusiasm.

EXERCISES

How accurately do you recall names and identify people? Make other tests of this kind for yourself. You will notice an enormous improvement in your powers of accurate observation if you drill yourself regularly.

Clip a few hundred portraits from current newspapers and magazines. Write the names on the back. Begin by looking at the portraits and trying to recall the names. After you have achieved considerable skill in this, reverse the process. Now look only at the names on the back of the portraits. Then try to describe the appearance of the person named. This will tax your powers considerably.

On the following pages you will find an outline of a project. Fill it out with great care, taking as much time as you need for a thorough job. Probably you will have to copy the outline on several sheets of paper, in order to make room for the details you will have to fill in.

EXERCISE

PROJECT

Number........   When started....................
                     When finished...................

What I wish to accomplish.......................................
....
....

For this I shall set aside...............hours every week, as follows:
....
I shall need the following supplies...................................
....
....
The best books to study are.......................................
....
....
The best magazines and journals are...............................
....
The main problems to be solved, during the first period of study, are
....
....
The leading authorities on the subject are........................
....
....

I am specially interested in the following aspects of the project........

....

....

I shall begin *today* investigating..........................with a

view to finding out whether I may not become interested in it.

EXERCISE

I have been interested in the subjects which I have checked off in the following list:

Architecture.
Metallurgy.
History of Russia.
Harmony and counterpoint.
Poultry raising.
Sanskrit.
Shipbuilding.
Boxing.
City politics.
Aviation.
Radio.
Economics.
Astronomy.
Bookkeeping.
Ancient history.
Carpentering.
Philosophy.
Painting.
Finance.
Advertising.
Engineering.
Making jewelry.
Tennis.
Riding horseback.
Playing a musical instrument.
Psychology.
Gardening.
Sailing.
Clay modeling.
Biology.
Home economics.
Modern European history.
Golf.
Making pottery.
Chemistry.
Physics.

Ethics.
Wrestling.
Polo.
Botany.
Agricultural engineering.

EXERCISE

1. Write a list of your strongest interests.

2. On this list check off those which you are now pursuing in a more than casual manner.

3. Next check off those you have never pursued.

4. Among these latter, check off those you have neglected because you could not afford the money required to pursue them properly.

5. Then check off those which you passed up because you lacked time.

6. Lastly, check off those you did not follow up because you lacked special training or native abilities.

After this record has been finished, reexamine it and answer the following questions:

1. How much would it cost to pursue each interest you have foregone because of its expense?

2. How much time would you have to devote to each interest you have dropped because of lack of time?

3. Which abilities are you sure you lack for the pursuit of those you dropped because of inability?

BOOK VII

EQUIPMENT, THE LESSER HALF OF METHOD

EQUIPMENT, THE LESSER HALF OF METHOD

To make a table, the carpenter must have the right tools. To learn how to make a table, the apprentice needs those tools much more than the experienced carpenter does. After skill has been acquired, the worker knows how to get along with inferior equipment, like the virtuoso who is able to play a tune on one string of his fiddle, using a stove poker as bow. But before mastery, one toils in the dark with too few instruments or with the wrong sort. The master may plane with a file, but not the fledgling.

Thus straight up the scale of accomplishments. Yet, oddly enough, few learners appreciate how thoroughly dependent they are on equipment. Did not Abe Lincoln study by the light of a tallow dip on the floor of his log cabin? See where he got! Well, that sounds convincing—until you begin to analyze the facts. Then you find several things; for instance, Lincoln quite certainly would have advanced much further than he did, had his learning equipment been better. The marvel is that he progressed as far as he did with what he had.

Then, too, do not overlook the fact that what men had to learn in the first half of the nineteenth century was immeasurably simpler than what we now must assimilate. What if Lincoln had been obliged to learn calculus, physiological chemistry, or international finance? Suppose he had endeavored to learn medicine instead of law? And suppose it had been a medical science as advanced as our own today. Could he? Not in a thousand years of candle light. And how much did he actually learn? Less than the average high school student must learn, in order to graduate from a first-rate institution. And most of what he learned was, I believe, law. Law, the most backward and ludicrous of all subjects! Law, mostly a set of primitive principles and a mass of court cases. Stuff which any bright boy could read by himself and understand well enough.

The attic genius passes simply because modern learning is all but impossible without adequate equipment. This is not an effect of the machine age. On the contrary, it grows out of the inner nature of the facts themselves which have made the machine age possible. Modern science is revolutionizing the art of learning. Even the subjects which we usually think of as elementary have expanded so greatly of late that, compared with fifty years ago, the learner requires many things.

Stick to Serious Periodicals.

Popular magazines are all well enough for mere pleasure reading. But the learner seldom finds a line in them worth the nickel or dime they cost him. Nor has he a right to expect more. Addressed to the millions, why should they fit the precious few who seek to expand their understanding?

No country on earth has special periodicals equal to our own. Almost everything worth learning is now covered by some of them; and as a rule they are well edited. You pick up in their columns current news about the subject and the experts in it, and you readily assimilate the technical terms through continuous reading. I regularly read more than a dozen journals in as many fields and can testify that they afford me endless stimulation. There are always articles which outrun my wit, but these serve the purpose of piquing my curiosity. The others give me information of every sort. You will find the same is true in your own field of inquiry.

Buy Books!

Americans read few books, and most of these profit the ragman far more than the reader. The best books are too costly for the average learner and, I fear, will long remain so. It is hard to draw up a list of required readings in any important field at a total cost of less than $100. No wonder the public libraries are filled with students!

Another difficulty is that one must watch his step lest he be inveigled into buying worthless books. Of late the market has been flooded with so-called "Introductions" to all sorts of subjects, from metaphysics to mumblety-peg, which help the serious student about as much as ragweed helps the hay-feverish. They truly serve a different group of readers, namely the skimmer, whose notion of being well read is to have touched one petal on each flower in the garden of literature, and the poseur who babbles a phrase and bluffs a whole volume.

Moral: If dollars mean much to you, buy introductions and textbooks only on the recommendation of an **expert**. Never follow a blurb.

The Choice of Books.

A brilliant book sometimes happens to be a bad one for the learner simply because its author knows too much and cannot escape from the fullness of his knowledge. Few great experts have the knack of passing down to the average reader the principles and facts of their specialties. Bertrand Russell, for example, is one of the world's outstanding mathematicians and logicians; but he has not popularized mathematics and logic. It is only in fields wherein he is not an authority that he shines—notably political philosophy. There he truly radiates bright beams of wit and wisdom. So too, in a somewhat qualified sense, with John Dewey, Robert Millikan, Einstein, and most other leaders of thought and discovery.

Hence the seeming paradox: You often learn more and learn faster from a book or a teacher who has much less to offer you, in the absolute sense, than from the masters themselves and their masterpieces. Many learners have trouble accepting this truth. They think that they must study only the best books—which they take to mean the solidest tomes of the greatest specialists. Trying it, they flounder and become discouraged. Then they marvel at the progress some friend makes by reading a cheap correspondence-school course or by hiring some shabby student to tutor him. It's just like the rich man who thinks he will catch the biggest trout in the brook if he buys a hundred-dollar fishing pole, all the flies known to the angler's art, and forty-dollar hip boots. The small urchin with a hand-whittled hickory pole and a tin of worms brings home the fish.

Some of the most brilliant teachers under whom I have sat have been also the poorest; and, lackaday, some dull old pedants whose brilliance was concentrated in their shiny pants and on their bald domes have enlightened me with ease, grace and precision. To become personal again, the two worst instructors I ever had in mathematics were themselves geniuses or near-geniuses. The greater of the pair was the late Alexander Ziwet, a most charming human being as well as a very great mathematician, according to the annals of fame. Unfortunately for most sophomores, however, Ziwet thought in terms of calculus as easily as they though in terms of football. He taught calculus most informally, without notes, without even a blackboard and chalk much of the time. It seemed beyond his grasp that most of us were doomed by Nature to be dunderheads in calculus. So his mind seldom met a sophomore's, and the sophomore learned little—at least back in the days of which I speak.

I mention all this for good reasons. You, the learner, must disabuse your mind of the notion that, especially in the beginning of a subject, you will advance fastest under a great authority or by reading his works. The order of learning is not the order of teacher's fame or achieving. It is determined solely by the relation between you and the subject matter.

Equip Your Study Properly!

Let me return to the matter of physical equipment. Scholars pooh-pooh this, but I deem them in the wrong. For nine out of every ten learners, the material aids to study help tremendously. Among these, the following are most important:

1. A typewriter. Handwriting is archaic and may soon be obsolete. The best of it is only half legible, the worst a hen track. Slow to pen, it is still slower to read. Life goes to waste over handwriting. I hope to see the day when it will be regarded as an insult to write a letter in long hand.

2. A filing cabinet. This must be self-evident. I've said enough about it already.

3. Shelves for arranging books, pamphlets, notes, specimens, and other material in some easily accessible system.

4. A commodious desk, well stocked with pens, pencils, colored crayons, erasers, and so on.

5. A large wall bulletin on which outlines may be posted, for quick inspection. The value of this device naturally depends upon the eyemindedness of the learner. I could hardly get along without it.

It is useless to specify anything beyond these elementals. What else one has will be determined by the special study If working on music or a foreign language, a recording phonograph is worth its weight in gold. In working over minerals or insects, one must have microscopes. And so on, without end.

The Trail of the Goat.

Today I saw:

Today I heard:

Today I learned:

Use Your Radio!

Keep a radio calendar posted in a conspicuous place. Opportunities of learning by radio are enormously increasing. You will find many helpful courses regularly offered. Read your daily paper to find out what they are.

If there is some subject you wish to study which never comes in over the air, write in to the major broadcasting companies and tell them about it. If many do this, the companies may be persuaded to furnish all with whatever they seek. Radio education is at its beginnings. It is up to you, the learner, to decide what shall be taught through this marvelous medium.

Equipment for the Three Major Subjects of Modern Life.

Now comes the list of books and other equipment needed by the beginner in the three most important subjects of twentieth-century civilization. You recall, I hope, that I explained, early in this book, how and why geography, psychology, and mathematics, each taken in the widest sense and scope, constitute the foundation of modern culture. To make the right start in these, follow the advice of the experts who have prepared the following recommendations for your special benefit. We look first at the lists drawn up by Prof. J. Russell Smith, of Columbia University, whose writings in general as well as in economic geography are nationally famous.

Studying Geography

I

(For the boy away from big schools who has not more than $10 or $15 to spend in a year.)

1. Begin by reading "Geography and Our Need of It," by J. Russell Smith, American Library Association, Chicago, 35 cents.

2. "New Physical Geography," by von Englen, Macmillan, $3. This book gives an understanding of the surface of the earth.

3. The student should early learn to read a contour (topographic) map. Get from the U. S. Geological Survey, Washington. D. C., a list of the maps

published by them covering territory to which the student has access. He should early go into the field, and, reading the topographic map, come to an understanding of the country to which he has physical access. In the same way he should go to the fields and see the things, as far as possible, that are mentioned in physical geography. If he lives in the flat country, he should by all means go to some hills and to broken land, even if it is only the bluffs along a mid-western stream. 50 cents.

4. A dollar globe.

5. "Why the Weather," by C. F. Brooks. Geography, which is a study of man's relationship to the earth, requires an understanding, both of the earth and of the air—two great environmental factors. This book by Brooks explains the weather so that one who understands it has an added daily interest. $2.50.

6. U. S. Weather Map. While studying the weather, students should subscribe to the U. S. Weather Map published nearest his home. See U. S. Weather Bureau, Washington, D. C. $1.25 for six months. Also secure from the Weather Bureau those sections of Bulletin W that cover the student's home and adjacent areas. 5 cents per section.

7. He should examine copies, perhaps subscribe for a short time, to the weekly weather and crop reports published by the U. S. Weather Bureau, Washington, D. C., which discuss conditions throughout the United States and their influence upon agriculture for the week.

8. Having acquired some understanding of the earth and its forms, the air and its performances, the next thing to master is some understanding of the world as a whole, which can best be secured by discovering that there are type climate regions which recur in the various continents. For this see: "Climates of the World," by Glenn Trewartha, Geographical Press, Columbia University, 35 cents.

9. This knowledge of climates will make an interesting background for "Atlas of World Agriculture," by V. C. Finch and C. E. Baker, Government Printing Office, $1.; and also for "Principles of Human Geography," by E. Hunting and D. Cushing.

These should not be read merely to be remembered, as we do the multiplication tables, but to be used as the detective uses the signs which, on being interpreted, tell him a story. The story is the way man gets along on this earth in the complicated process of making it his home.

10. An Atlas. "Appleton's School Atlas" will be very helpful in building up in the student's mind a map of the world which is such an important basis in the study of geography. $3.

This course of study makes an excellent year's work. An interesting review of it can be had by getting a few bound volumes or loose back numbers of the National Geographic Magazine. Skim through the articles, classifying them as to the climatic regions each one tells about. It cannot be too strongly emphasized that the understanding of these climatic regions is the real basis of geography. (See Jones and Whittlesey, Section III, which follows.)

II

(A suggested course of study for the student who wishes to spend about $30 or $40 a year.)

The student who has more money to spend should, if possible, travel enough while reading the physical geography to see all of the processes that are to be seen within 50 or 100 miles, and that is usually a surprising amount.

1. Include the references given above, under Section I.

2. Buy a better atlas.

3. Buy some sets of topographic maps published by the U. S. Geological Survey showing typical landscapes and physiographic types.

4. The student who can afford it will enjoy being in contact with the current flow of geographical material by subscribing to the following journals:

National Geographic Magazine, Washington, D. C. Popular, pictorial, unsystematic, but interesting.

Economic Geography, Worcester, Massachusetts. A magazine whose name describes it.

Geographic Review, American Geographical Society, New York. Scholarly and scientific articles with a record of geographical events and careful reviews of new publications.

III

(For the student who wishes more liberal equipment.)

A person with more money to spend will want early to possess a good library globe twelve to eighteen inches in diameter, a good American atlas (as good as there are—a Rand McNally or a Hammond) to show detailed locations in America, and a good European atlas, such as the London Times Atlas, or Andrée (a German atlas but usable), which give details of foreign countries not to be obtained in maps published in America.

The studies thus far have given an introduction to the world environment, and should be followed by:

"Industrial and Commercial Geography," by J. Russell Smith. The world industries are presented in this book, which is widely used as a college text, but easy enough for any high school student to understand.

At this point the study of geography may be followed in any of three ways, depending upon the taste of the reader. For want of other names, call these methods: (*a*) philosophic; (*b*) continental and political; and (*c*) regional.

a. Philosophic.

A French book translated into English, "Principles of Human Geography," by J. Brunhes. This book reaches about the world, regardless of country, continent or type of climate, and discusses geographic subjects in a philosophic but interesting way.

"The Human Habitat," by Ellsworth Huntington, and "From Pole to Pole," by Sven Hedin, are books by men of wide experience in travel and exploration, giving a general discussion of geography, much like that of Brunhes' book, but with different methods, facts, and points of view.

b. Continental and political.

The easiest book with which to begin this study is "North America," by J. Russell Smith, published by Harcourt, Brace & Company. Then read "South America," by Clarence Jones, published by Henry Holt & Company "Europe," by D. H. Smith. While this book gives only a moderately good treatment of the subject, there is none better. Follow this with "Asia," by Dudley Stamp, an English book which is a mine of information but short on the economic side; and "Australia," by Griffith Taylor.

"England," by W. Dibelius, published by Harper & Brothers in 1930, is not essentially a geography but a critical evaluation of all phases of English life and economy by a German professor. It should supplement D. H. Smith's "Economic Geography." "Geography of France," by Blanchard and Todd, published in 1919 by Rand McNally & Company, is the only book on France available in English and does not cover the more recent post-war developments. The agricultural conditions of the country up to date are covered in the U. S. Department of Agriculture Technical Bulletin No. 37, "France," by L. G. Michael. This is available through the Superintendent of Documents, Washington, D. C., 25 cents.

The student should also acquaint himself with the "Commerce Year Book," Vol. II, published by the Government Printing Office, Washington, D. C. This source is valuable for its trade and production figures, and has useful maps.

Political geography is the study of problems that have a geographic origin and must be settled by political methods, *i.e.*, by governments. A river that runs through two countries creates problems which man can settle only through the action of government. This very complicated subject is covered excellently by Isaiah Bowman in "The New World," published by the World Book Company. This book deals with the problems that vex nations, and will explain nine of the next ten, if not, indeed, all of the next ten international flare-ups that appear in the daily press. It is not a book that one is likely to read from cover to cover, but it will be consulted from time to time as interest in geography grows and reading habits involve more understanding of international problems and frictions.

c. Regional.

(For world regions, see "Climates," by Glenn Trewartha, or "Economic Geography," by Jones and Whittlesey. The selected readings in this last book give vivid pictures of the regions. *"Influences of Geographic Environment,"* by E. C. Semple, published by Henry Holt & Company, is an exceptionally interesting book of broad scope. Many people consider that Miss Semple carries her interpretation of environmental influence too far. Nevertheless the book contains an astonishing variety of examples of environmental influences in all fields of human activity, and most of Miss Semple's claims are justifiable.)

Important books:

1. The Equatorial Forest. "Natural Man," by Charles Hose, published by The Macmillan Company, gives an account of primitive peoples in the forests of Borneo. "The Conquest of the Tropics" (the story of the United Fruit Company), by F. U. Adams, gives an account of their plantations.

2. Tropic Grasslands. "People of the Small Arrow," by J. H. Dreiberg, is human geography in story form, and scientifically correct.

3. The Desert's Edge. "The Manners and Customs of the Kevala Bedouins," by Alois Musil, published by the American Geographical Society. New York. "Arabia Deserta," 2 volumes, by C. Doughty, was written on the spot forty years ago and is regarded as a classic. It has recently been reprinted. It tells about people who change but little.

4. The Mid-latitude Grasslands. "The Mongols," by F. A. Larson, Duke of Mongolia, is a wonderful story of men of the dry grassland.

5. The Farm Lands of East Asia. "Farmers of Forty Centuries," by F. H. King, published by Harcourt, Brace & Company. This book is a classic, giving an interesting and minute description of the age-old hand agriculture and manufacture by which China, Japan, and Korea have supported themselves for millenia.

A contrasting book, "Japan's Economic Position," by J. E. Orchard, published by Whittlesey House, McGraw-Hill Book Company, Inc., is a careful and scientific study of the achievements of the one oriental country that has tried to westernize its economic life.

6. Lands of Mediterranean Climate. "Mediterranean Lands," by M. Newbigin.

7. Northwest Europe. "Growth of the Soil," by Knut Hamsun. This book is fiction, but gives an excellent picture of man's fight for home space in a land that had drawbacks.

Manufacturing Man in Northwest Europe and the United States. "Denmark, a Co-operative Commonwealth," by F. C. Howe, published by Harcourt, Brace & Company. "American Economic Life," by Ingwell, Munro and Stryker, published by Harcourt, Brace & Company.

8. The Arctic. "Hunters of the Great North," by Stefansson, and "Across the Arctic," by Knud Rasmussen.

The Geologist's Primary Equipment.

Should you wish to press on beyond the foundations of geography into the fascinating fields of geology, here is how to start. Professors Berkey and Lobeck have kindly furnished the following information.

The list of really necessary equipment is very simple. One needs a *hammer* so that pieces of rock or minerals may be broken from ledges, a *knife blade* to be used for testing hardness of minerals, a *compass* for orientation in determining the strike of formations or for guiding one's self across the country. One needs also a *lens* or small magnifier so that the finer grained constituents of rock can be seen more plainly and one needs a *collecting bag* for carrying material. In case specimens are collected one ought to have small paper bags so that each specimen may be labeled and wrapped and kept separate. The extra paper of the bag serves both purposes. One needs a *local map* preferably U. S. *topographical sheet* such as is now available for most of the settled districts. If such a map is not available some other reliable map should be obtained.

If a *geological map* is available so much the better.

It is not practicable to carry equipment for elaborate tests of any kind in the field. This kind of investigation is cared for in the laboratory and belongs neither to the work of the beginner nor to the field.

It is entirely practicable for a beginner who has some natural liking for the subject and suitable educational background to make considerable progress both in geological understanding and observation. One may readily become a successful collector of minerals, or rocks, or fossils, and of typical views of surface features of structural conditions such as one may see in quarries or excavations or along road cuts or other outcrops of rock formations. It is a comparatively easy thing to begin to make observations of this kind and to start collections. The difficult thing is to gain enough breadth of experience and understanding of the possibilities to make sound interpretations of the data that one can so easily gather.

The beginner may take up the following fundamental books, noting well the comment on each:

"Elements of Geology," by William H. Norton, Ginn & Company, 1905. This book will probably be found to be one of the most readable and readily understood introductory books in geology. It takes the reader by the hand, as it were, and introduces him to the science of geology by imaginary visits to quarries and the open country. It makes geology appear very much simpler than it actually is, but this is as it should be for the beginner. This book, in other words, is really too simple for use as a college text book. The ordinary reader, however, would probably learn much more from it than from a more comprehensive volume in which the details obscure the ideas of broader significance. This book includes economic as well as historical geology.

"Geology, Physical and Historical," by Herdman F. Cleland, American Book Company, 1916. This is one of the standard but more elementary books widely used in introductory college courses in geology.

"College Geology," by Chamberlin and Salisbury, Part I, Processes, Revised by R. T. Chamberlin and Paul MacClintock, Henry Holt & Company, 1927. A very satisfactory and thoroughly reliable text book, known all over the world. It is simple, well written, and dignified, and very logical in its treatment. This should appeal to the average reader not having a teacher at hand.

"Textbook of Geology," by Pirsson and Schuchert, Part I, Physical geology, revised 1929, John Wiley & Sons, 1929. Probably the best introductory textbook in geology for college use. Somewhat more comprehensive and detailed than Chamberlin and Salisbury. Nevertheless it can easily be understood by the general reader. The arrangement is very logical and scientific. The reader with a studious turn of mind will find this book thoroughly satisfying, and with no real insurmountable difficulties.

"An Introduction to Earth History," by Hervey W. Shimer, Ginn & Company, 1925. This book is more matter of fact in its presentation than Norton's, which it otherwise resembles. Though simple, it has something of a technical flavor, and is somewhat cold and impersonal. Treats of all aspects of geology, including the historical.

"A Textbook of Geology," by Amadeus W. Grabau, Part I, General Geology, D. C. Heath & Company, 1920, 824 pages. Rich in examples and illustrations. Too profuse for the ordinary reader but a splendid reference book for the student of geology. Inspiring in its suggestions and ideas.

"An Introduction to Geology," by William B. Scott, The Macmillan Company, 1907. For many years one of the standard textbooks on geology in introductory college courses. A very satisfactory text book, well written, but rather profuse, being 800 pages long, including historical geology. A bit pretentious for the average reader.

"Principles of Geology," by Lyell, 1853.

"Manual of Geology," by Dana, 1863.

"Textbook of Geology," by Geike, 1882.

"Elements of Geology," by LeConte, 1882. These four books should be known by every student of geology. Each one is a classic. Hardly suited, however, to use as a modern text.

Books on historical geology are not suggested in this list except in so far as historical geology is treated in connection with the physical aspects of geology and the two combined in one book, as in Norton, Cleland, and Shimer.

The Equipment for Psychology.

If you are a good learner, you recall that this book regards all the sciences of human nature as integral parts of psychology, even though the commoner and more precise usage would call the entire group anthropology. The beginner will profit, in the long run, if he gets the wider view of mankind as seen by the anthropologists well before he plunges into the endless mazes of psychology.

So I advise him to tackle at the outset the following volumes:

"Are We Civilized?" by Robert H. Lowie.
"Primitive Society," by Robert H. Lowie.
"The Mind of Primitive Man," by Franz Boas.
"Anthropology and Modern Life," by Franz Boas.
"Early Civilization," by Alexander Goldenweiser.
"Anthropology," by A. L. Kroeber.
"Men of the Old Stone Age," by Henry Fairfield Osborn.

While it is well to read, sooner or later, all seven books, the learner who seeks more special knowledge of human nature may safely press on to other texts, while reading in general anthropology. For in the latter there is not much which must be thoroughly mastered prior to taking up the basic works on individual psychology.

We move on, now, toward that goal, first pausing on our way to consider man as a social creature analyzed psychologically. Whereas the first list of books, given above, present you with a picture of man's external organizations, the next list emphasizes rather the social stimulus and response. These volumes should be read in the order mentioned:

"Social Psychology," by Floyd H. Allport.
"The Psychology of Social Institutions," by C. H. Judd.
"Social Change," by W. F. Ogburn.
"Human Nature and Conduct," by John Dewey.

Do not despair if you find long passages in Dewey dark! Do your best with them and pass on to other things. Later— maybe years later—you will return to Dewey and see a new light.

As the basis of all higher social activity, as well as of all intellectual progress, is language, you should next spend some time studying this amazing phenomenon. I warn you that it may overtax you, at this stage of your progress. But it is better to get, as soon as possible, a glimpse of the part which speech plays in culture. Even the glimpse will put you on guard against easy errors. Whenever possible, come back to this subject for a while. Attack the following books in the order named:

"Language," by Edward Sapir.
"Semantics," by M. Bréal.
"Language," by Otto Jespersen.
"The English Language," by L. P. Smith.

At times you may fear that you have wandered far from psychology, but you haven't. Indeed, no view of human nature is well founded unless it presents a clear picture of the part played by the larynx and its noises in the rise of society and intellectual opinions.

If you wade through as much as one-quarter of Jespersen's monumental work, you will do well. Pick the chapters according to your own interest.

It seems to me that, before the learner attempts to absorb a large systematic presentation of psychology, he will do best to catch the bird's-eye view of its vaster dominions. To this end I recommend, as the next move, a quick survey of the seven ages of man as a personality. This is called "developmental psychology" and embraces an immense deal of special studies, few of which need concern you. Get rather a broad view as drawn for you by H. L. Hollingworth in his book, "Mental Growth and Decline" (New York, 1927). Practically every line of it can be understood without a previous knowledge of general psychology. At this point I should—as a matter of personal preference—turn aside long enough to read a book in social biology which discloses, not the normal trend of an individual from birth to death, but rather the actual tendencies now visible among the peoples of the Western World as a whole. An excellent approach to this difficult subject is found in S. J. Holmes' "The Trend of the Race" (New York, 1921). You may find much of it pretty stiff, but that need not prevent you from getting the bird's-eye view. Skim what you find unduly hard. Then come back to psychology.

You should now be ready for a general study, which must be more than a bird's-eye view. Read and reread as thoughtfully as you can a standard college textbook such as R. S. Woodworth's "Psychology" (New York, 1925, and later editions). Drill yourself thoroughly, chapter by chapter.

My recommendation for the next step may be challenged by psychologists as being too severe; and I admit that for some learners it may not work well. But it is a good practice to jump off into deep water and see how well you can swim. So here goes! Tackle that huge volume, "The Foundations of Experimental Psychology," edited by Carl Murchison and written by twenty-three leading psychologists (Clark University, 1929). Understand at the outset that you will almost certainly be unable to assimilate more than a quarter of it. But return to it after you have mastered other books.

To learn one of the latest and most illuminating views about the nature of human experience, study with care Wolfgang Köhler's "Gestalt Psychology" (New York, 1929)—not an easy volume, perhaps, but worthy of your best efforts, and highly significant. You may best prepare yourself for it by reading, just before it, the same psychologist's famous study, "The Mentality of Apes," in which he reports his long first-hand studies of these fascinating creatures.

Doubtless you will wish to learn about the new technique of mental testing. Read then, as your first book in this difficult field, Sidney and Luella Pressey's "Introduction to the Use of Standard Tests." Having completed this imposing array of volumes, you will surely be able to select your own line of study beyond them. It will inevitably lead you to some specialty. For no subject breaks up into more special lines than psychology.

No matter in which direction you veer, from here on, you ought to extend your reading in biology; for without a fair knowledge of life and its creature forms you will be at a grave disadvantage in understanding the deeper problems of human nature. Now, the literature of biology is colossal and changing pretty fast. Scores of excellent books may be found helpful; but the following short list will suffice until you are able to pick and choose for yourself.

Get the bird's-eye view first of all. Perhaps the best way to do that is to tackle the huge two-volume work entitled "The Science of Life," which is just coming off the presses. This has been written by H. G. Wells, in collaboration with his son, G. P. Wells, and Julian Huxley. It is a popularized survey of the whole range of biology. The deft touch of H. G. Wells lightens many a difficult passage.

Next attack something stiffer yet essentially popular. Read "Human Biology and Racial Welfare," edited by Edmund V. Cowdry. Here is a collection of essays by twenty-eight leaders of research and interpretation in the whole realm of biology, eugenics, and education. From these you gain a broad picture of the significance of all that men have learned about the nature of life.

Having finished these two large works, you are more than ready to take up special studies, like the seven following:

"The Biological Basis of Human Nature," by H. S. Jennings.
"Prometheus" (a short essay), by H. S. Jennings.
"Animal Biology," by Haldane and Huxley.
"Evolution and Genetics," by T. H. Morgan.
"Heredity and Environment," by E. G. Conklin.
"What Is Evolution?" by G. H. Parker.
"The Green Leaf," by D. T. McDougall.

The Mathematician's Lean Equipment.

Emil Lengyel went to interview Einstein for the *New York Times*, not long ago, and, on being ushered into the study of the great mathematician, "was surprised, even disappointed, not to see any instruments in the room." Then, he adds:

> Professor Einstein apparently guessed my thoughts, tapped his forehead and said with a smile: "Here are my instruments."

To be sure, the ordinary learner is not quite so independent of physical accoutrement as the genius Einstein. But, as compared with most other learners, he goes it alone and empty-handed. Paper and pencil suffice, once he has made a start with some textbook. He can invent his own problems endlessly. To list his needs, then, is merely a matter of knowing at which level of learning he wishes to start, for, unlike geography, each level determines its own prerequisites severely. To attack the theory of probabilities before mastering algebra and calculus is folly.

There are books which the beginner can study at home at leisure, carrying himself as far as he is able to go. The one best recommended is

> "Practical Mathematics for Home Study," by Claude I. Palmer.

This, of course, is strictly, a drill book in every type of mathematical calculation from addition up to trigonometry. It should be paralleled with a few books about mathematics, such as

> "Number, The Language of Science," by Tobias Dantzig. This is a fascinating story of the rise of man's insight into the key ideas and methods of mathematics, told by a mathematician who can bring these abstruse matters down to the grasp of the cultured non-mathematical reader. In many ways an amazing piece of work.
>
> "Introduction to Mathematics," by A. N. Whitehead. Very short but brilliantly clear and helpful.
>
> "The Principle of Relativity," by A. N. Whitehead. A pretty stiff dose; yet the learner must come, sooner or later, to this, the key subject of modern physics.

The Physical Sciences.

In a precise sense, the physical sciences are those which enable man to control things in his environment through the medium of applied mathematics, and the physiological sciences are those which enable him to do likewise with things inside of himself and his fellows. The physiological sciences are, alas, much too difficult to be discoursed upon here. But the physical may be approached by almost any reader who has found elementary algebra within his grasp. (Approached, I say; not necessarily mastered!) Here are well approved works for the beginner in physics and chemistry. They have been selected by Prof. Frederick Barry, who specializes in the history of science; he has been advised by the various departments at Columbia most concerned with each sub-list.

Popular Literature on General Science.
"The Outline of Science: A Plain Story Simply Told," J. Arthur Thompson (editor).
"An Introduction to Physical and Chemical Science," by William C. D. Whetham.
"Contemporary Science," Benjamin Harrow (editor).
"Foundations of the Universe," by M. Luckiesh.

Popular Introductory works on Physics.
"Concerning the Nature of Things," by Sir William Bragg.
"Science of Today," by Sir Oliver Lodge.
"Atoms and Rays," by Sir Oliver Lodge.
"Introduction to Contemporary Physics," by Karl K. Darrow.
"The Nature of the Physical World," by A. S. Eddington.

Elementary Textbooks on Physics.
"Physics," by Oscar M. Stewart.
"Practical Physics," by N. Henry Black and Harvey Nathaniel Davis.
"General Physics for Students: A Text-Book on the Fundamental Properties of Matter," by Edwin Edser.
"General Physics," by Henry Crew.

Popular Presentations of Elementary Chemistry.
"Triumphs and Wonders of Modern Chemistry," by Martin Geoffrey, Revised edition.
"Chemistry in Daily Life," by Dr. Lassar-Cohn, Fifth edition.

"Chemistry in Familiar Things," by Samuel S. Sadtler, Fourth edition revised.

"Chemistry in Modern Life," by Svante A. Arrhenius.

"Chemistry in the Service of Man," by Alexander Findlay.

"Chemistry in the World's Work," by Harrison E. Howe.

"Conversations on Chemistry," by William Ostwald.

"An Introduction to the Study of Chemical Philosophy," by William A. Tilden.

"Inorganic Chemistry for Colleges," by Lyman C. Newell.

The above books are arranged in the order of simpler and more easily understood to more thorough.

THE READER'S NOTEBOOK

In Which Are Recorded
His Impressions and Reactions
Concerning the
Art of Learning

How Much Have You Learned from This Book?

Now that you have finished your first survey of the art of learning, why not examine yourself? Can you persuade You, the teacher, to grant a diploma to You, the learner?

Write on the following pages, your reactions to various aspects of the volume. These are roughly indicated in each heading.

If you read the book again, write a fresh set of notes.

If some friend of yours has also read the book, exchange copies with him and see how his reactions differ from yours. Discuss these differences with him.

If you are strongly moved to criticize anything I have said, I should be glad to hear from you about it.

WHAT I HAVE LEARNED FROM THIS BOOK

The most important things I haved learned are

1.

2.

3.

4.

5.

6.

7.

8.

9.

10.

I disagree with the author on the following matters:

1.

2.

3.

4.

5.

6.

7.

8.

9.

10.

The following matters have not been sufficiently explained or argued:
1.

2.

3.

4.

5.

6.

7.

8.

I should like to learn more about the following matters:
1.

2.

3.

4.

5.

6.

7.

8.

9.

10.

My strongest traits as a learner seem to be:

1.

2.

3.

4.

5.

6.

7.

8.

9.

10.

My own chief weaknesses as a learner now seem to be:
1.

2.

3.

4.

5.

6.

7.

8.

I intend to begin learning the following things at once:

1.

2.

3.

INDEX

A

Abilities, discovering special, 89
  needed for learning, 74
Adolescent learners, 200
Adult, average and superior, 83
Adult learners, 201
Adult learning, 17
Age and learning, 14
Aggressive learning, 210
Aldrich, Thomas Bailey, 287
Alekhine, 165, 251
Amassing facts, 163
Amateur research, 337
Ambition must lead to learning, 71
American attitude toward learning, 328
American Telephone and Telegraph Company, study of telephone conversations, 253
Americans as esthetes, 306
Anderson, Roy N., 120
Anderson, Sherwood, 107
Animal learning, 81
Aquinas, Thomas, 126
Archimedes, 41
Architecture, opportunities for study in America, 347
Aristotle, 41, 66
Art, appreciation of, 311
  mistaken conceptions of learning of, 309
Artists, distinguished from performers, 305
Attic genius, passing of, 370
Attitudes favorable to learning, 183

B

Background necessary for learning, 68
Barr, Martin W., 82
Barry, Frederick, 387
Barrymore, John, 305
Beethoven, 305
Berger, Barton, 71
Berkey, Professor C. P., 379
Berol, 281
Biography, need for scientific, 355
Book, W. F., 243
Books, choice of, 371
  use of, 262
Boswell, 356
Botany, problems of, 339
Briefs, preparation of, 265
Broun, Heywood, 273
Browsing, value of, 191
Bryan, W. J., 165, 207
Byron, 290

C

Carpenter, E. E., 99
Caruso, 18, 301
Chemistry, need for research in, 388
Chesterton, G. K., 328
Cody, Sherwin, 249
Cold, common, need for study of, 355
Collectors, amateur, 357
College graduates, superiority of, 186
Community movies, 352
Compliance and learning, 184
Concentration, how to learn, 118, 119, 120
  importance of, 117
Consumer psychology, need for, 341
Conversation an aid to learning, 297
Crime in America, study of, 356